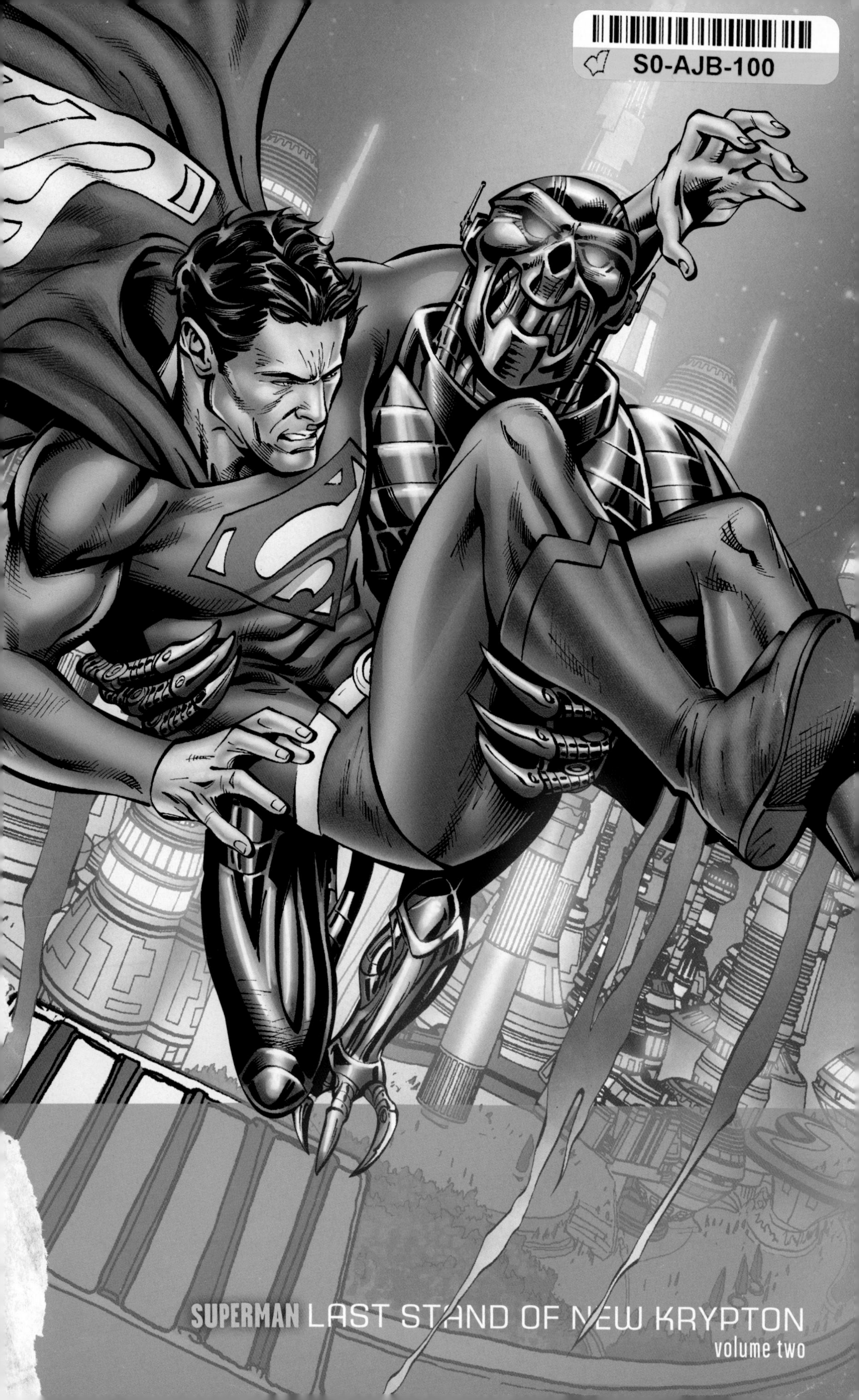

SUPERMAN LAST STAND OF NEW KRYPTON

volume two

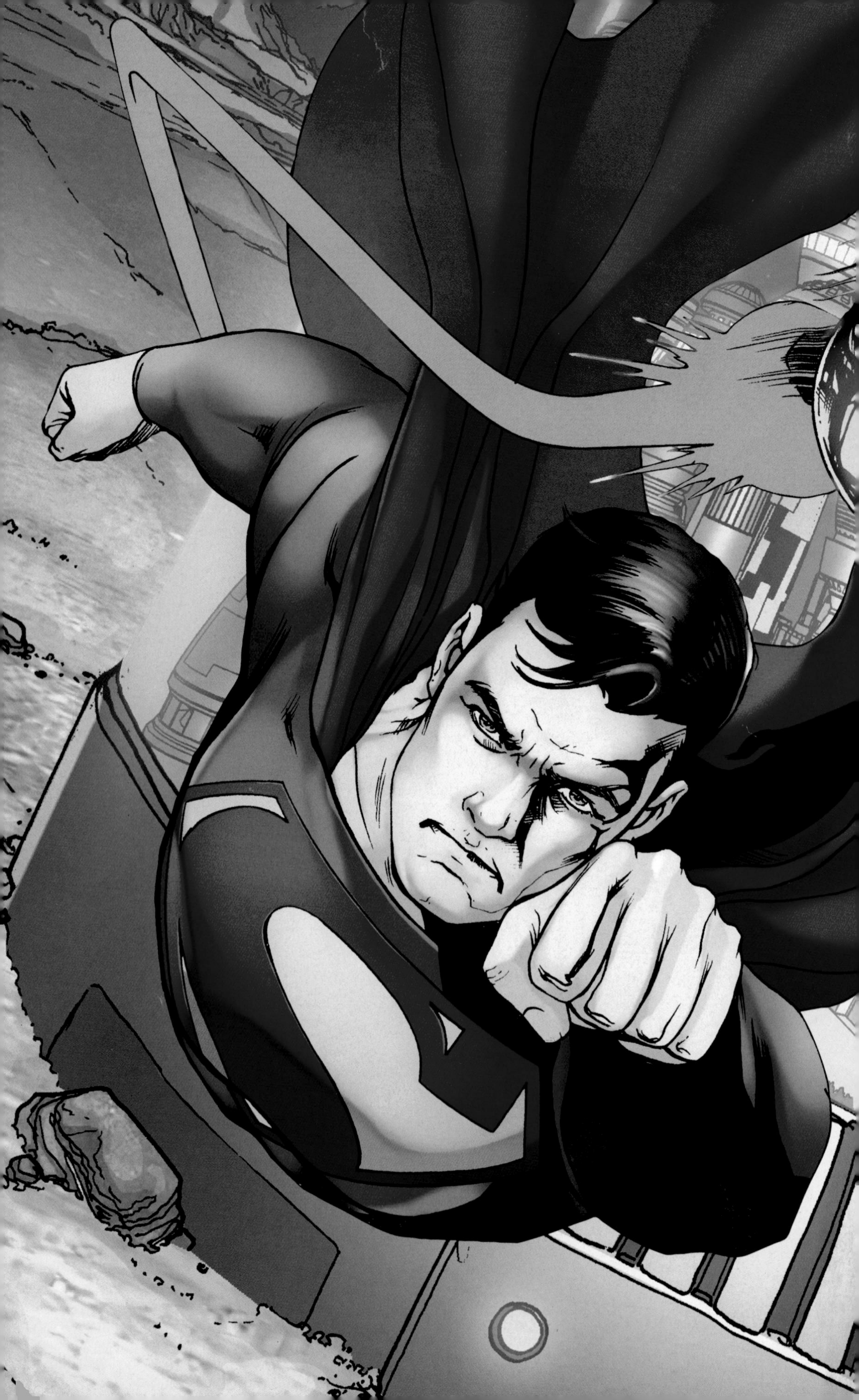

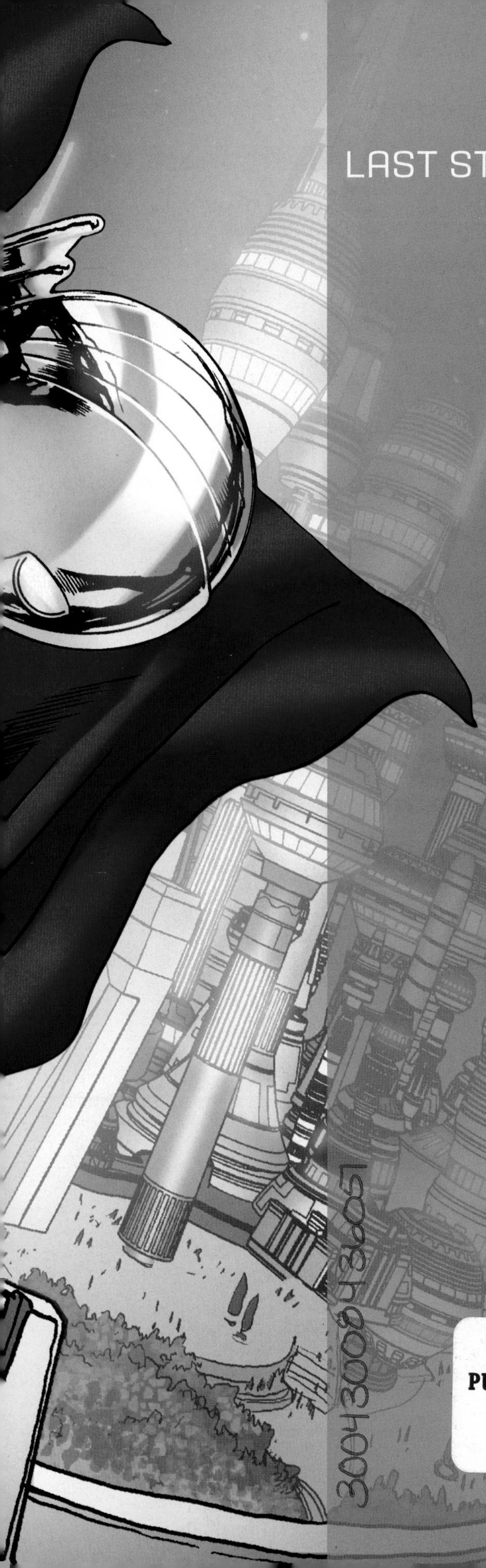

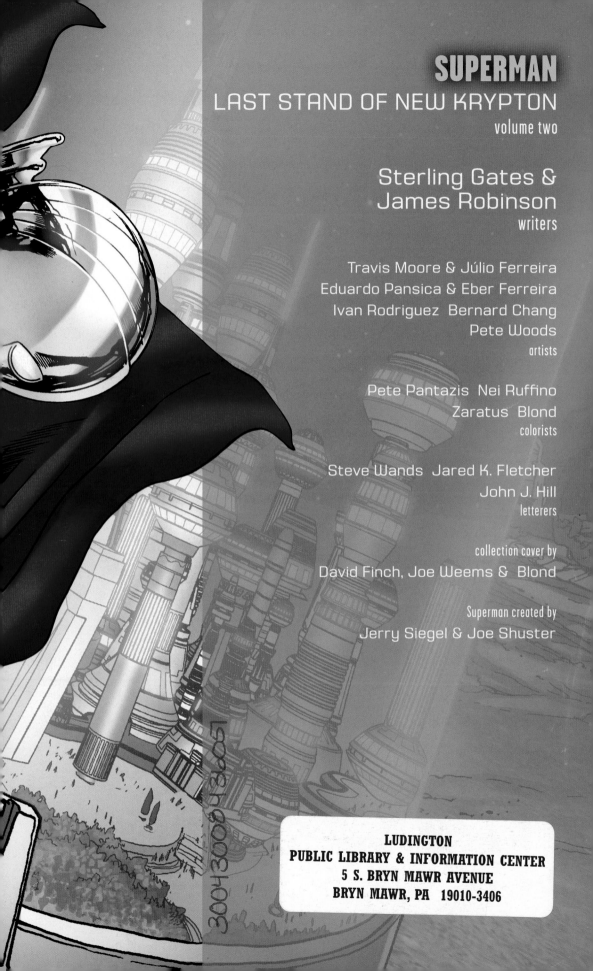

SUPERMAN

LAST STAND OF NEW KRYPTON

volume two

Sterling Gates &
James Robinson
writers

Travis Moore & Júlio Ferreira
Eduardo Pansica & Eber Ferreira
Ivan Rodriguez Bernard Chang
Pete Woods
artists

Pete Pantazis Nei Ruffino
Zaratus Blond
colorists

Steve Wands Jared K. Fletcher
John J. Hill
letterers

collection cover by
David Finch, Joe Weems & Blond

Superman created by
Jerry Siegel & Joe Shuster

MATT IDELSON Editor-original series WIL MOSS Assistant Editor-original series IAN SATTLER Director – Editorial, Special Projects and Archival Editions
SEAN MACKIEWICZ Editor ROBBIN BROSTERMAN Design Director – Books ROBBIE BIEDERMAN Publication Design

EDDIE BERGANZA Executive Editor BOB HARRAS VP – Editor-in-Chief

DIANE NELSON President DAN DIDIO and JIM LEE Co-Publishers GEOFF JOHNS Chief Creative Officer JOHN ROOD Executive VP – Sales, Marketing and Business Development
AMY GENKINS Senior VP – Business and Legal Affairs NAIRI GARDINER Senior VP – Finance JEFF BOISON VP – Publishing Operations
MARK CHIARELLO VP – Art Direction and Design JOHN CUNNINGHAM VP – Marketing TERRI CUNNINGHAM VP – Talent Relations and Services
ALISON GILL Senior VP – Manufacturing and Operations DAVID HYDE VP – Publicity HANK KANALZ Senior VP – Digital
JAY KOGAN VP – Business and Legal Affairs, Publishing JACK MAHAN VP – Business Affairs, Talent NICK NAPOLITANO VP – Manufacturing Administration
SUE POHJA VP – Book Sales COURTNEY SIMMONS Senior VP – Publicity BOB WAYNE Senior VP – Sales

SUPERMAN: LAST STAND OF NEW KRYPTON Volume 2

DC Comics, 1700 Broadway, New York, NY 10019. A Warner Bros. Entertainment Company
Printed by RR Donnelley, Salem, VA, USA. 2/3/12. First Printing.
SC ISBN: 978-1-4012-3037-1

SUSTAINABLE FORESTRY INITIATIVE
Certified Chain of Custody
At Least 25% Certified Forest Content
www.sfiprogram.org
SFI-01042
APPLIES TO TEXT STOCK ONLY

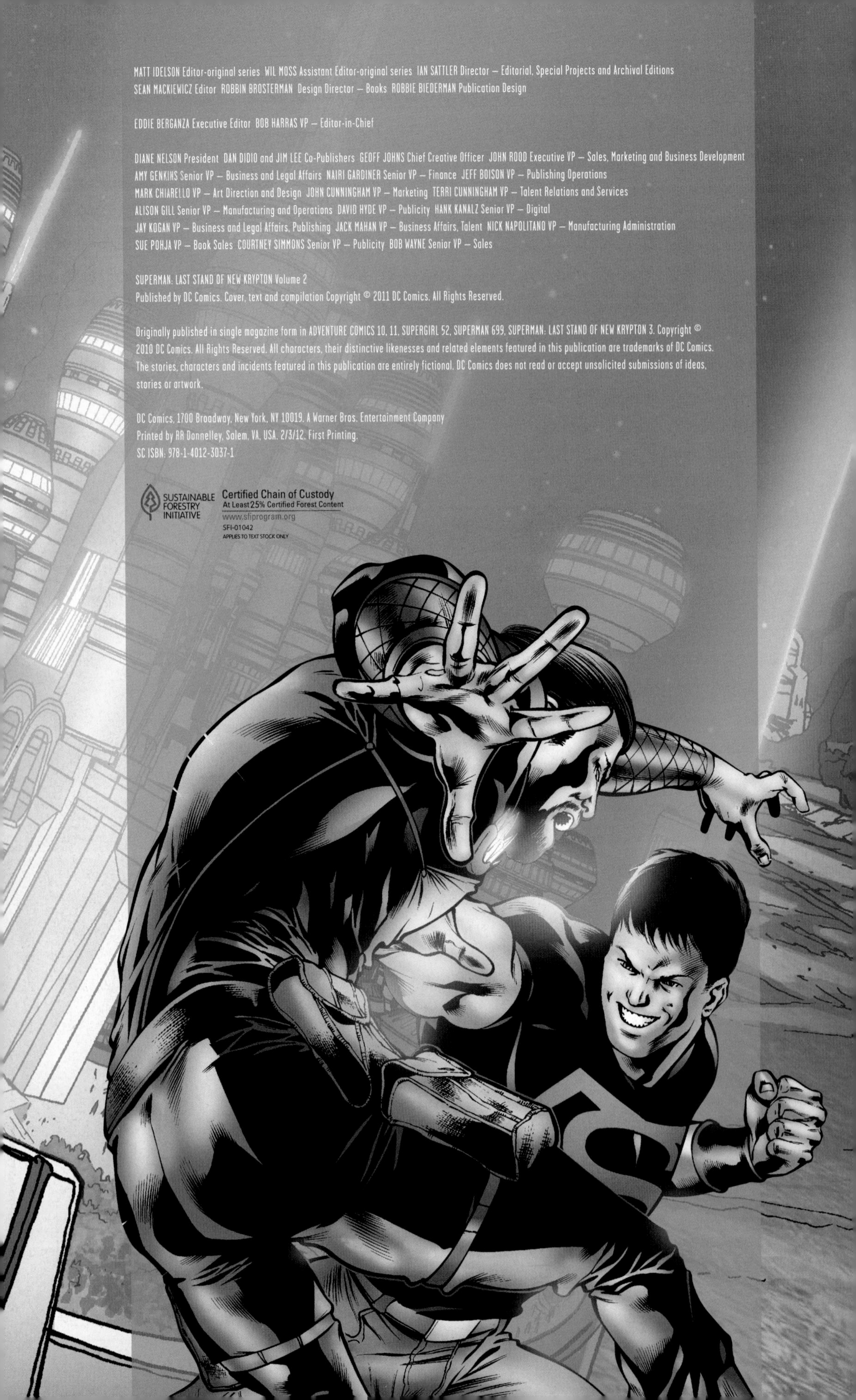

cover by **JOE QUINONES**

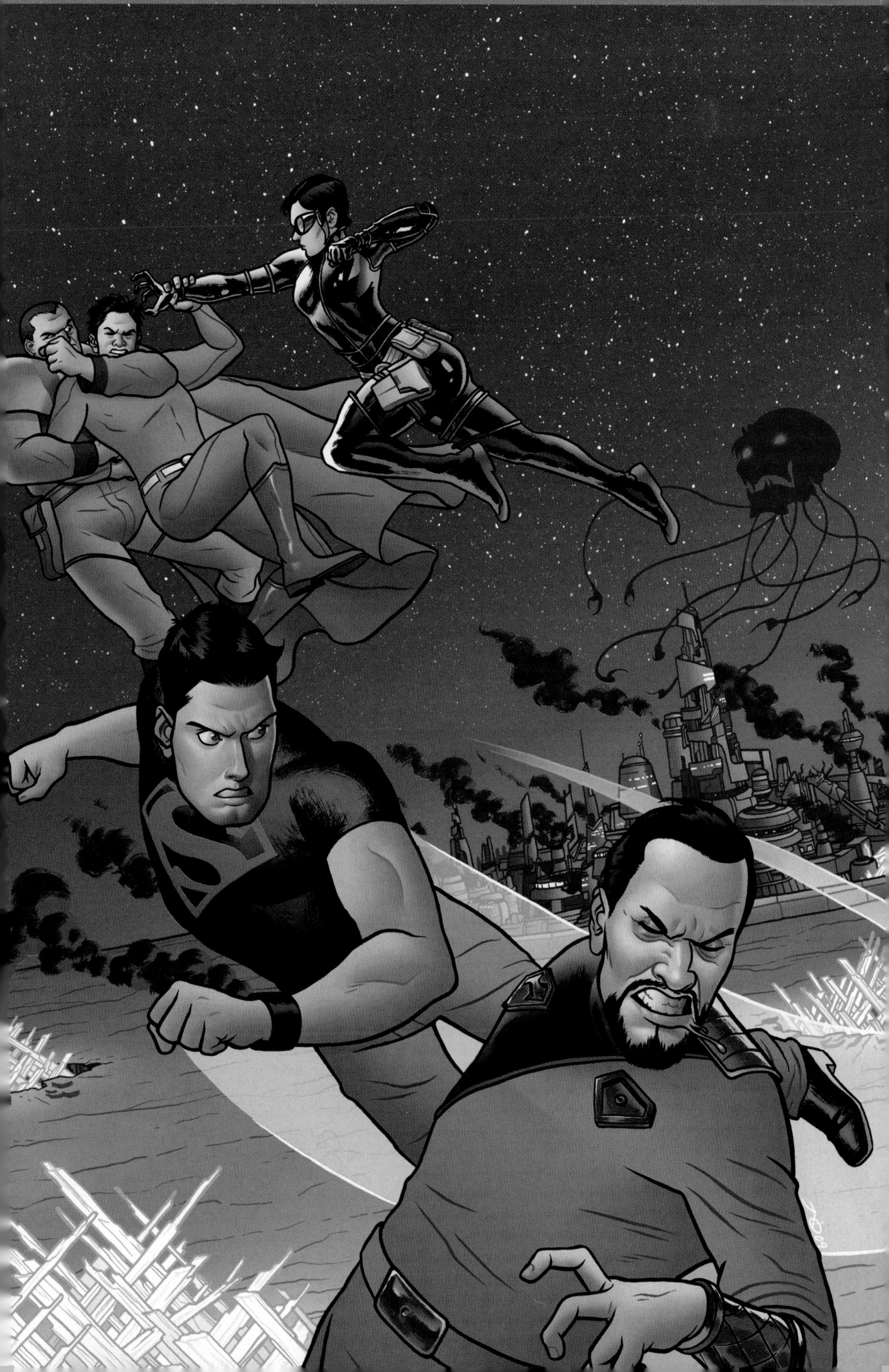

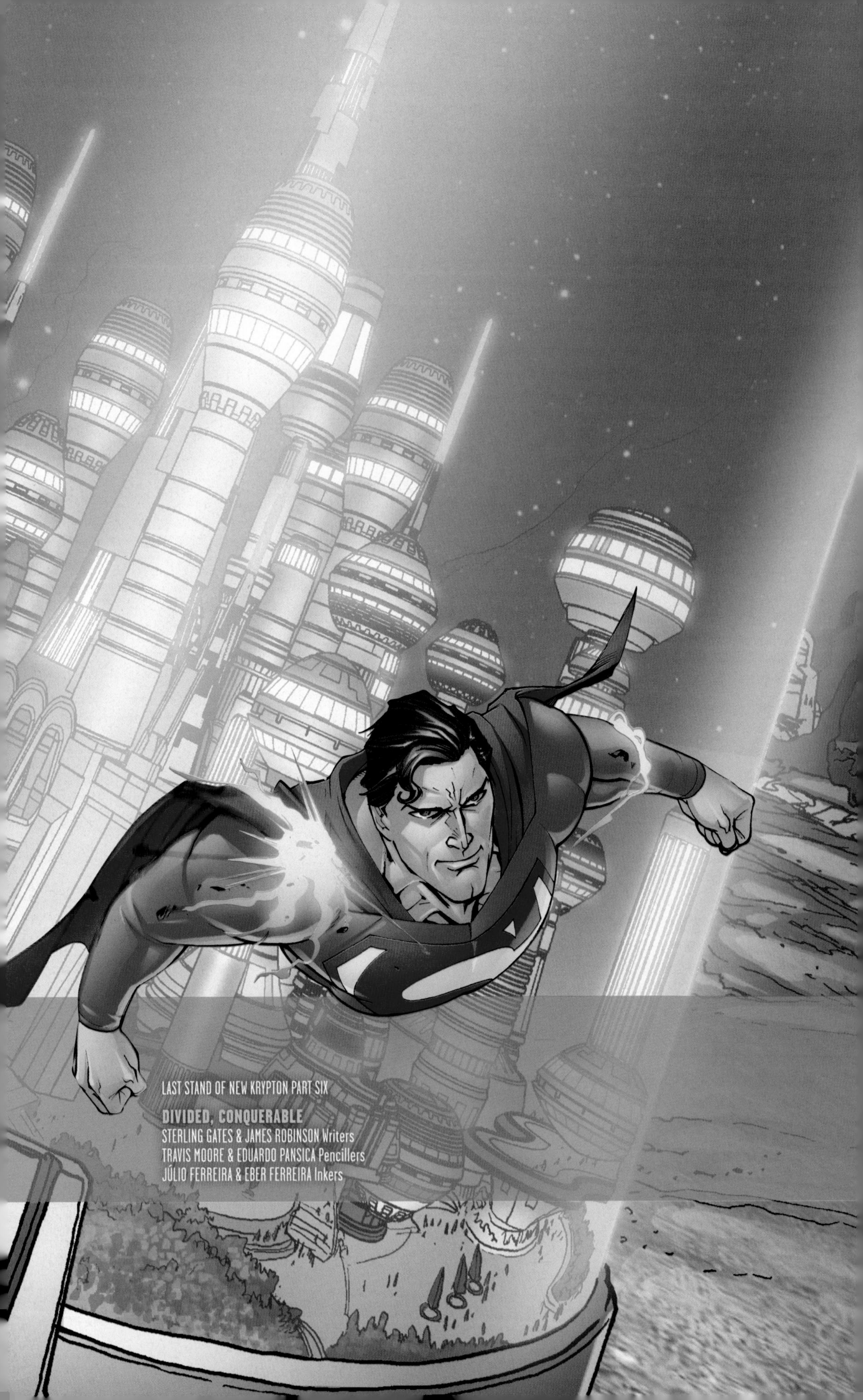
LAST STAND OF NEW KRYPTON PART SIX
DIVIDED, CONQUERABLE
STERLING GATES & JAMES ROBINSON Writers
TRAVIS MOORE & EDUARDO PANSICA Pencillers
JÚLIO FERREIRA & EBER FERREIRA Inkers

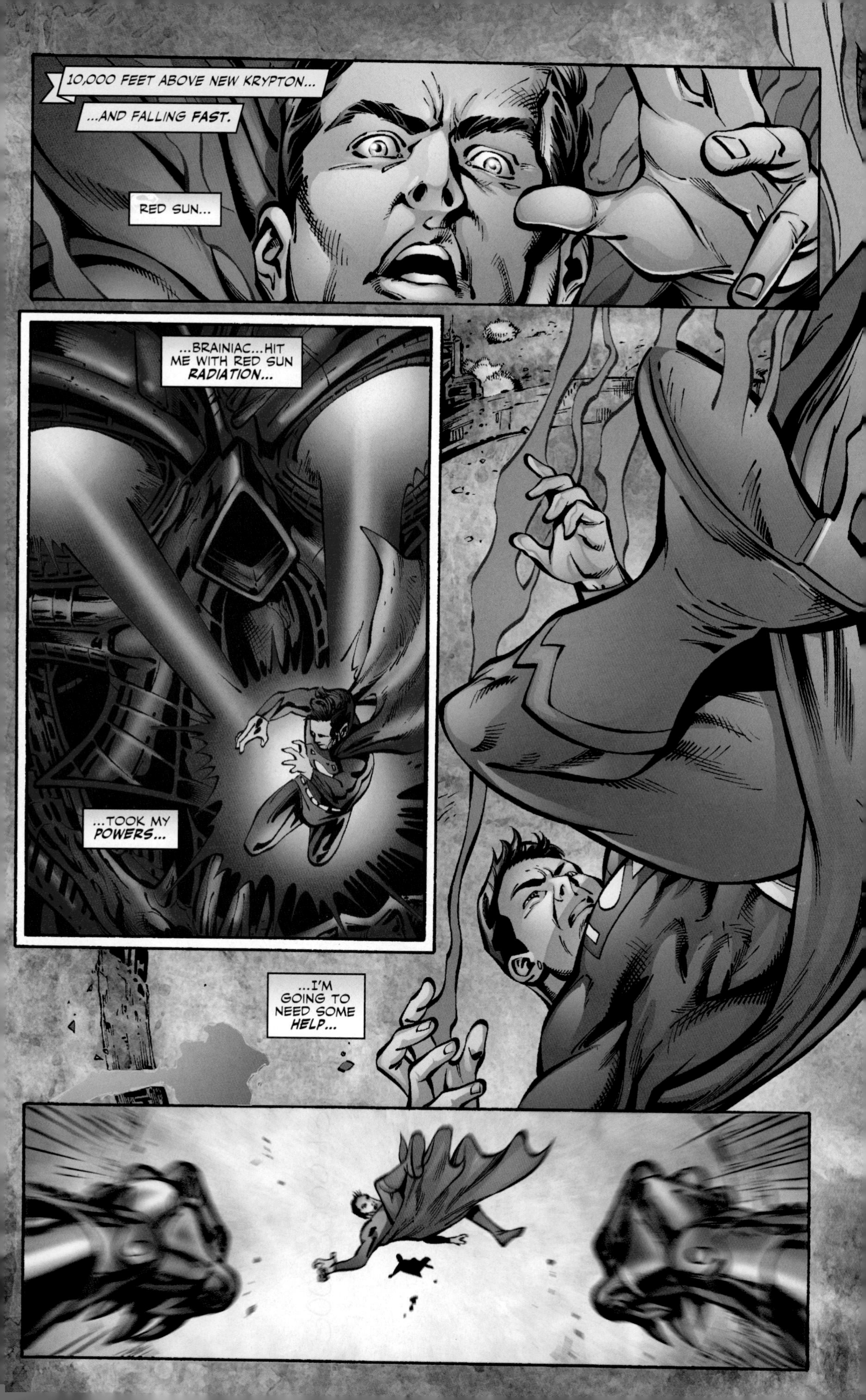
10,000 FEET ABOVE NEW KRYPTON...
...AND FALLING FAST.
RED SUN...
...BRAINIAC...HIT ME WITH RED SUN RADIATION...
...TOOK MY POWERS...
...I'M GOING TO NEED SOME HELP...

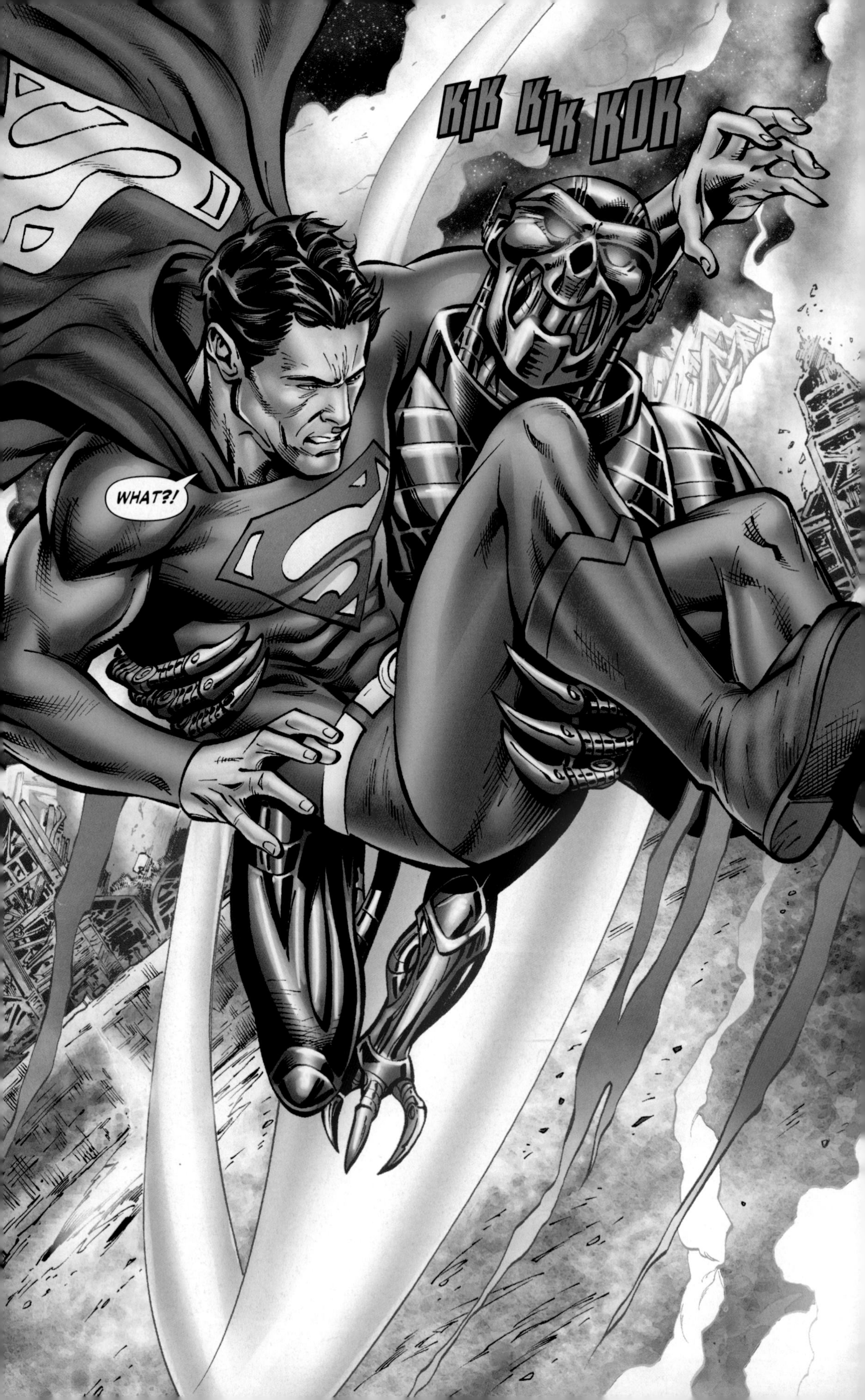
KIK KIK KOK
WHAT?!

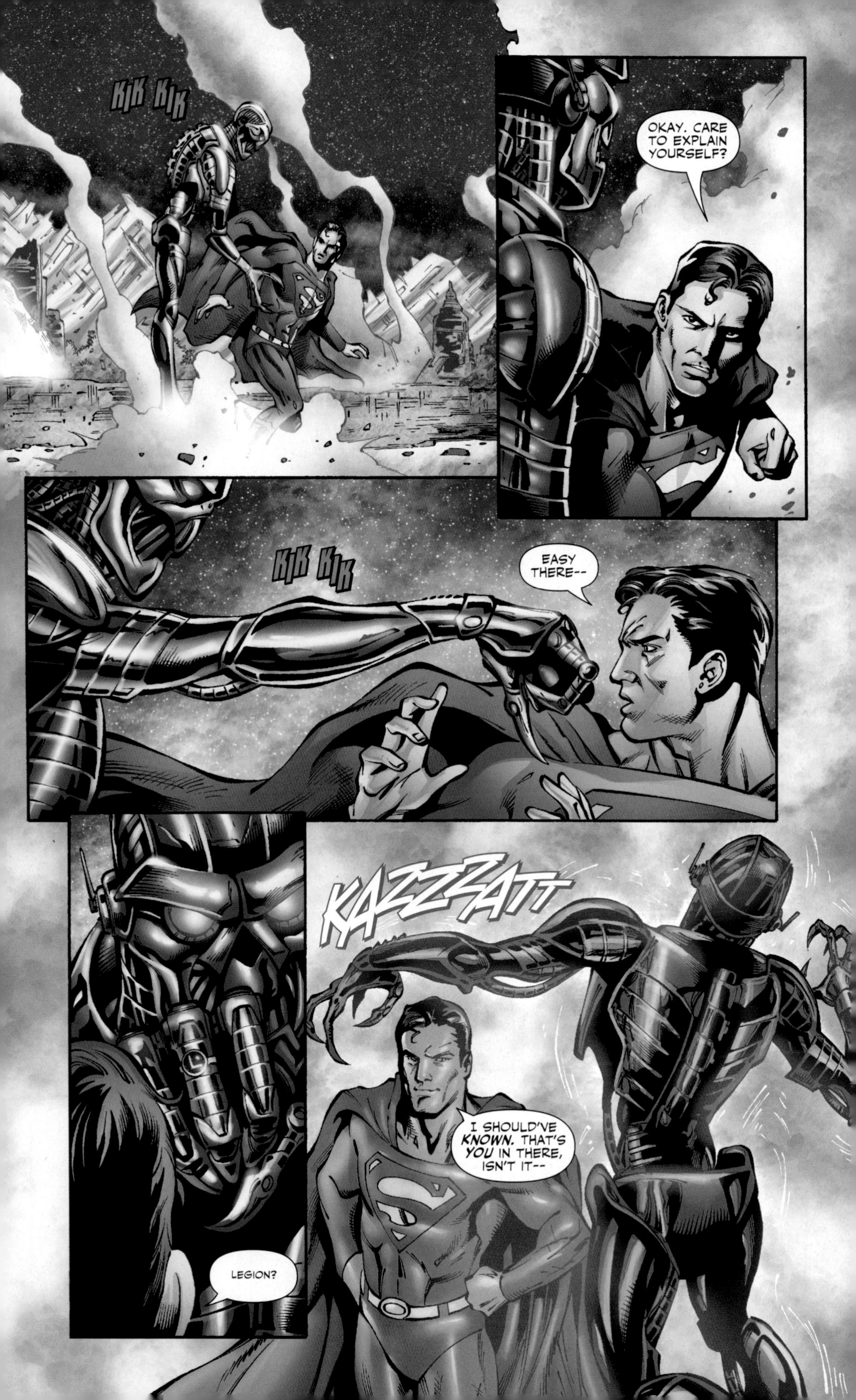
KIK KIK
OKAY. CARE TO EXPLAIN YOURSELF?
KIK KIK
EASY THERE--
LEGION?
KAZZZATT
I SHOULD'VE *KNOWN.* THAT'S *YOU* IN THERE, ISN'T IT--

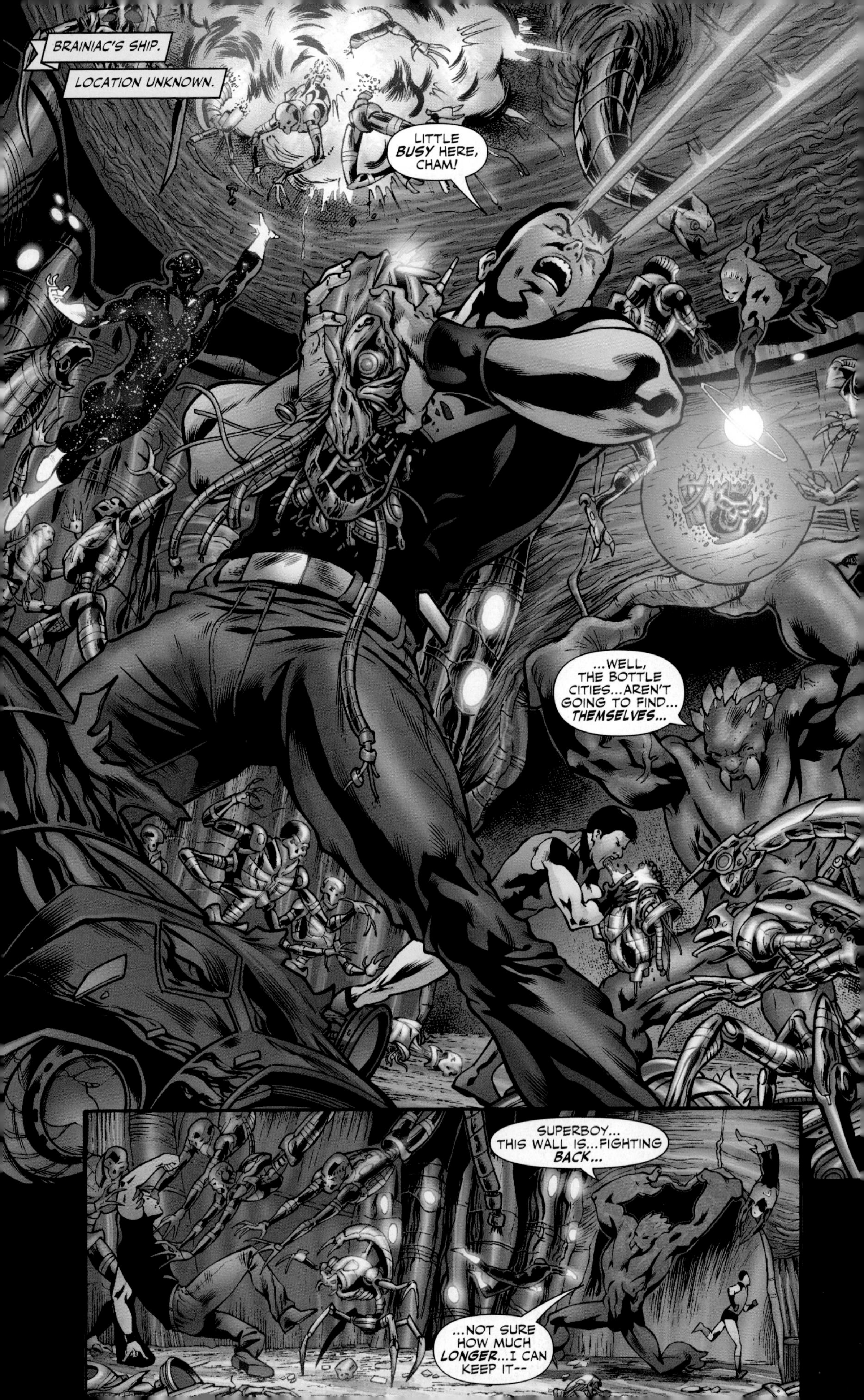
BRAINIAC'S SHIP.
LOCATION UNKNOWN.
LITTLE BUSY HERE, CHAM!
...WELL, THE BOTTLE CITIES...AREN'T GOING TO FIND... THEMSELVES...
SUPERBOY... THIS WALL IS...FIGHTING BACK...
...NOT SURE HOW MUCH LONGER...I CAN KEEP IT--

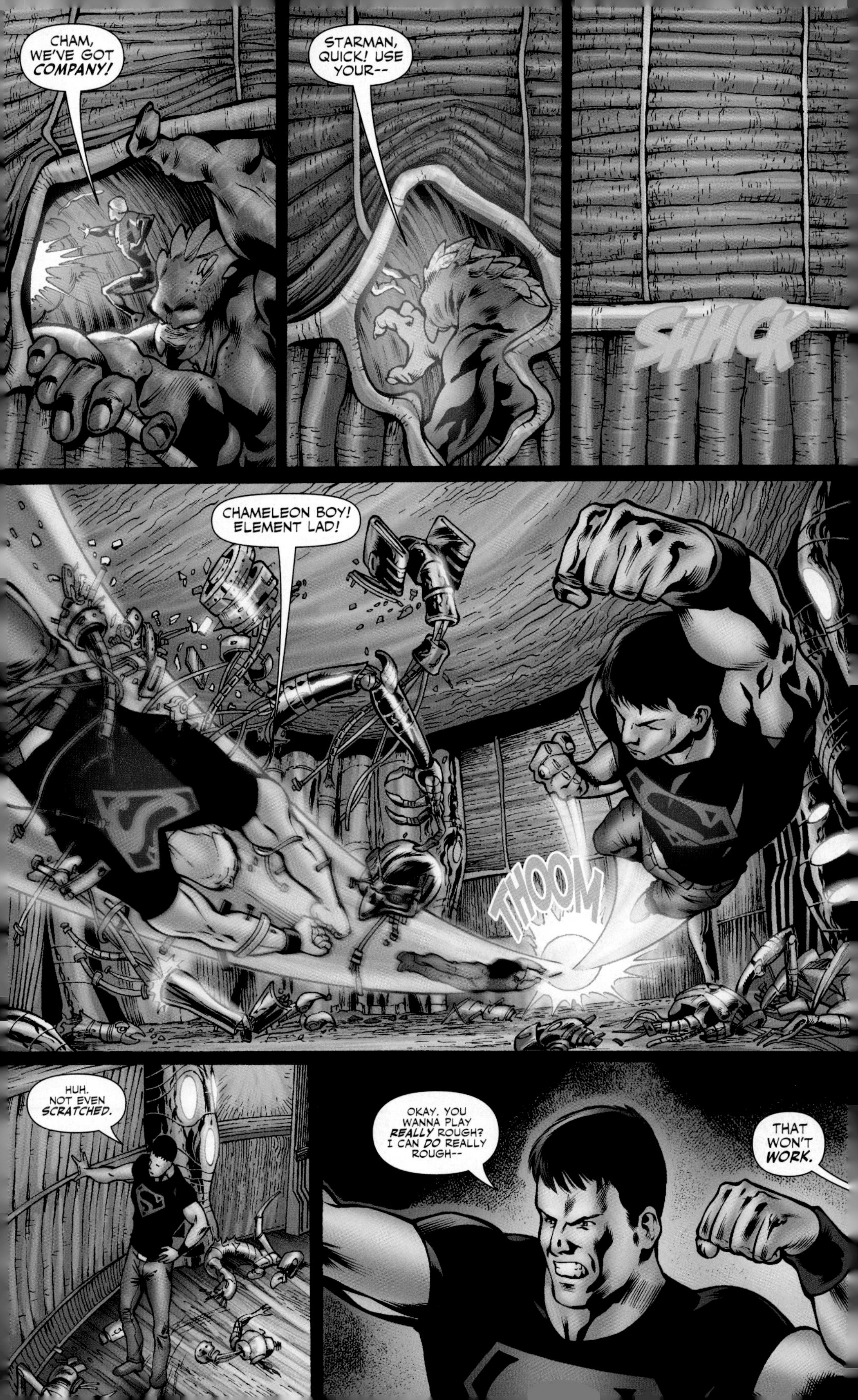
CHAM, WE'VE GOT *COMPANY!*
STARMAN, QUICK! USE YOUR--
SHHCK
CHAMELEON BOY! ELEMENT LAD!
THOOM
HUH. NOT EVEN *SCRATCHED.*
OKAY. YOU WANNA PLAY *REALLY* ROUGH? I CAN *DO* REALLY ROUGH--
THAT WON'T *WORK.*

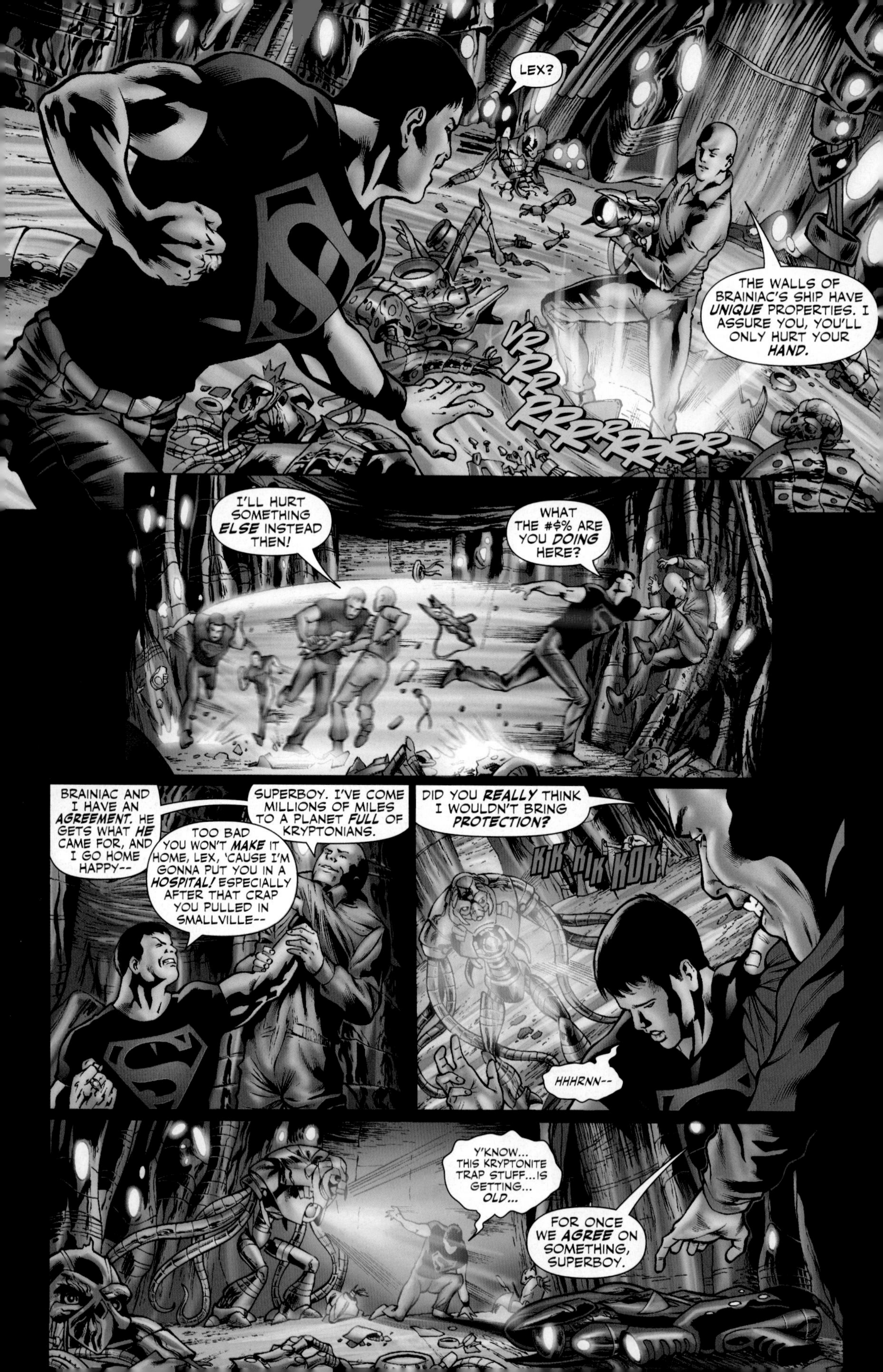

LEX?
THE WALLS OF BRAINIAC'S SHIP HAVE *UNIQUE* PROPERTIES. I ASSURE YOU, YOU'LL ONLY HURT YOUR *HAND.*
VRRRRRRRRRRRR
I'LL HURT SOMETHING *ELSE* INSTEAD THEN!
WHAT THE #$% ARE YOU *DOING* HERE?
SUPERBOY. I'VE COME MILLIONS OF MILES TO A PLANET *FULL* OF KRYPTONIANS.
BRAINIAC AND I HAVE AN *AGREEMENT.* HE GETS WHAT *HE* CAME FOR, AND I GO HOME HAPPY--
TOO BAD YOU WON'T *MAKE* IT HOME, LEX, 'CAUSE I'M GONNA PUT YOU IN A *HOSPITAL!* ESPECIALLY AFTER THAT CRAP YOU PULLED IN SMALLVILLE--
DID YOU *REALLY* THINK I WOULDN'T BRING *PROTECTION?*
KIK KIK KOK
HHHRNN--
Y'KNOW... THIS KRYPTONITE TRAP STUFF...IS GETTING... *OLD...*
FOR ONCE WE *AGREE* ON SOMETHING, SUPERBOY.

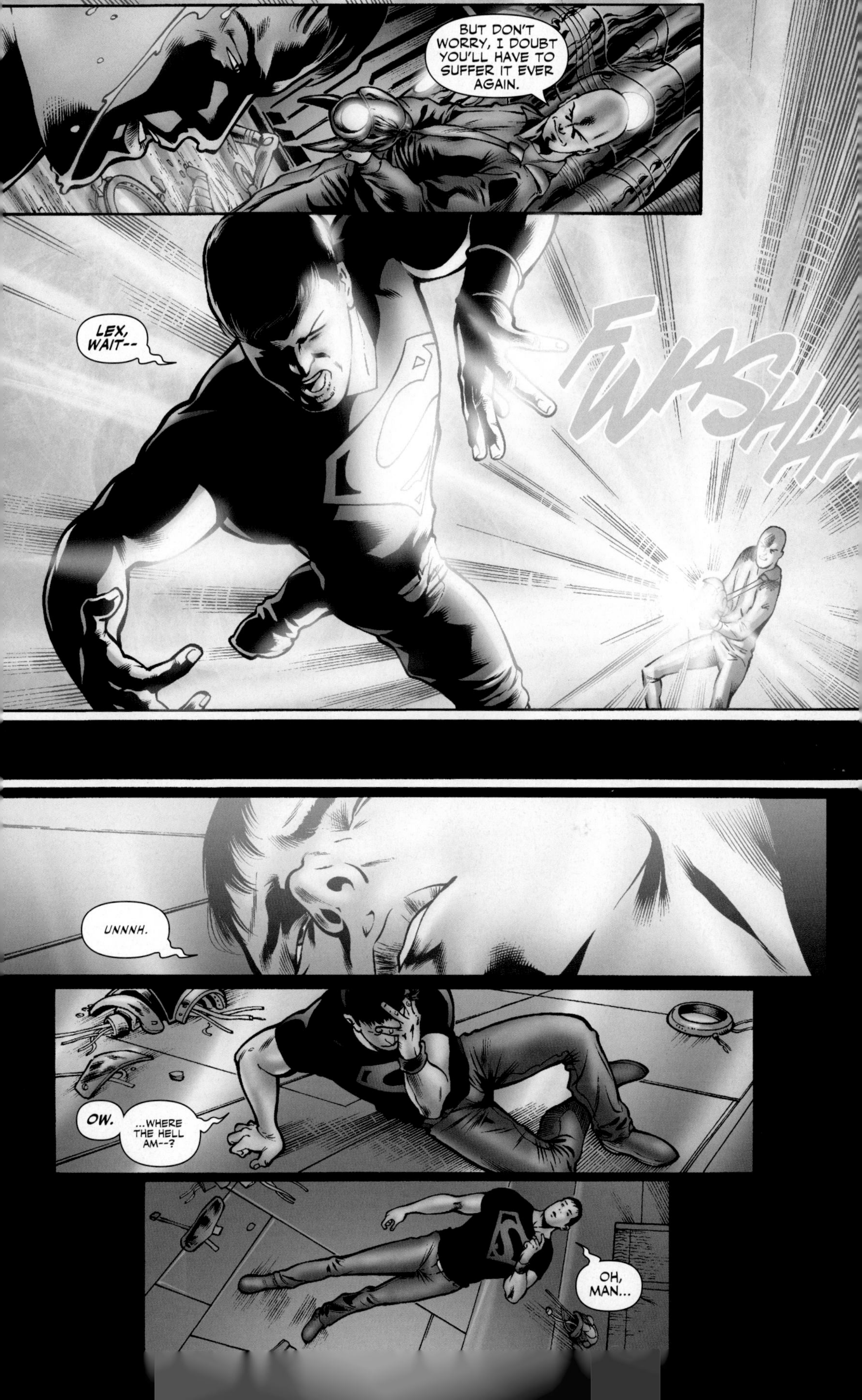
BUT DON'T WORRY, I DOUBT YOU'LL HAVE TO SUFFER IT EVER AGAIN.
LEX, WAIT--
FWASHHH
UNNNH.
OW.
...WHERE THE HELL AM--?
OH, MAN...

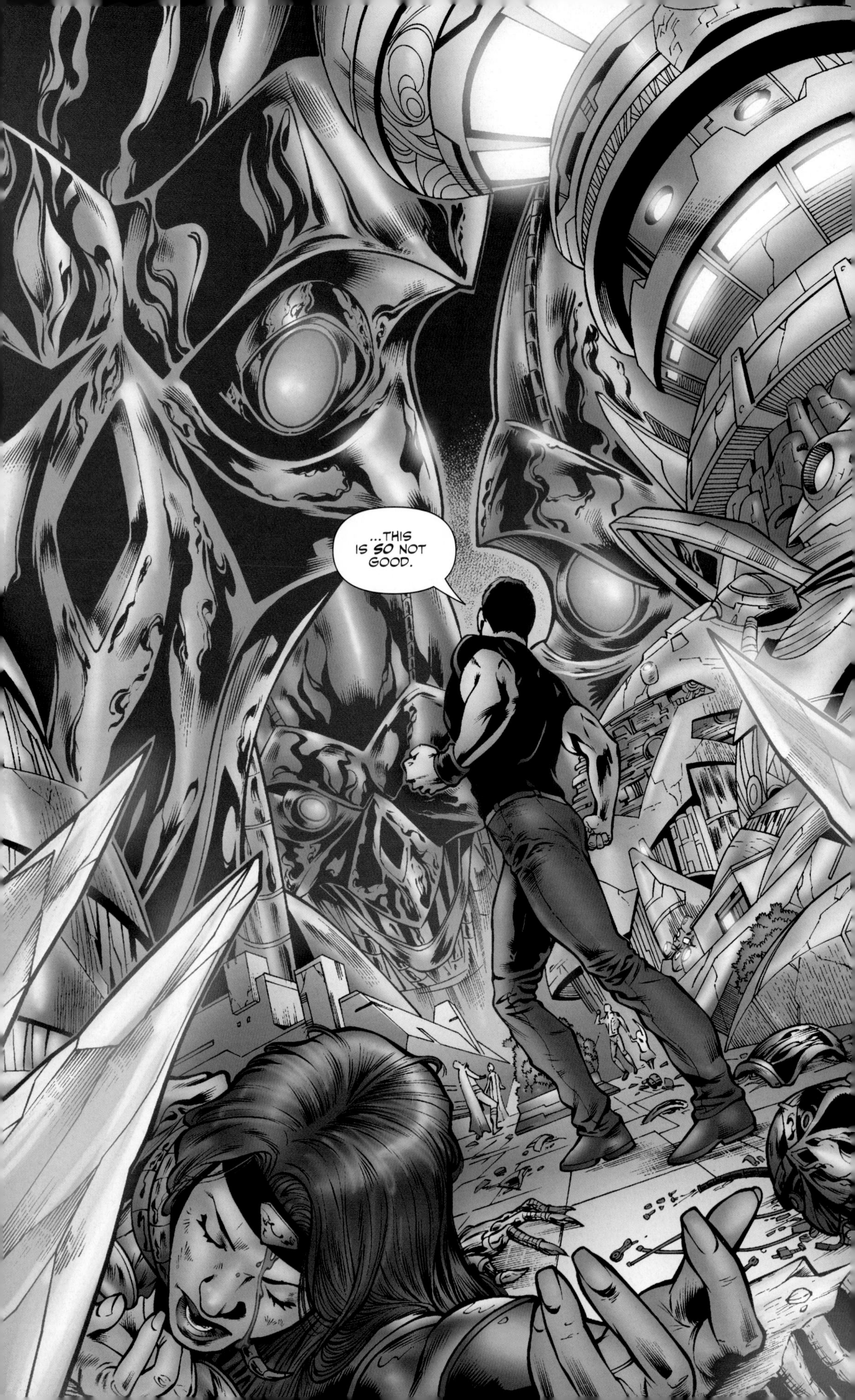
...THIS IS SO NOT GOOD.

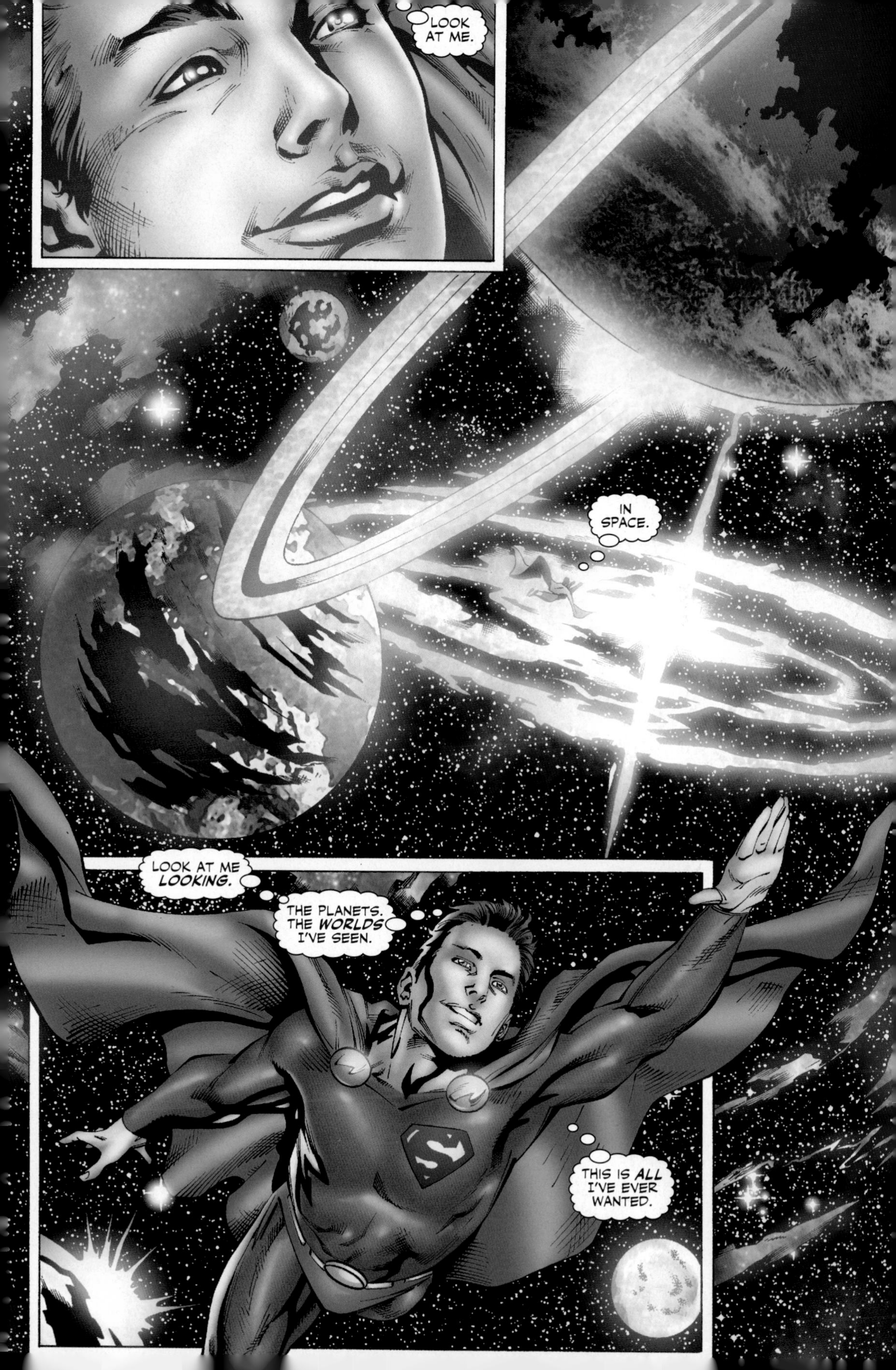

LOOK AT ME.
IN SPACE.
LOOK AT ME LOOKING.
THE PLANETS. THE WORLDS I'VE SEEN.
THIS IS ALL I'VE EVER WANTED.

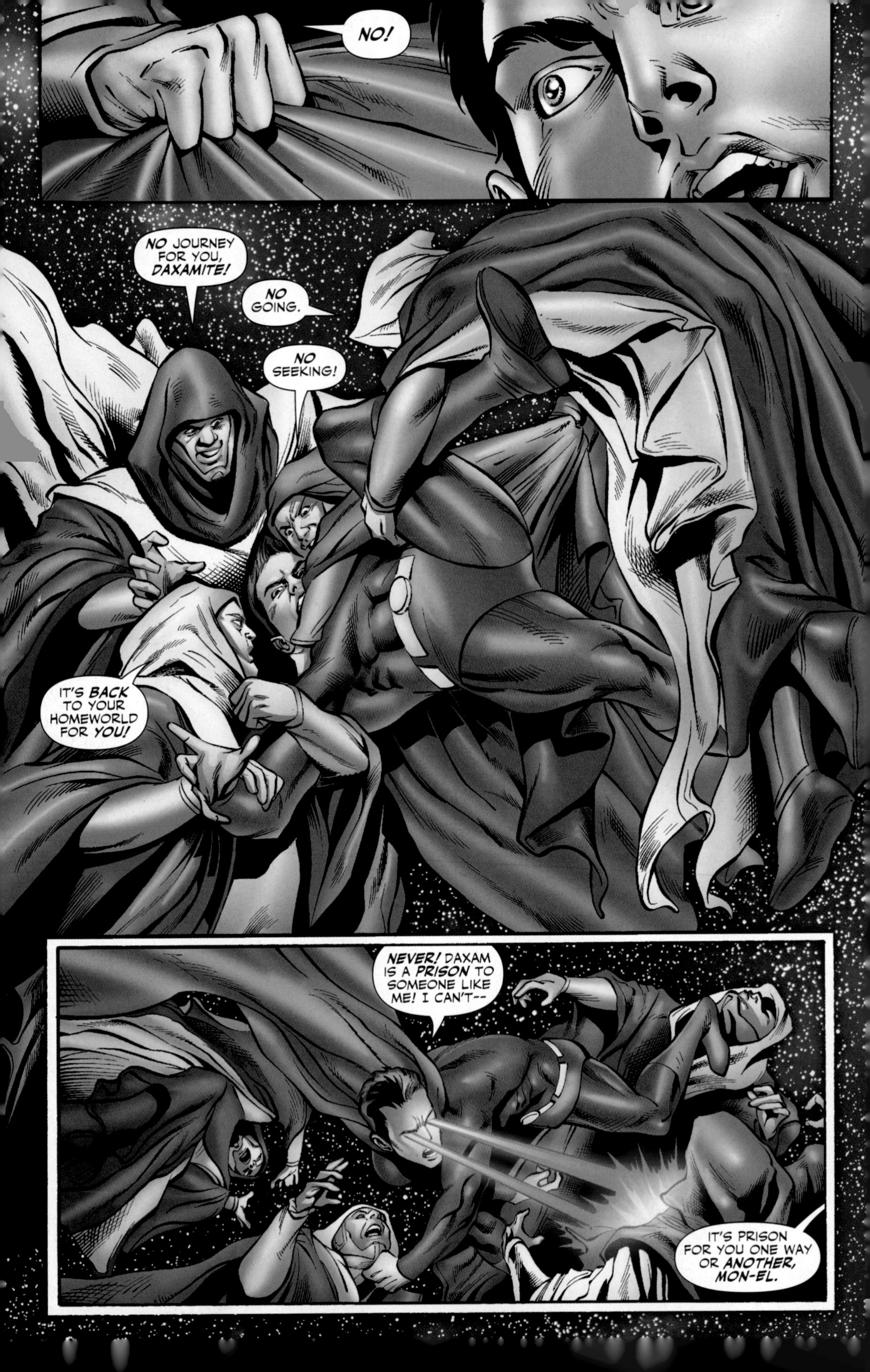
NO!
NO JOURNEY FOR YOU, DAXAMITE!
NO GOING.
NO SEEKING!
IT'S BACK TO YOUR HOMEWORLD FOR YOU!
NEVER! DAXAM IS A PRISON TO SOMEONE LIKE ME! I CAN'T--
IT'S PRISON FOR YOU ONE WAY OR ANOTHER, MON-EL.

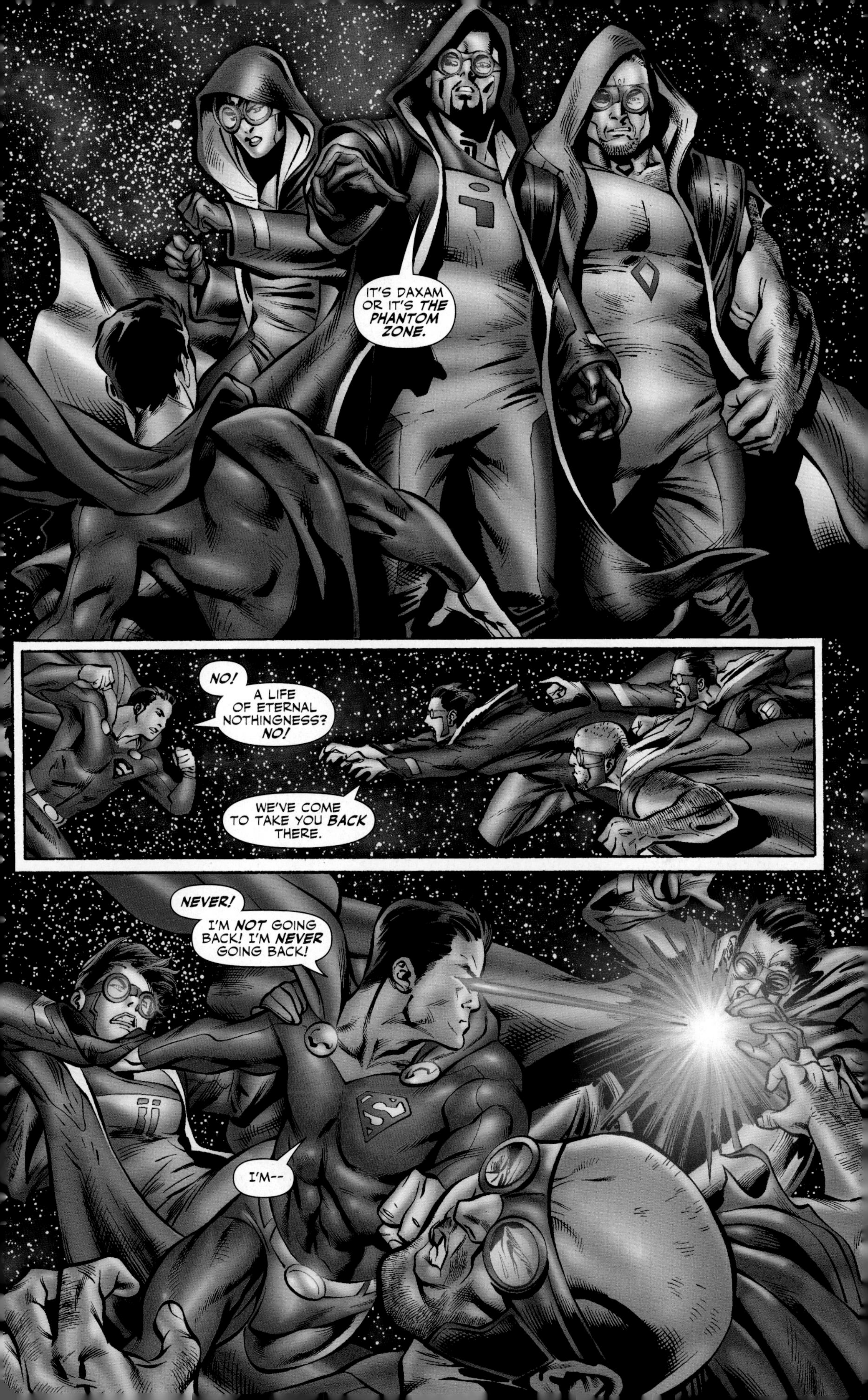
IT'S DAXAM OR IT'S THE PHANTOM ZONE.
NO!
A LIFE OF ETERNAL NOTHINGNESS? NO!
WE'VE COME TO TAKE YOU BACK THERE.
NEVER!
I'M NOT GOING BACK! I'M NEVER GOING BACK!
I'M--

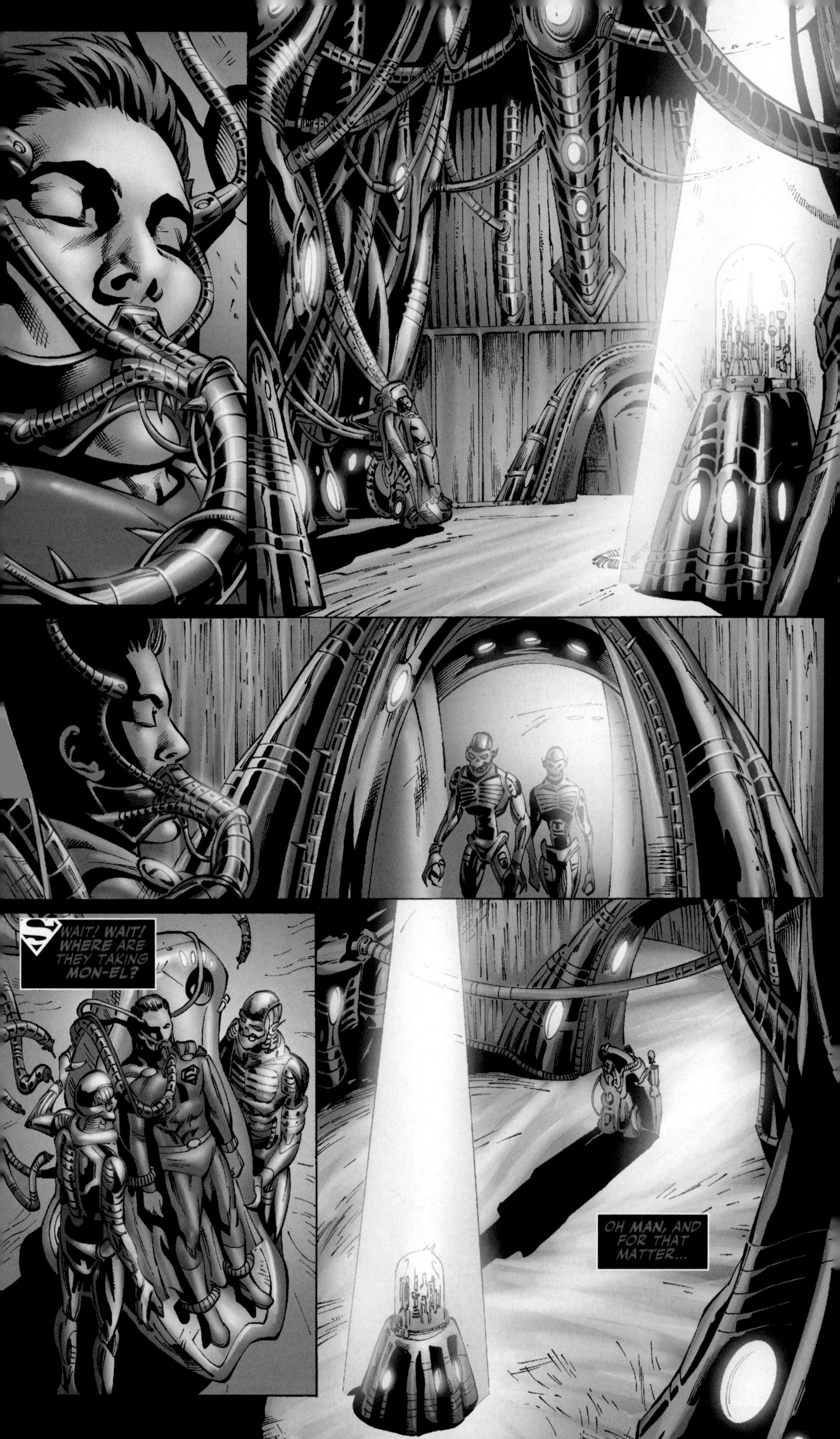
WAIT! WAIT! WHERE ARE THEY TAKING MON-EL?
OH MAN, AND FOR THAT MATTER...

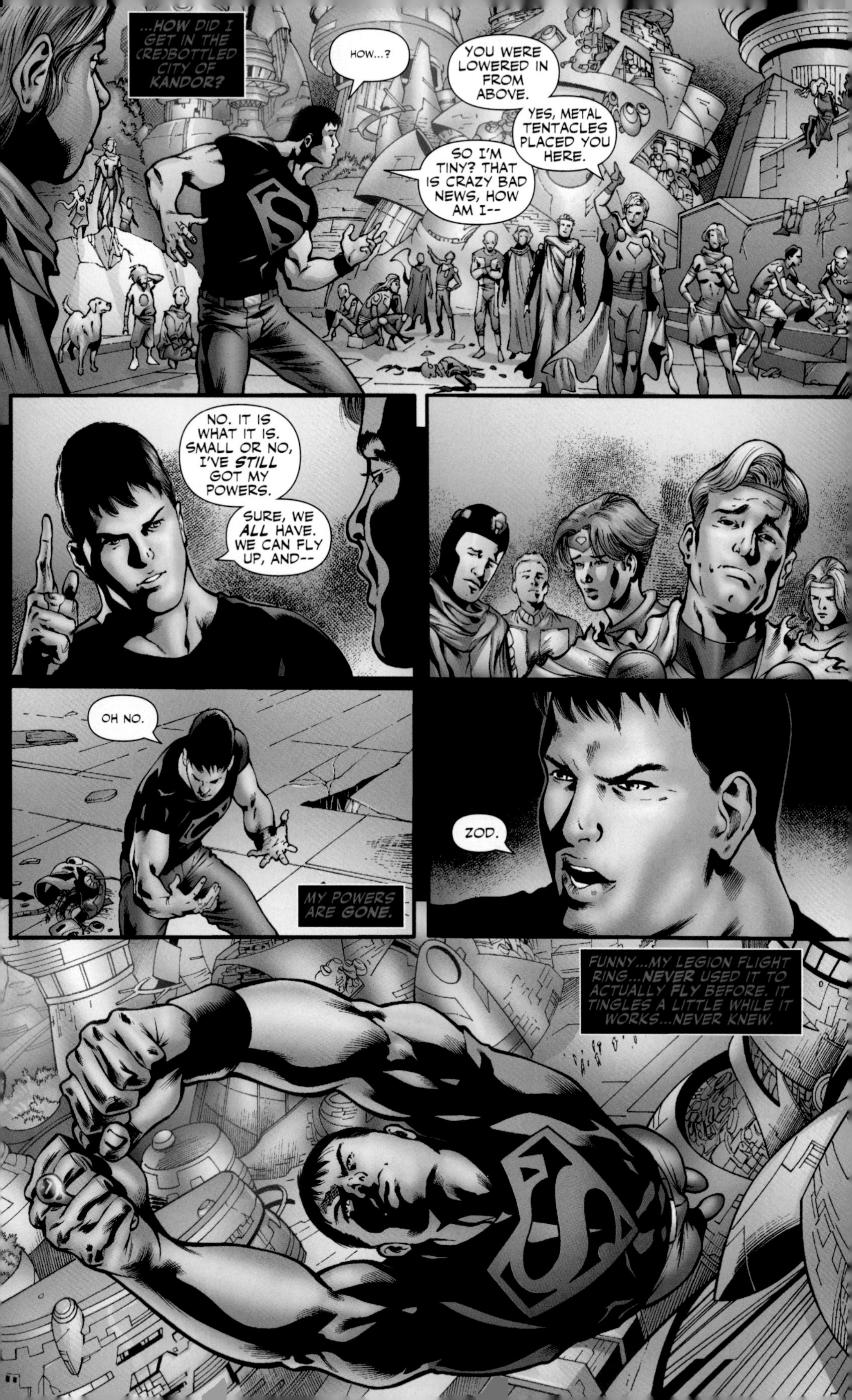
...HOW DID I GET IN THE (RE)BOTTLED CITY OF KANDOR?
HOW...?
YOU WERE LOWERED IN FROM ABOVE.
YES, METAL TENTACLES PLACED YOU HERE.
SO I'M TINY? THAT IS CRAZY BAD NEWS, HOW AM I--
NO. IT IS WHAT IT IS. SMALL OR NO, I'VE STILL GOT MY POWERS.
SURE, WE ALL HAVE. WE CAN FLY UP, AND--
OH NO.
MY POWERS ARE GONE.
ZOD.
FUNNY...MY LEGION FLIGHT RING...NEVER USED IT TO ACTUALLY FLY BEFORE. IT TINGLES A LITTLE WHILE IT WORKS...NEVER KNEW.

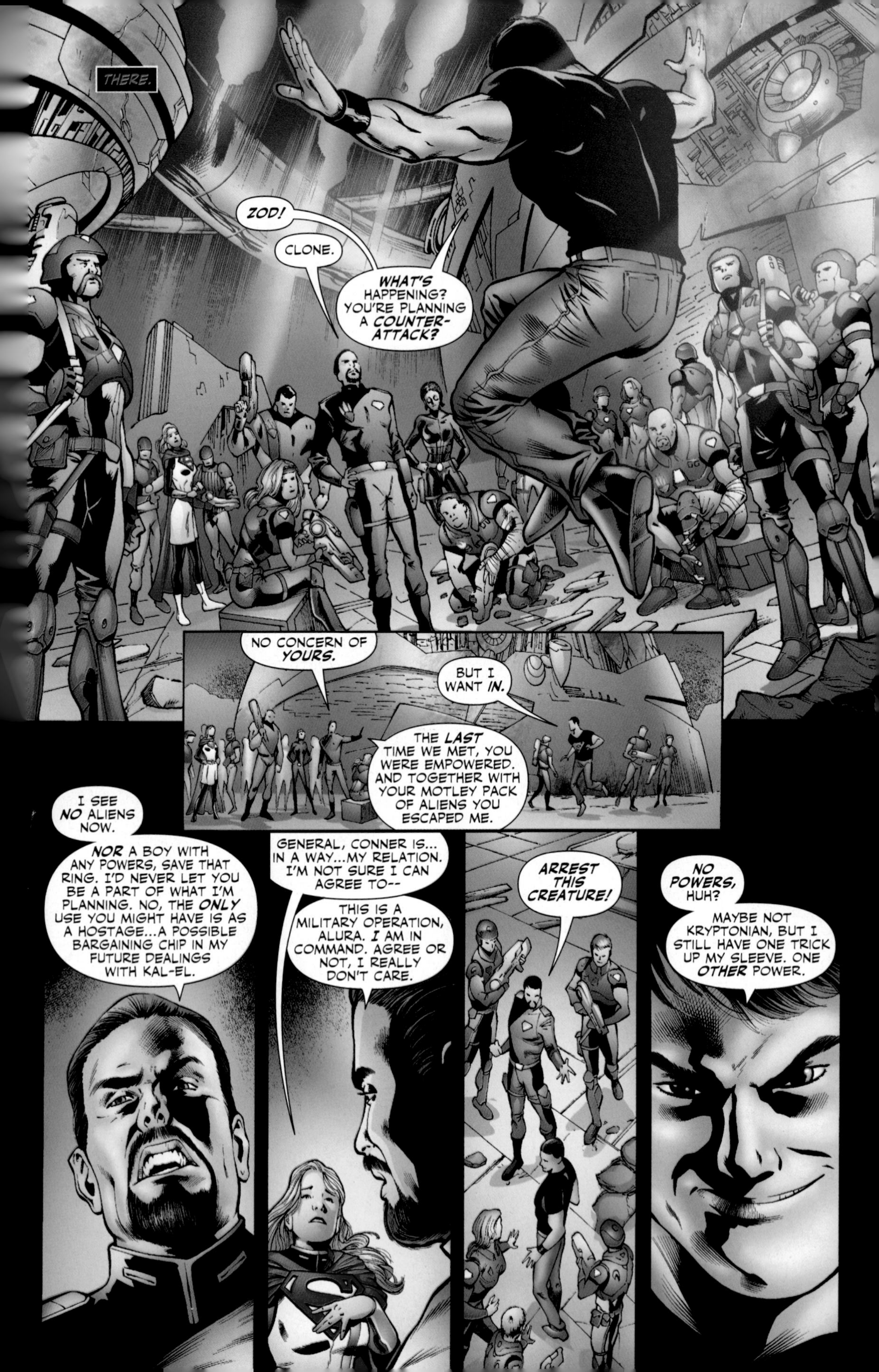
THERE.
ZOD!
CLONE.
WHAT'S HAPPENING? YOU'RE PLANNING A COUNTER-ATTACK?
NO CONCERN OF YOURS.
BUT I WANT IN.
THE LAST TIME WE MET, YOU WERE EMPOWERED. AND TOGETHER WITH YOUR MOTLEY PACK OF ALIENS YOU ESCAPED ME.
I SEE NO ALIENS NOW.
NOR A BOY WITH ANY POWERS, SAVE THAT RING. I'D NEVER LET YOU BE A PART OF WHAT I'M PLANNING. NO, THE ONLY USE YOU MIGHT HAVE IS AS A HOSTAGE...A POSSIBLE BARGAINING CHIP IN MY FUTURE DEALINGS WITH KAL-EL.
GENERAL, CONNER IS... IN A WAY...MY RELATION. I'M NOT SURE I CAN AGREE TO--
THIS IS A MILITARY OPERATION, ALURA. I AM IN COMMAND. AGREE OR NOT, I REALLY DON'T CARE.
ARREST THIS CREATURE!
NO POWERS, HUH?
MAYBE NOT KRYPTONIAN, BUT I STILL HAVE ONE TRICK UP MY SLEEVE. ONE OTHER POWER.

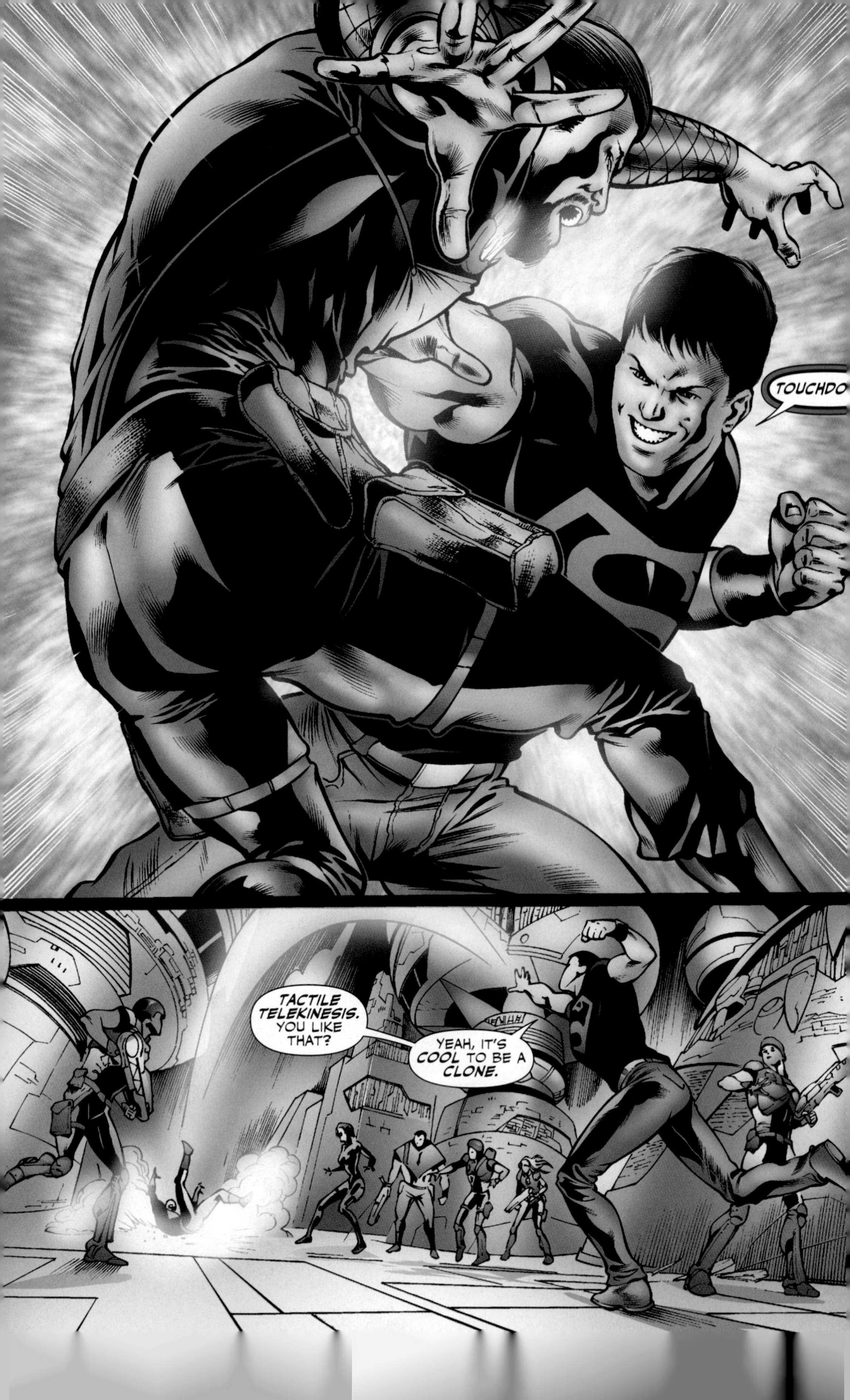
TOUCHDO
TACTILE TELEKINESIS. YOU LIKE THAT?
YEAH, IT'S COOL TO BE A CLONE.

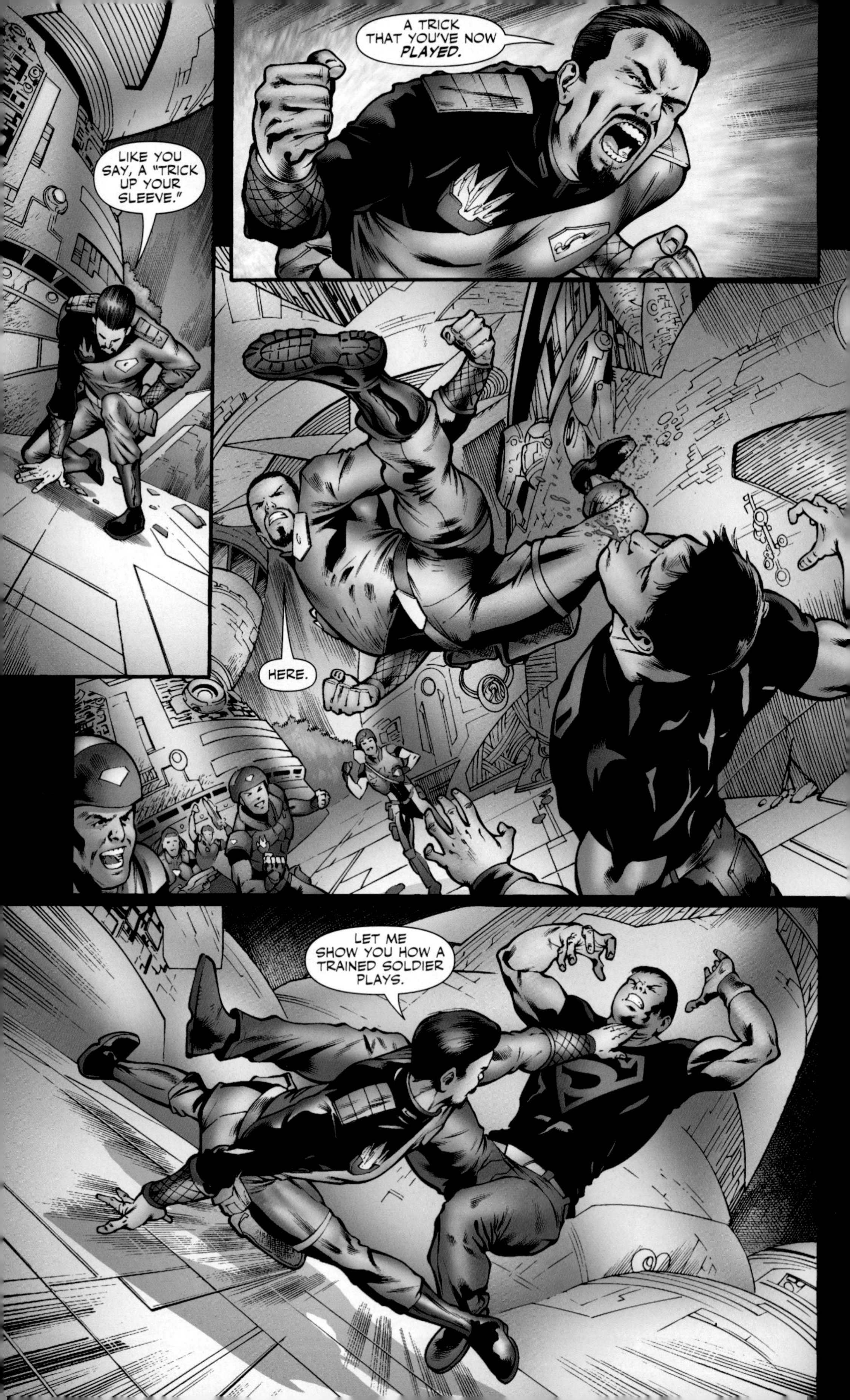
LIKE YOU SAY, A "TRICK UP YOUR SLEEVE."
A TRICK THAT YOU'VE NOW *PLAYED.*
HERE.
LET ME SHOW YOU HOW A TRAINED SOLDIER PLAYS.

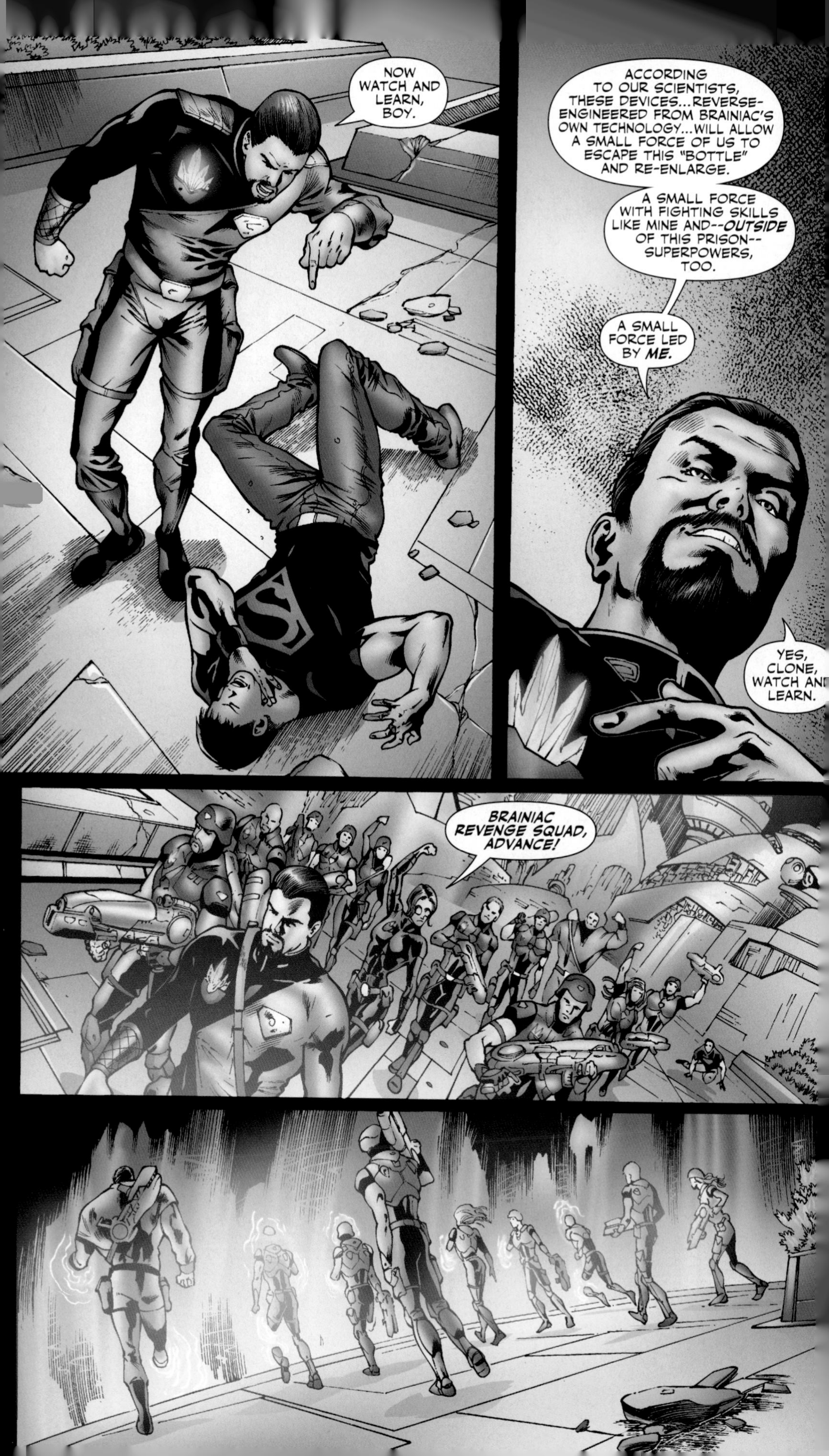
NOW WATCH AND LEARN, BOY.
ACCORDING TO OUR SCIENTISTS, THESE DEVICES...REVERSE-ENGINEERED FROM BRAINIAC'S OWN TECHNOLOGY...WILL ALLOW A SMALL FORCE OF US TO ESCAPE THIS "BOTTLE" AND RE-ENLARGE.
A SMALL FORCE WITH FIGHTING SKILLS LIKE MINE AND--OUTSIDE OF THIS PRISON--SUPERPOWERS, TOO.
A SMALL FORCE LED BY ME.
YES, CLONE, WATCH AND LEARN.
BRAINIAC REVENGE SQUAD, ADVANCE!

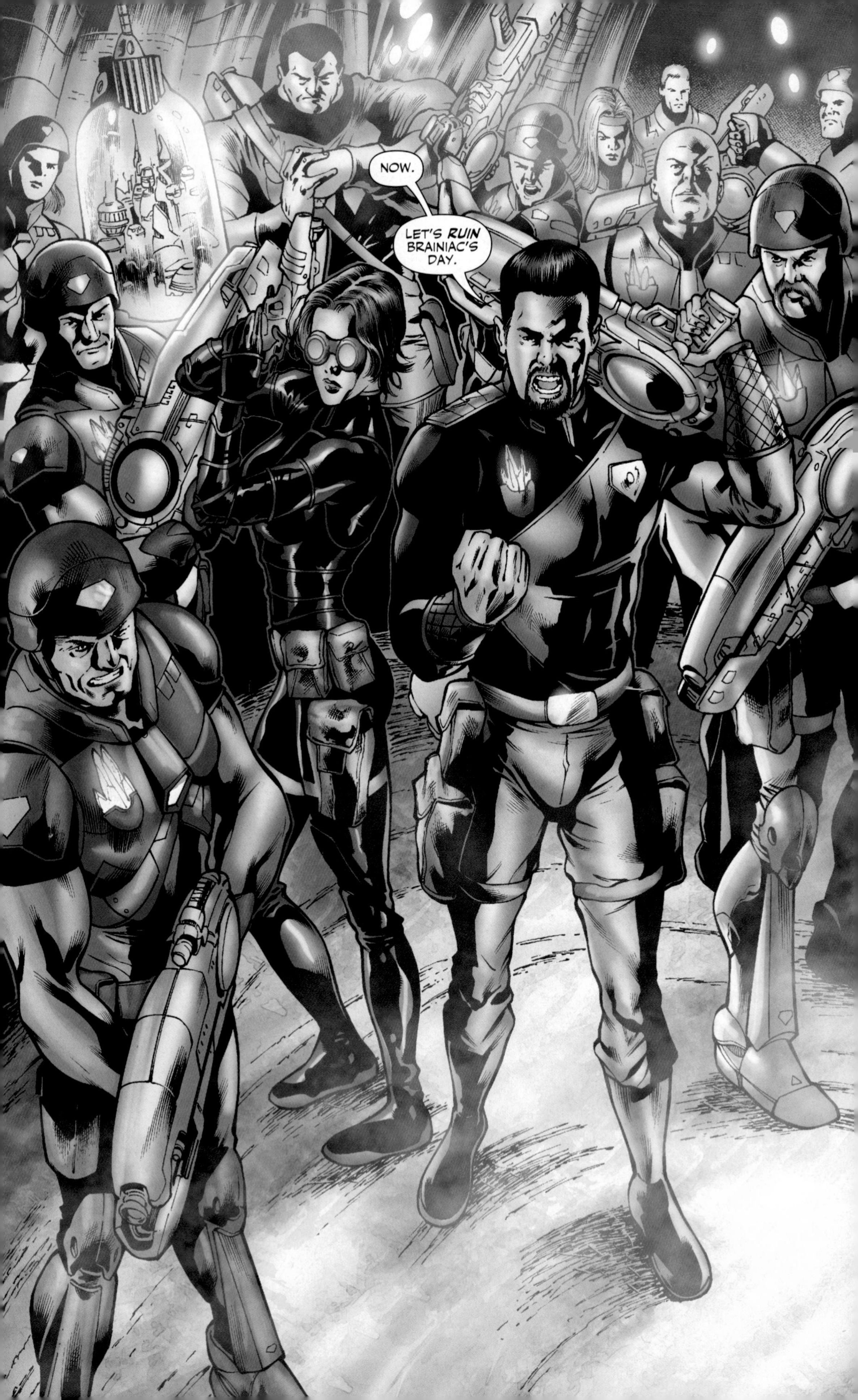
NOW.
LET'S RUIN BRAINIAC'S DAY.

cover by **MATT CAMP** & **NEI RUFFINO**

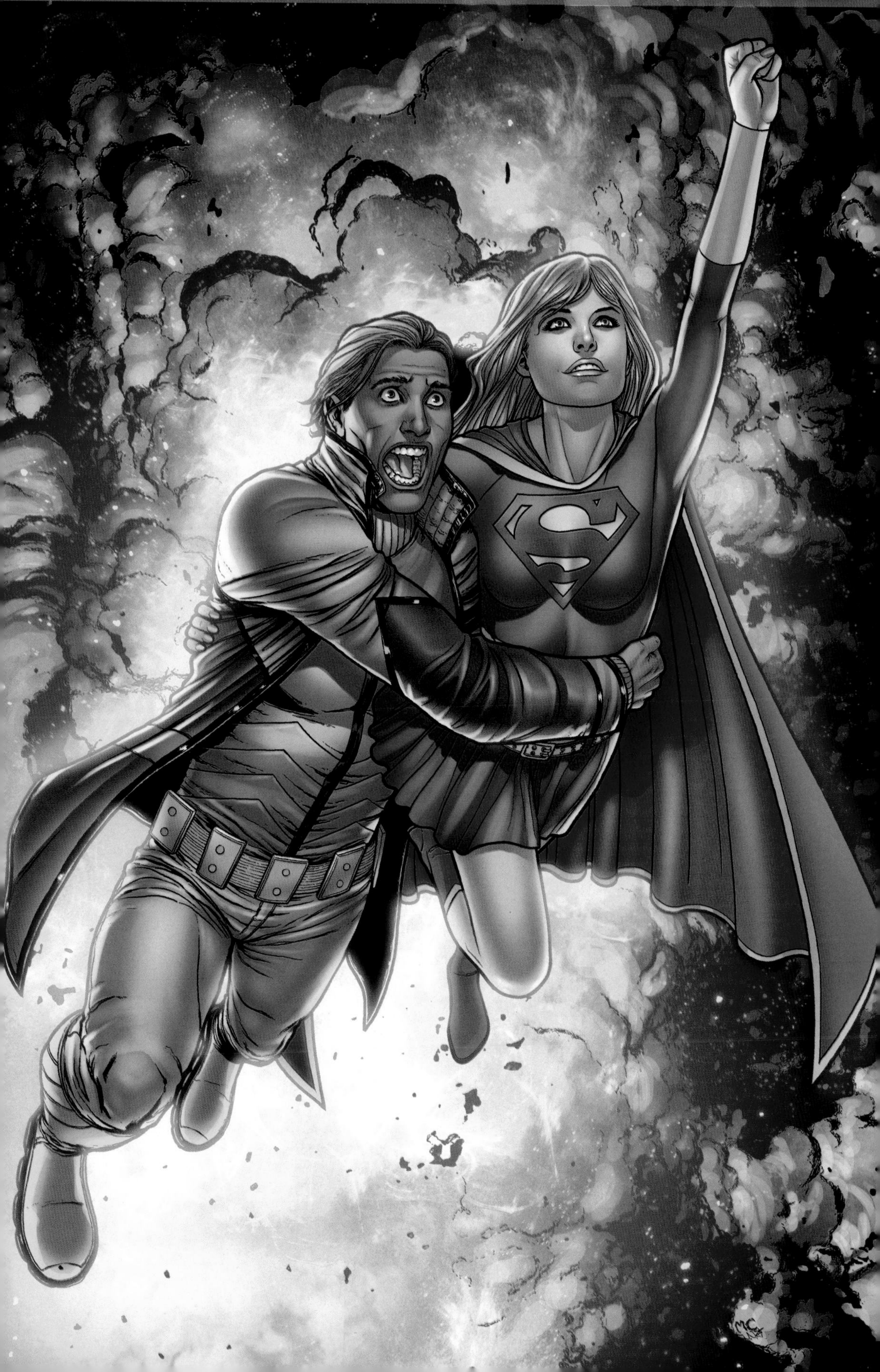

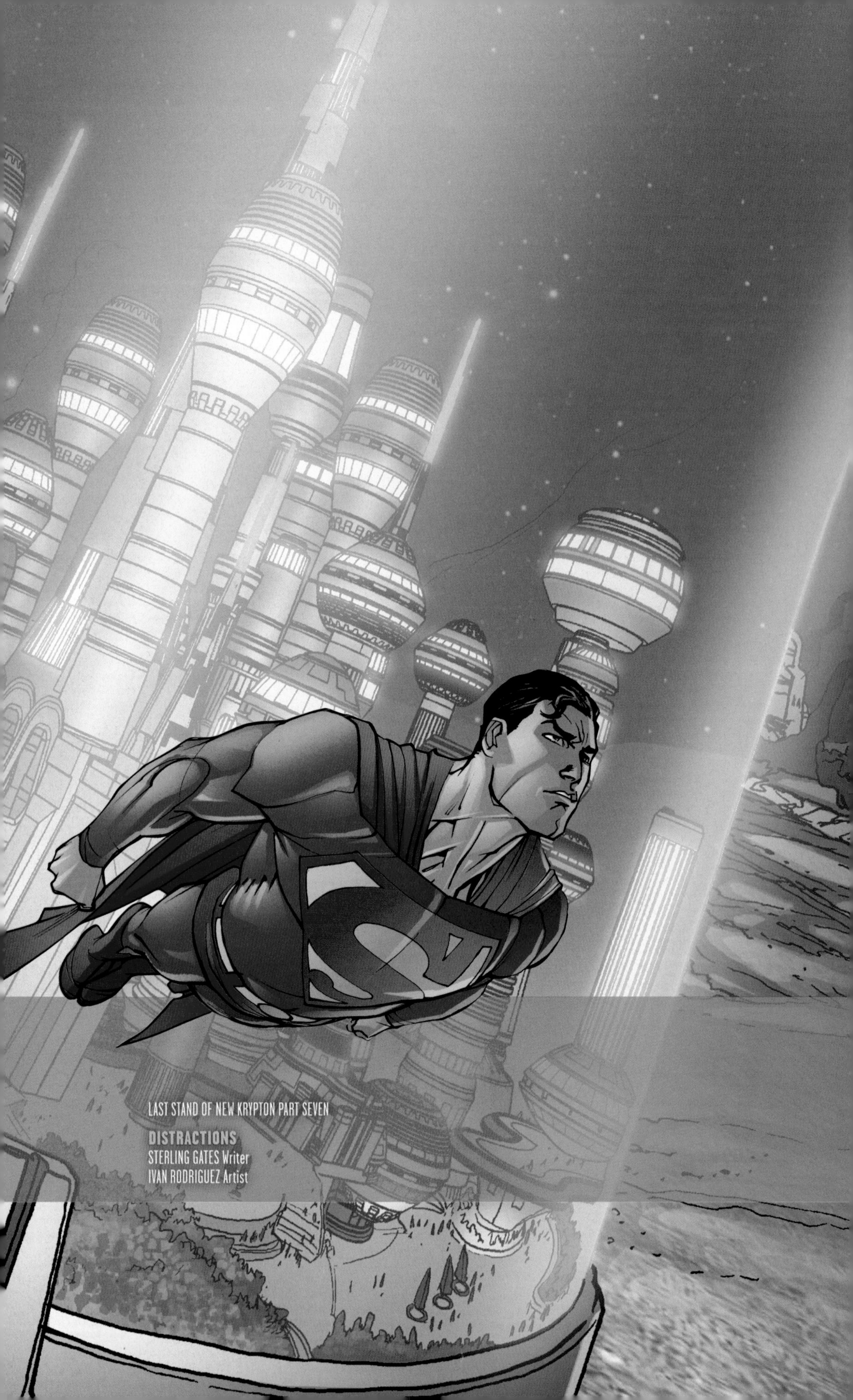
LAST STAND OF NEW KRYPTON PART SEVEN
DISTRACTIONS
STERLING GATES Writer
IVAN RODRIGUEZ Artist

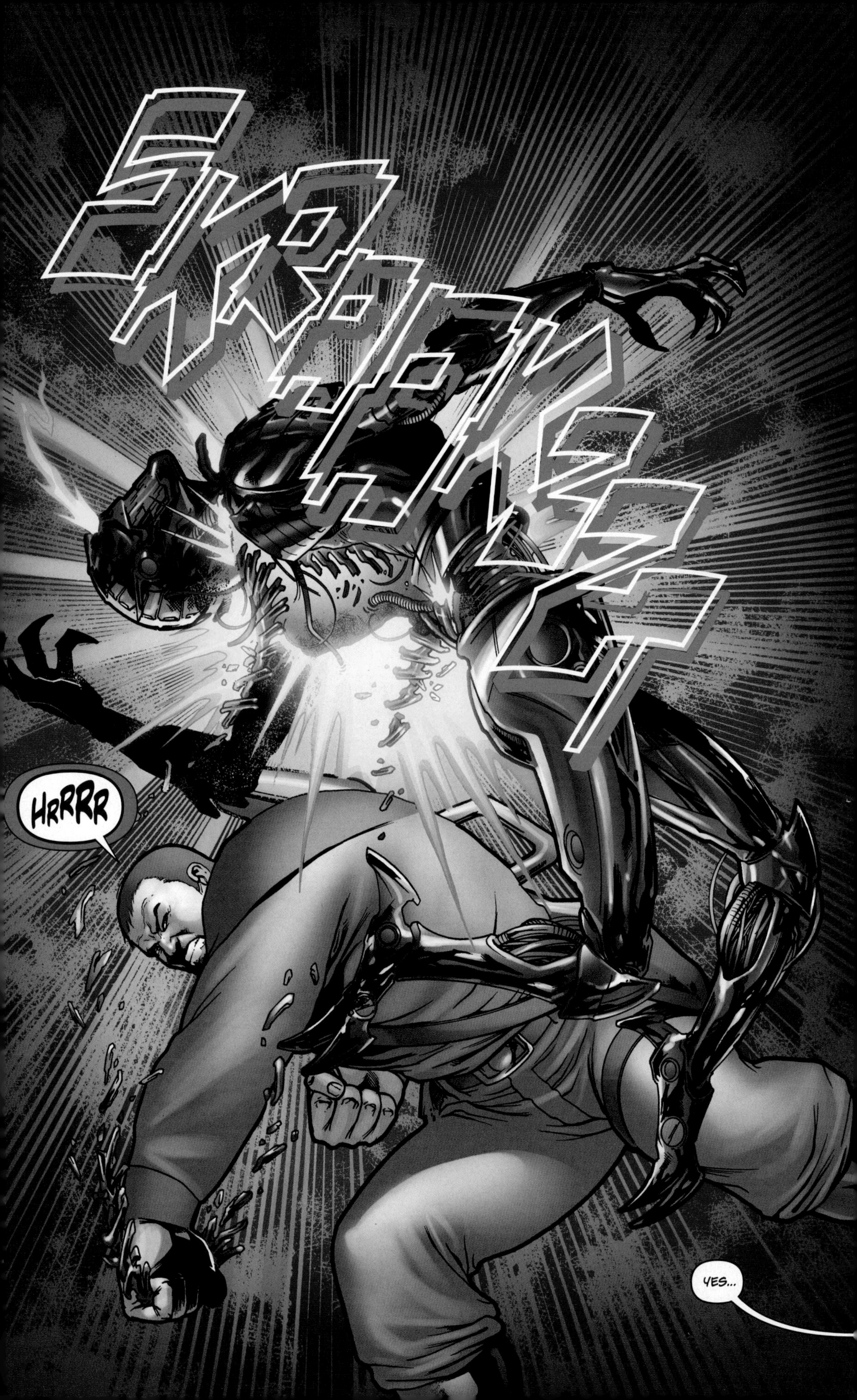
HRRRR
YES...

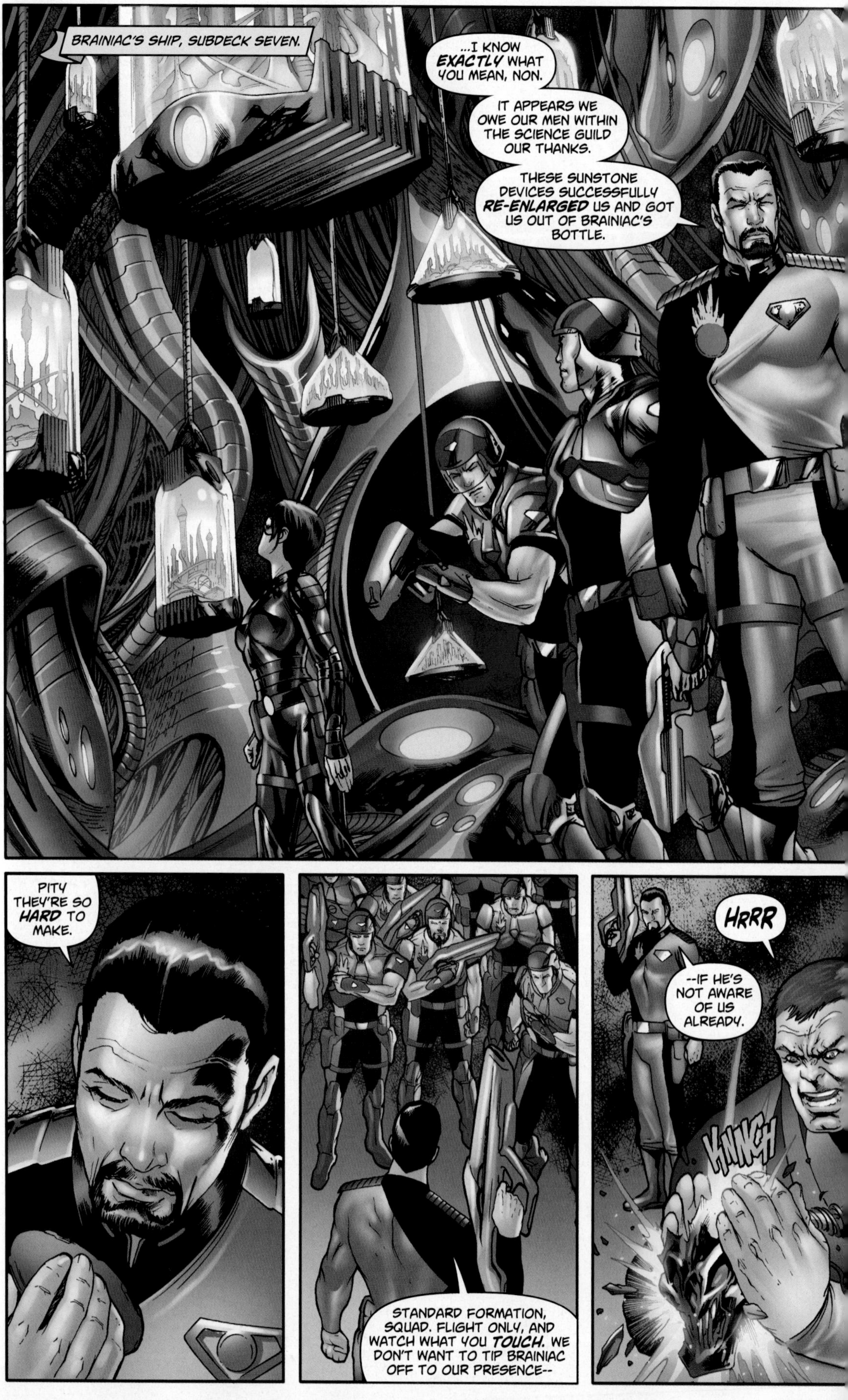
BRAINIAC'S SHIP, SUBDECK SEVEN.
...I KNOW EXACTLY WHAT YOU MEAN, NON.
IT APPEARS WE OWE OUR MEN WITHIN THE SCIENCE GUILD OUR THANKS.
THESE SUNSTONE DEVICES SUCCESSFULLY RE-ENLARGED US AND GOT US OUT OF BRAINIAC'S BOTTLE.
PITY THEY'RE SO HARD TO MAKE.
STANDARD FORMATION, SQUAD. FLIGHT ONLY, AND WATCH WHAT YOU TOUCH. WE DON'T WANT TO TIP BRAINIAC OFF TO OUR PRESENCE--
HRRR
--IF HE'S NOT AWARE OF US ALREADY.
KNNCH

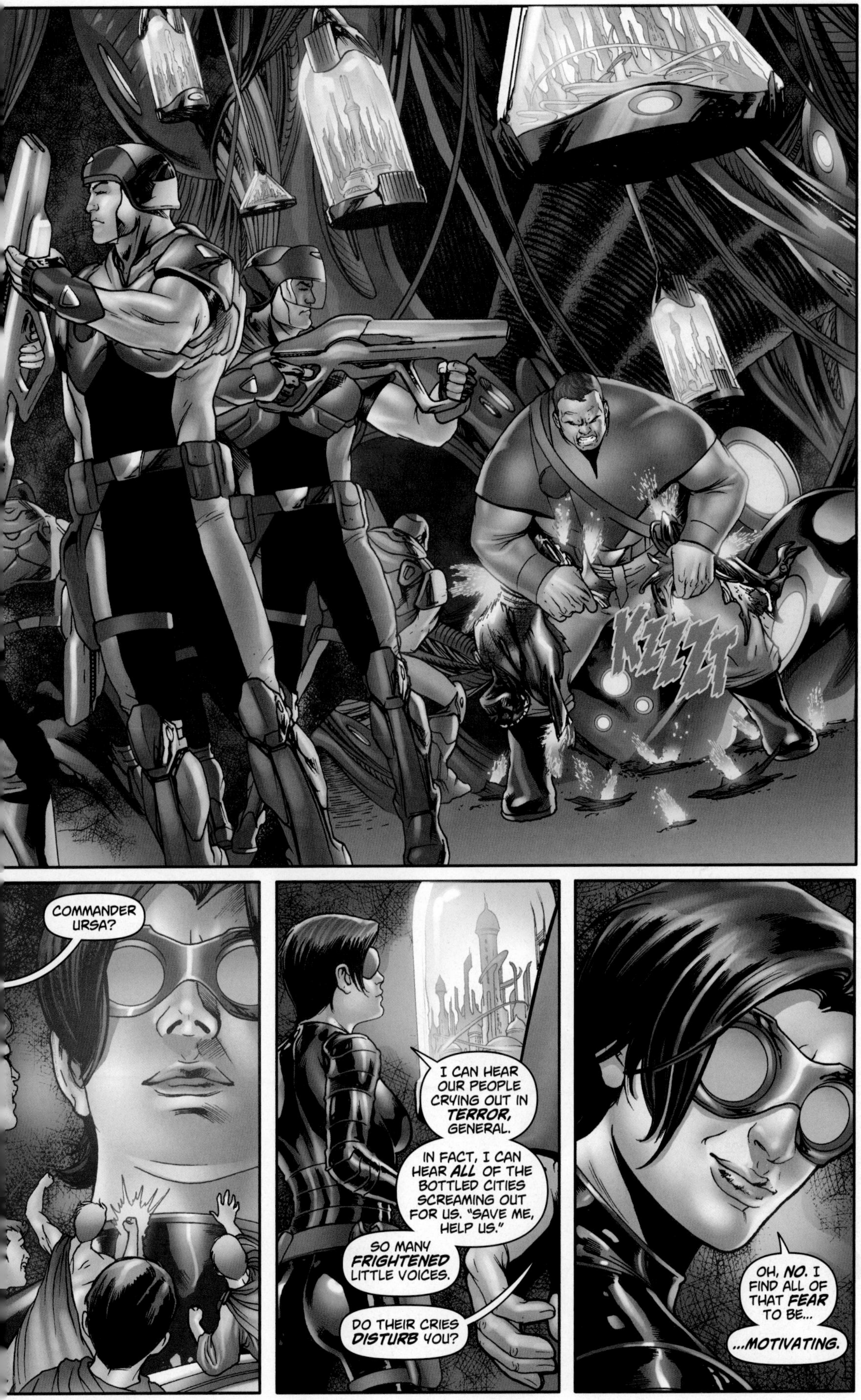
KZZZT
COMMANDER URSA?
I CAN HEAR OUR PEOPLE CRYING OUT IN TERROR, GENERAL.
IN FACT, I CAN HEAR ALL OF THE BOTTLED CITIES SCREAMING OUT FOR US. "SAVE ME, HELP US."
SO MANY FRIGHTENED LITTLE VOICES.
DO THEIR CRIES DISTURB YOU?
OH, NO. I FIND ALL OF THAT FEAR TO BE...
...MOTIVATING.

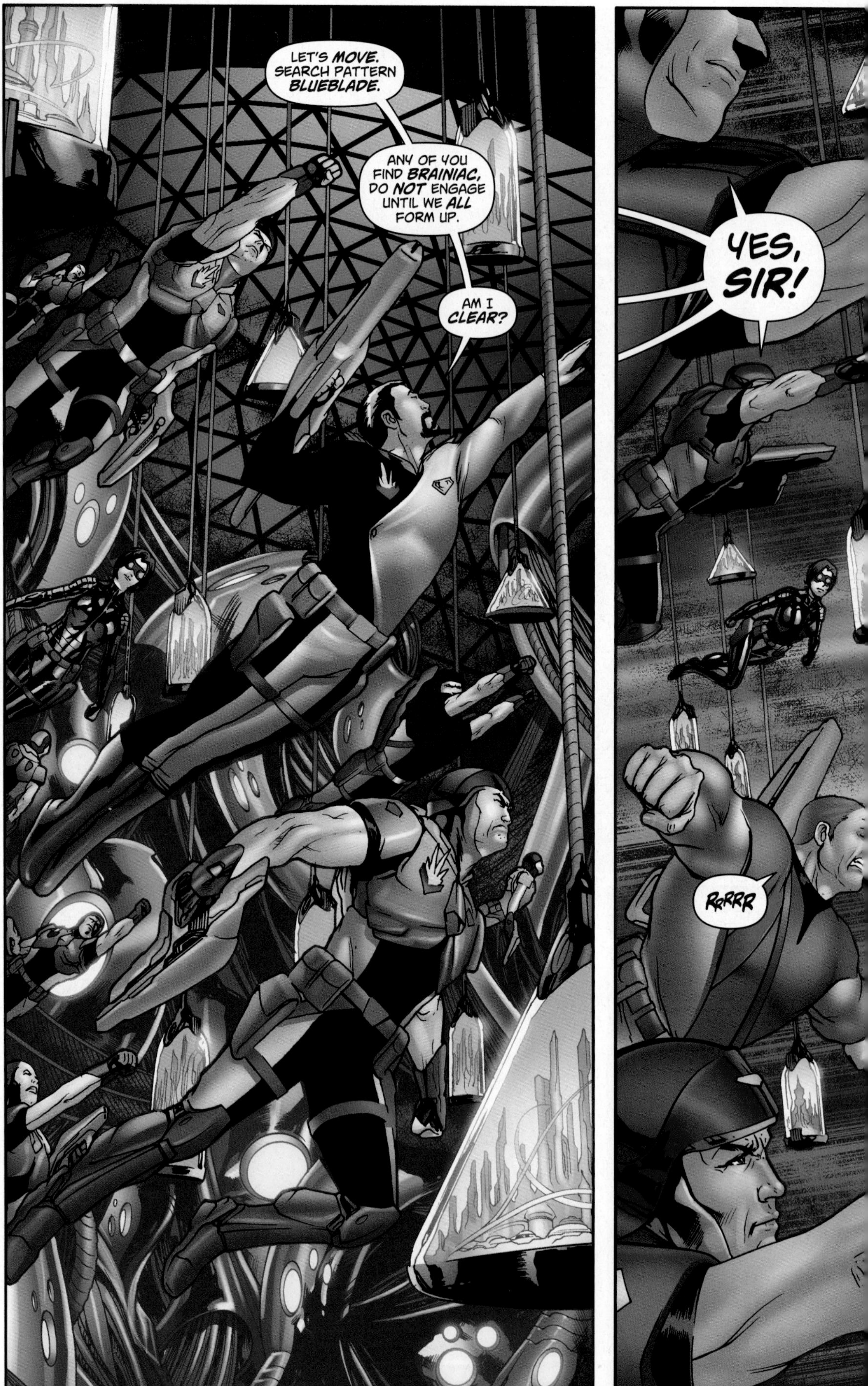
LET'S MOVE. SEARCH PATTERN BLUEBLADE.
ANY OF YOU FIND BRAINIAC, DO NOT ENGAGE UNTIL WE ALL FORM UP.
AM I CLEAR?
YES, SIR!
RRRRR

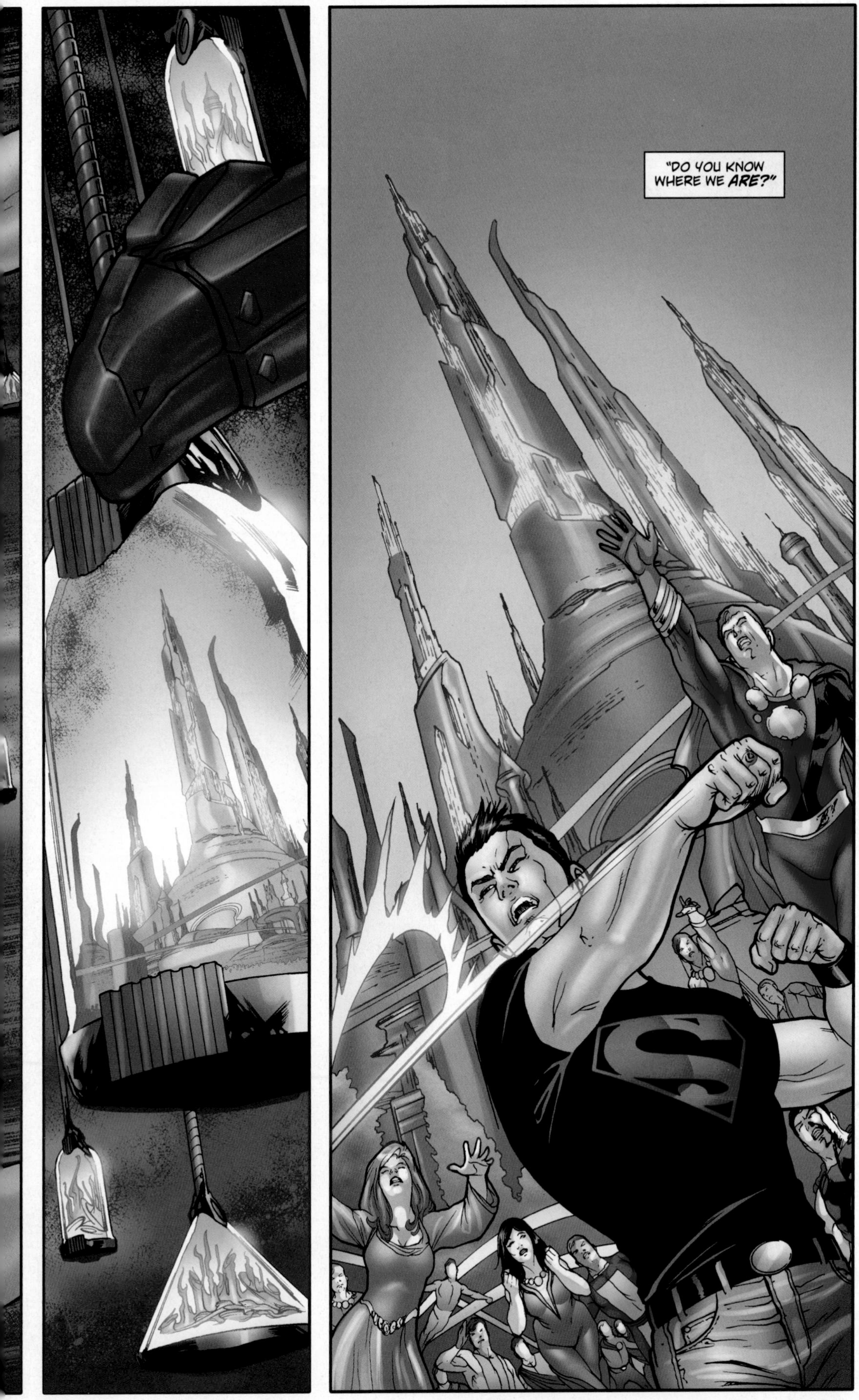
"DO YOU KNOW WHERE WE ARE?"

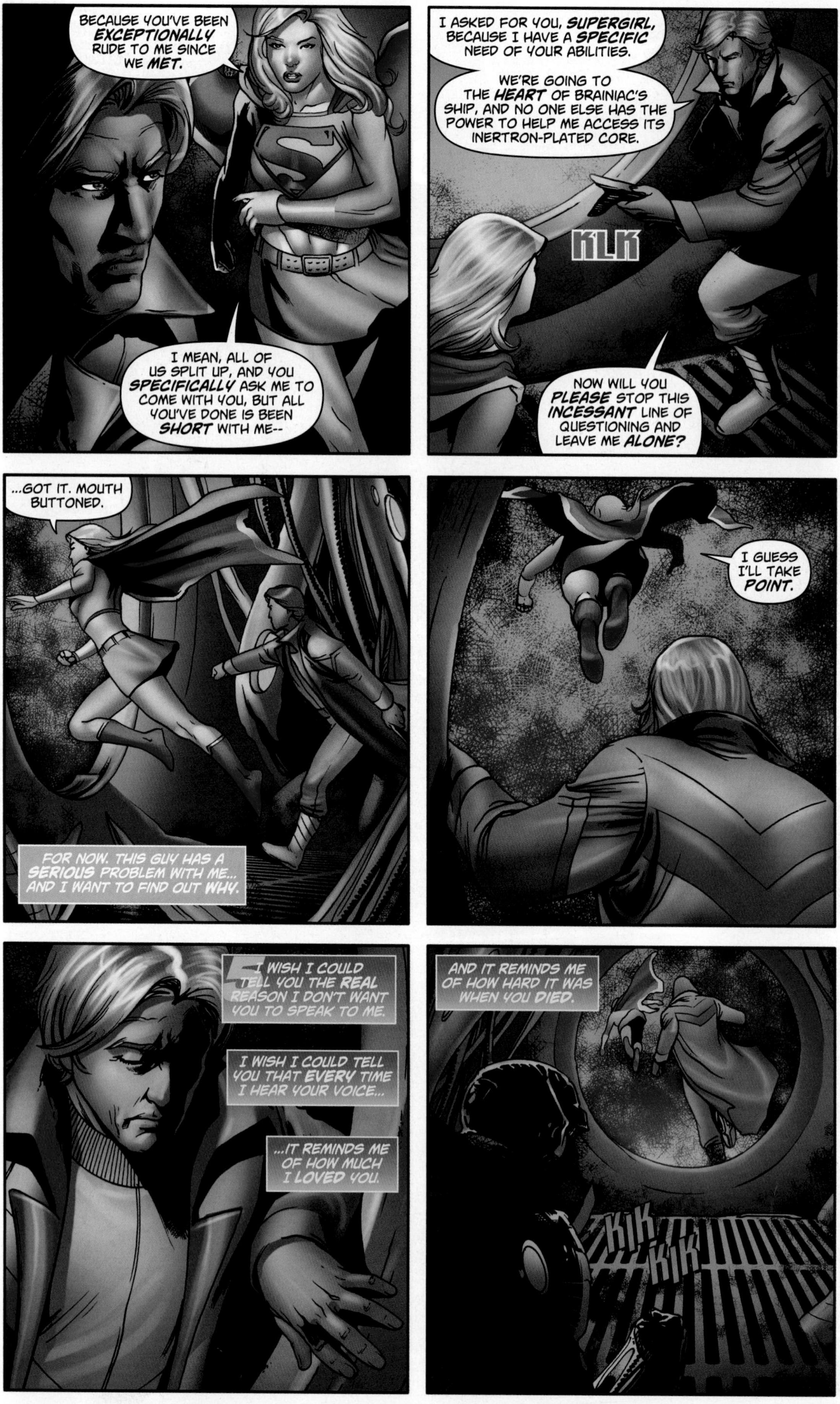
BECAUSE YOU'VE BEEN EXCEPTIONALLY RUDE TO ME SINCE WE MET.
I MEAN, ALL OF US SPLIT UP, AND YOU SPECIFICALLY ASK ME TO COME WITH YOU, BUT ALL YOU'VE DONE IS BEEN SHORT WITH ME--
I ASKED FOR YOU, SUPERGIRL, BECAUSE I HAVE A SPECIFIC NEED OF YOUR ABILITIES.
WE'RE GOING TO THE HEART OF BRAINIAC'S SHIP, AND NO ONE ELSE HAS THE POWER TO HELP ME ACCESS ITS INERTRON-PLATED CORE.
KLK
NOW WILL YOU PLEASE STOP THIS INCESSANT LINE OF QUESTIONING AND LEAVE ME ALONE?
...GOT IT. MOUTH BUTTONED.
FOR NOW. THIS GUY HAS A SERIOUS PROBLEM WITH ME... AND I WANT TO FIND OUT WHY.
I GUESS I'LL TAKE POINT.
I WISH I COULD TELL YOU THE REAL REASON I DON'T WANT YOU TO SPEAK TO ME.
I WISH I COULD TELL YOU THAT EVERY TIME I HEAR YOUR VOICE...
...IT REMINDS ME OF HOW MUCH I LOVED YOU.
AND IT REMINDS ME OF HOW HARD IT WAS WHEN YOU DIED.
KIK KIK

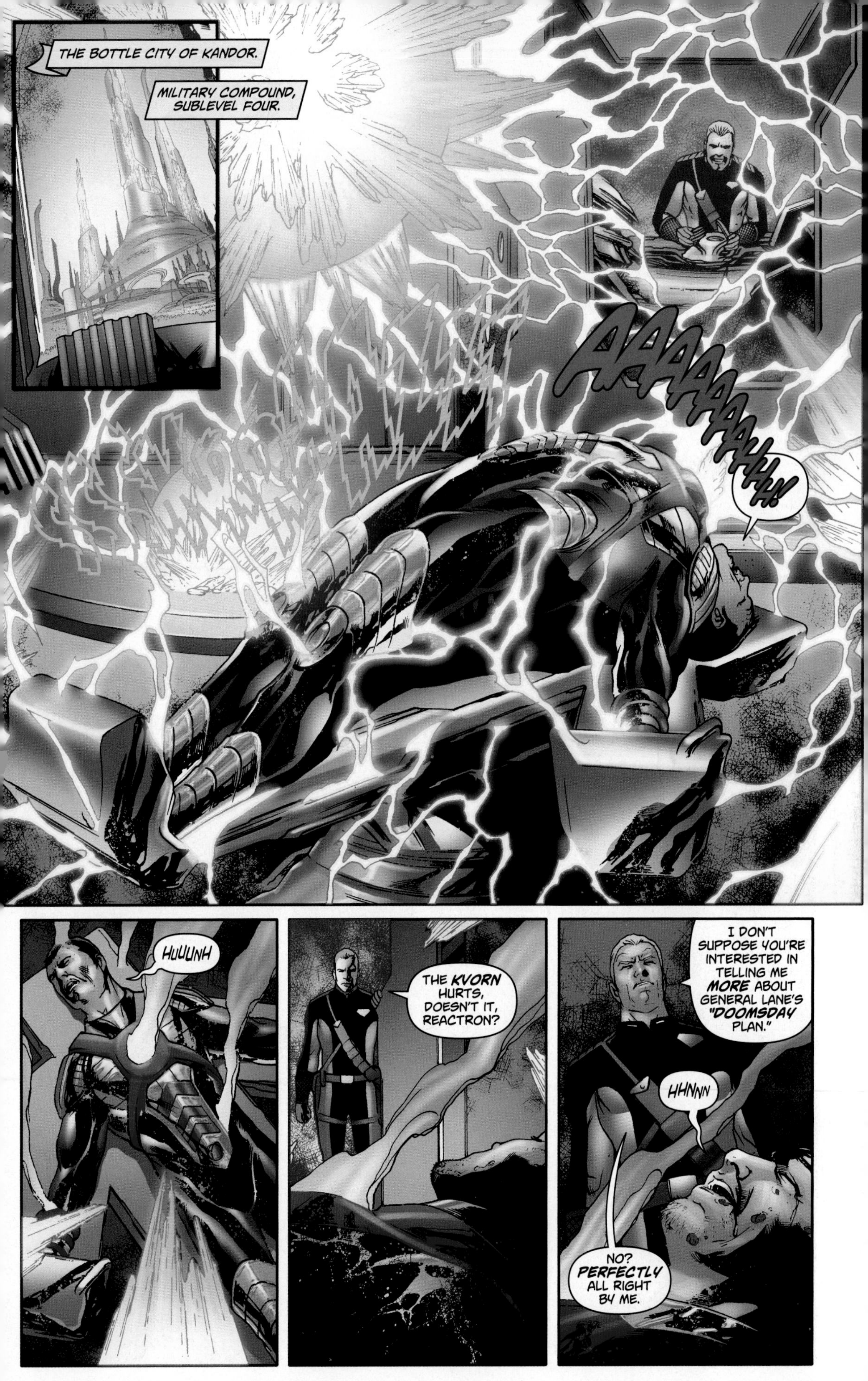
THE BOTTLE CITY OF KANDOR.
MILITARY COMPOUND, SUBLEVEL FOUR.
AAAAAAAAHHH!
HUUUNH
THE KVORN HURTS, DOESN'T IT, REACTRON?
I DON'T SUPPOSE YOU'RE INTERESTED IN TELLING ME MORE ABOUT GENERAL LANE'S "DOOMSDAY PLAN."
HHNNN
NO? PERFECTLY ALL RIGHT BY ME.

AS YOU KNOW, ALURA HAS GIVEN ME THE *FREEDOM* TO DO WHATEVER I *WANT* TO YOU. NO ONE KNOWS YOU'RE *DOWN* HERE BUT SHE AND I.

AND SHE DOESN'T NEED YOUR *BODY*. SHE JUST WANTS THE *INFORMATION* IN YOUR *HEAD*.

I'LL... HNNNH... I'LL... K-K-KLL YOU... GOR...

THREATS?

NO, YOU TRIED THOSE LAST WEEK, REMEMBER? ALL *THAT* GOT YOU WAS AN EXTRA FIFTEEN MINUTES UNDER THE *KVORN*.

MAYBE YOU *DON'T* REMEMBER.

MAYBE I SHOULD GIVE YOU ANOTHER FEW MINUTES NOW. JUST TO *REFRESH* YOUR MEMORY.

PLS... NO...GR... *PLEASE*...

≷SNF≷

IT'S *COMMANDER* GOR. TO YOU.

WRRRRR

AH. MISTRESS ALURA. COME TO *CHECK* ON ME?

ARE THE *CATTLE* STILL PANICKING AND *HAMMERING* AWAY AT THE FORCE FIELD?

DON'T THEY REALIZE THAT'S *POINTLESS*, AND THAT GENERAL *ZOD* WILL *SAVE* US--

FZZT

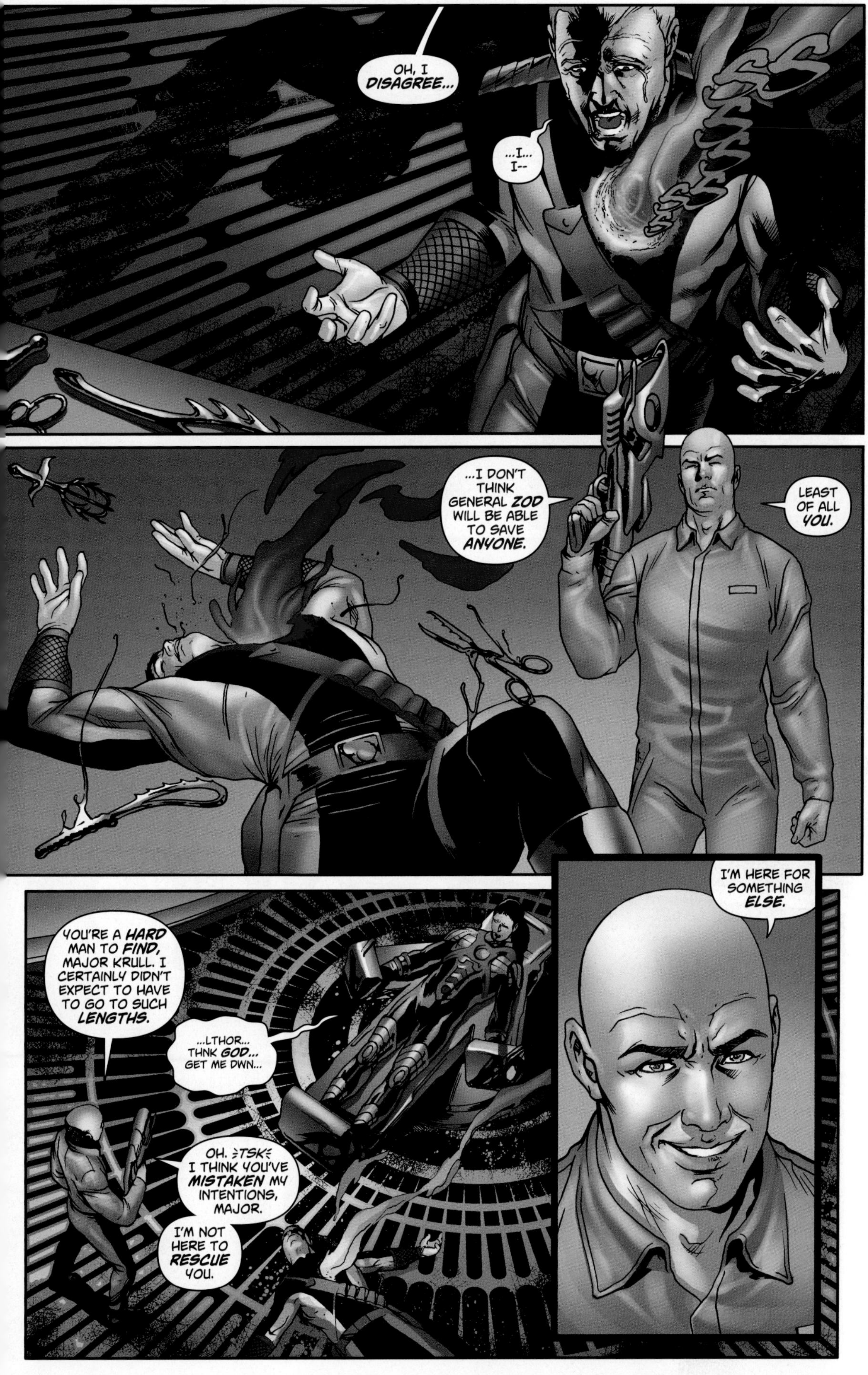
OH, I DISAGREE...
...I... I--
...I DON'T THINK GENERAL ZOD WILL BE ABLE TO SAVE ANYONE.
LEAST OF ALL YOU.
YOU'RE A HARD MAN TO FIND, MAJOR KRULL. I CERTAINLY DIDN'T EXPECT TO HAVE TO GO TO SUCH LENGTHS.
...LTHOR... THNK GOD... GET ME DWN...
OH. TSK I THINK YOU'VE MISTAKEN MY INTENTIONS, MAJOR.
I'M NOT HERE TO RESCUE YOU.
I'M HERE FOR SOMETHING ELSE.

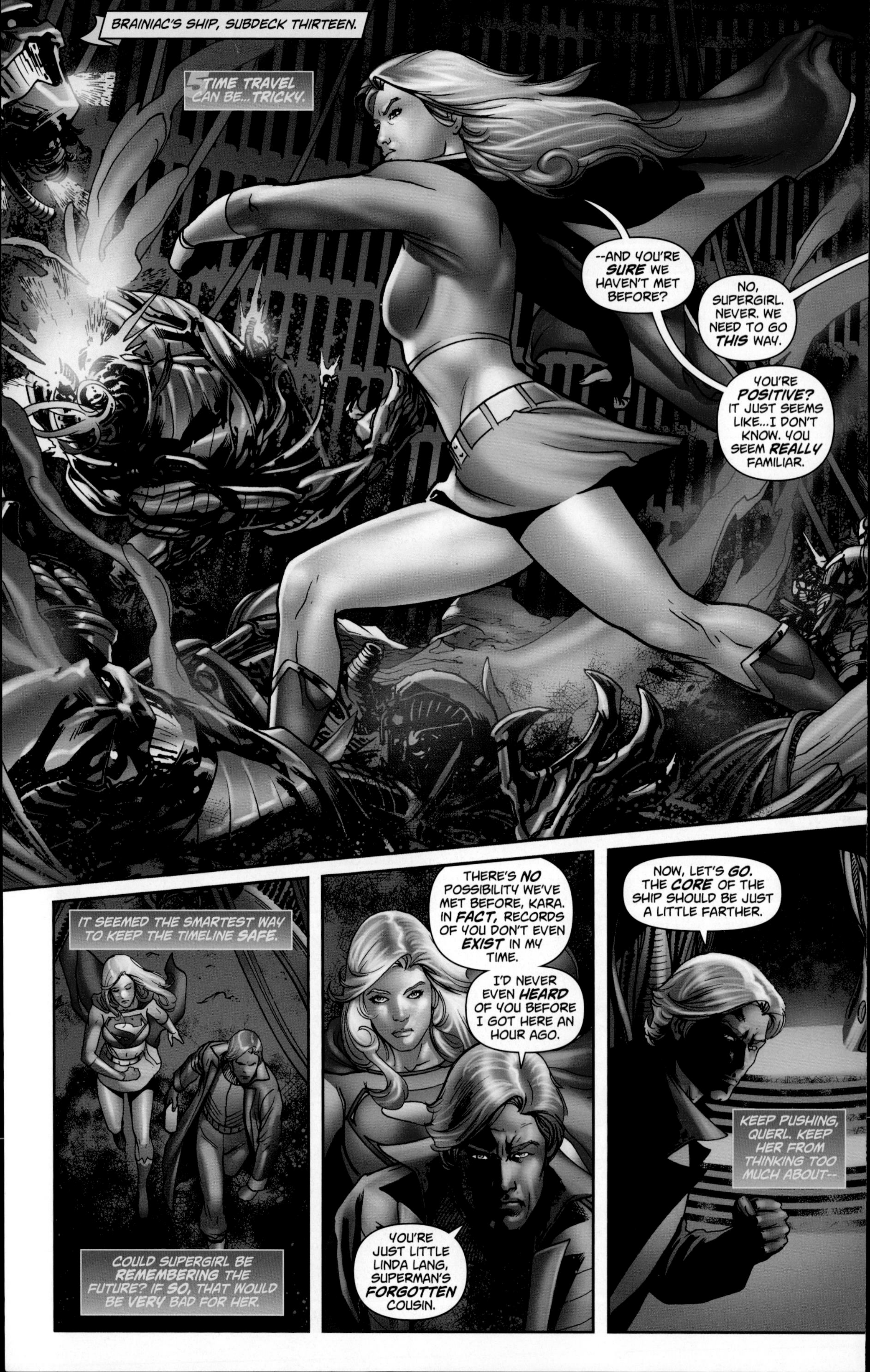

BRAINIAC'S SHIP, SUBDECK THIRTEEN.
5TIME TRAVEL CAN BE...TRICKY.
--AND YOU'RE SURE WE HAVEN'T MET BEFORE?
NO, SUPERGIRL. NEVER. WE NEED TO GO THIS WAY.
YOU'RE POSITIVE? IT JUST SEEMS LIKE...I DON'T KNOW. YOU SEEM REALLY FAMILIAR.
IT SEEMED THE SMARTEST WAY TO KEEP THE TIMELINE SAFE.
COULD SUPERGIRL BE REMEMBERING THE FUTURE? IF SO, THAT WOULD BE VERY BAD FOR HER.
THERE'S NO POSSIBILITY WE'VE MET BEFORE, KARA. IN FACT, RECORDS OF YOU DON'T EVEN EXIST IN MY TIME.
I'D NEVER EVEN HEARD OF YOU BEFORE I GOT HERE AN HOUR AGO.
YOU'RE JUST LITTLE LINDA LANG, SUPERMAN'S FORGOTTEN COUSIN.
NOW, LET'S GO. THE CORE OF THE SHIP SHOULD BE JUST A LITTLE FARTHER.
KEEP PUSHING, QUERL. KEEP HER FROM THINKING TOO MUCH ABOUT--

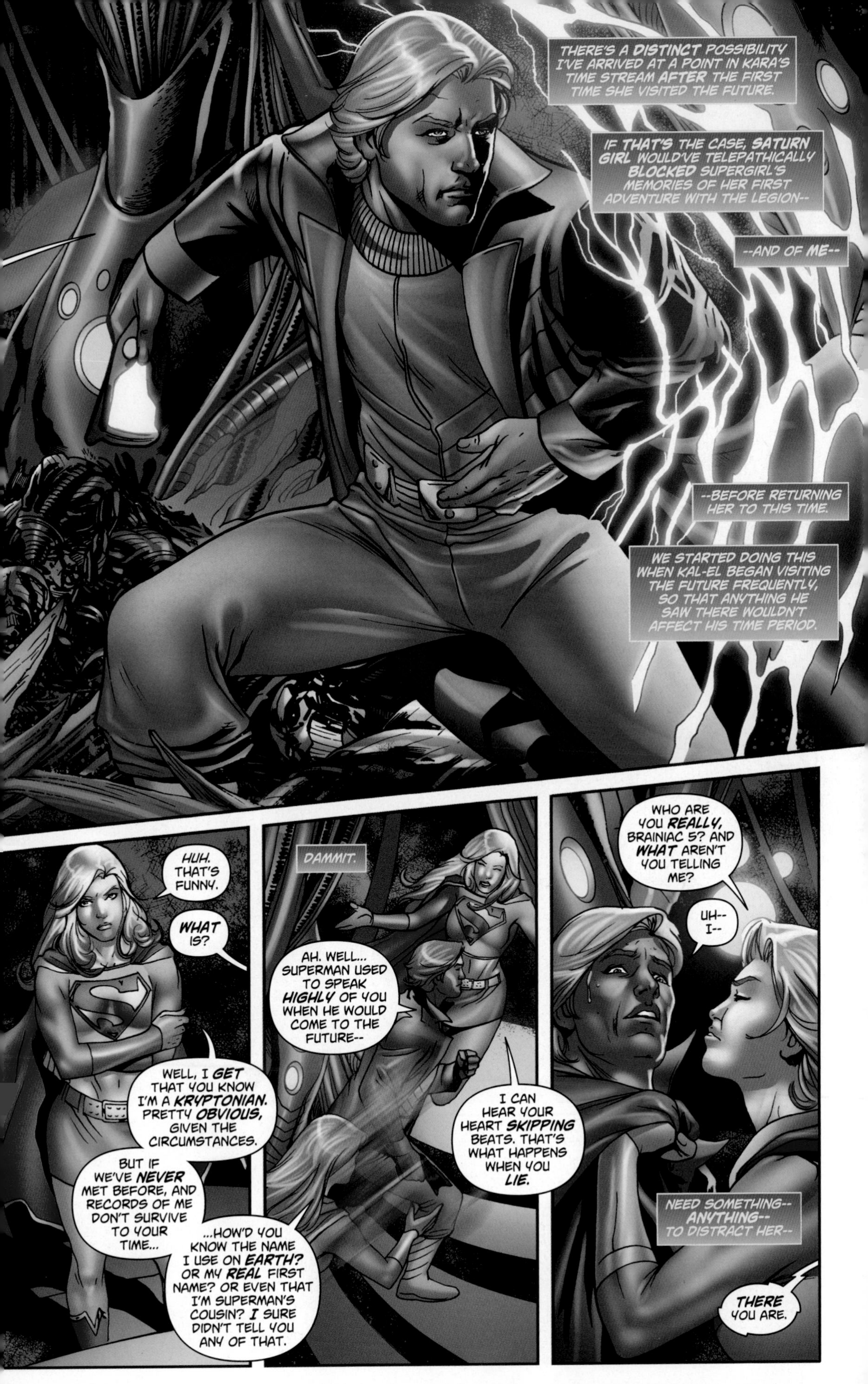
THERE'S A DISTINCT POSSIBILITY I'VE ARRIVED AT A POINT IN KARA'S TIME STREAM AFTER THE FIRST TIME SHE VISITED THE FUTURE.
IF THAT'S THE CASE, SATURN GIRL WOULD'VE TELEPATHICALLY BLOCKED SUPERGIRL'S MEMORIES OF HER FIRST ADVENTURE WITH THE LEGION--
--AND OF ME--
--BEFORE RETURNING HER TO THIS TIME.
WE STARTED DOING THIS WHEN KAL-EL BEGAN VISITING THE FUTURE FREQUENTLY, SO THAT ANYTHING HE SAW THERE WOULDN'T AFFECT HIS TIME PERIOD.
HUH. THAT'S FUNNY.
WHAT IS?
WELL, I GET THAT YOU KNOW I'M A KRYPTONIAN. PRETTY OBVIOUS, GIVEN THE CIRCUMSTANCES.
BUT IF WE'VE NEVER MET BEFORE, AND RECORDS OF ME DON'T SURVIVE TO YOUR TIME...
...HOW'D YOU KNOW THE NAME I USE ON EARTH? OR MY REAL FIRST NAME? OR EVEN THAT I'M SUPERMAN'S COUSIN? I SURE DIDN'T TELL YOU ANY OF THAT.
DAMMIT.
AH. WELL... SUPERMAN USED TO SPEAK HIGHLY OF YOU WHEN HE WOULD COME TO THE FUTURE--
I CAN HEAR YOUR HEART SKIPPING BEATS. THAT'S WHAT HAPPENS WHEN YOU LIE.
WHO ARE YOU REALLY, BRAINIAC 5? AND WHAT AREN'T YOU TELLING ME?
UH-- I--
NEED SOMETHING-- ANYTHING-- TO DISTRACT HER--
THERE YOU ARE.

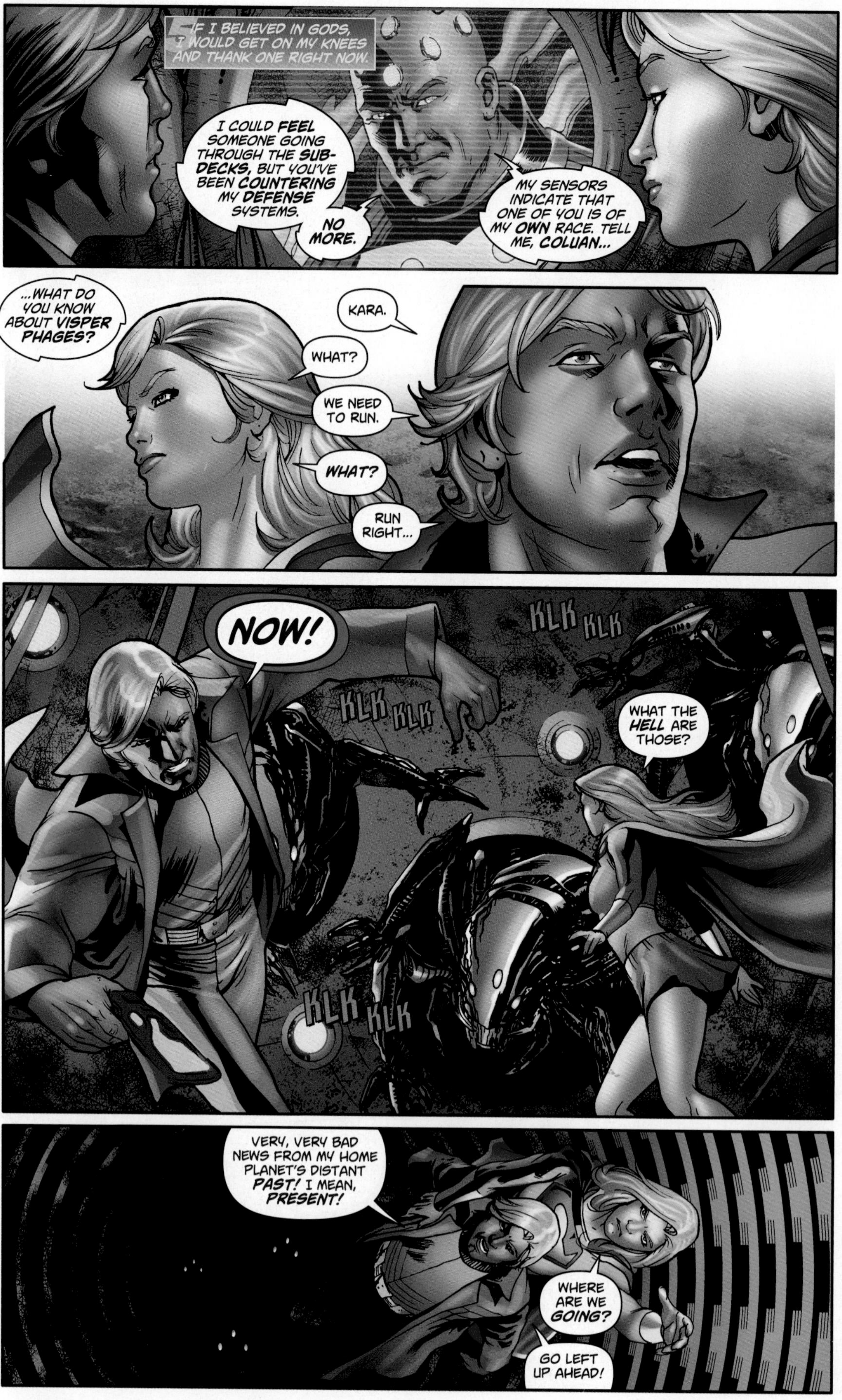

5
IF I BELIEVED IN GODS, I WOULD GET ON MY KNEES AND THANK ONE RIGHT NOW.
I COULD FEEL SOMEONE GOING THROUGH THE SUB-DECKS, BUT YOU'VE BEEN COUNTERING MY DEFENSE SYSTEMS.
NO MORE.
MY SENSORS INDICATE THAT ONE OF YOU IS OF MY OWN RACE. TELL ME, COLUAN...
...WHAT DO YOU KNOW ABOUT VISPER PHAGES?
KARA.
WHAT?
WE NEED TO RUN.
WHAT?
RUN RIGHT...
NOW!
KLK KLK
KLK KLK
WHAT THE HELL ARE THOSE?
KLK KLK
VERY, VERY BAD NEWS FROM MY HOME PLANET'S DISTANT PAST! I MEAN, PRESENT!
WHERE ARE WE GOING?
GO LEFT UP AHEAD!

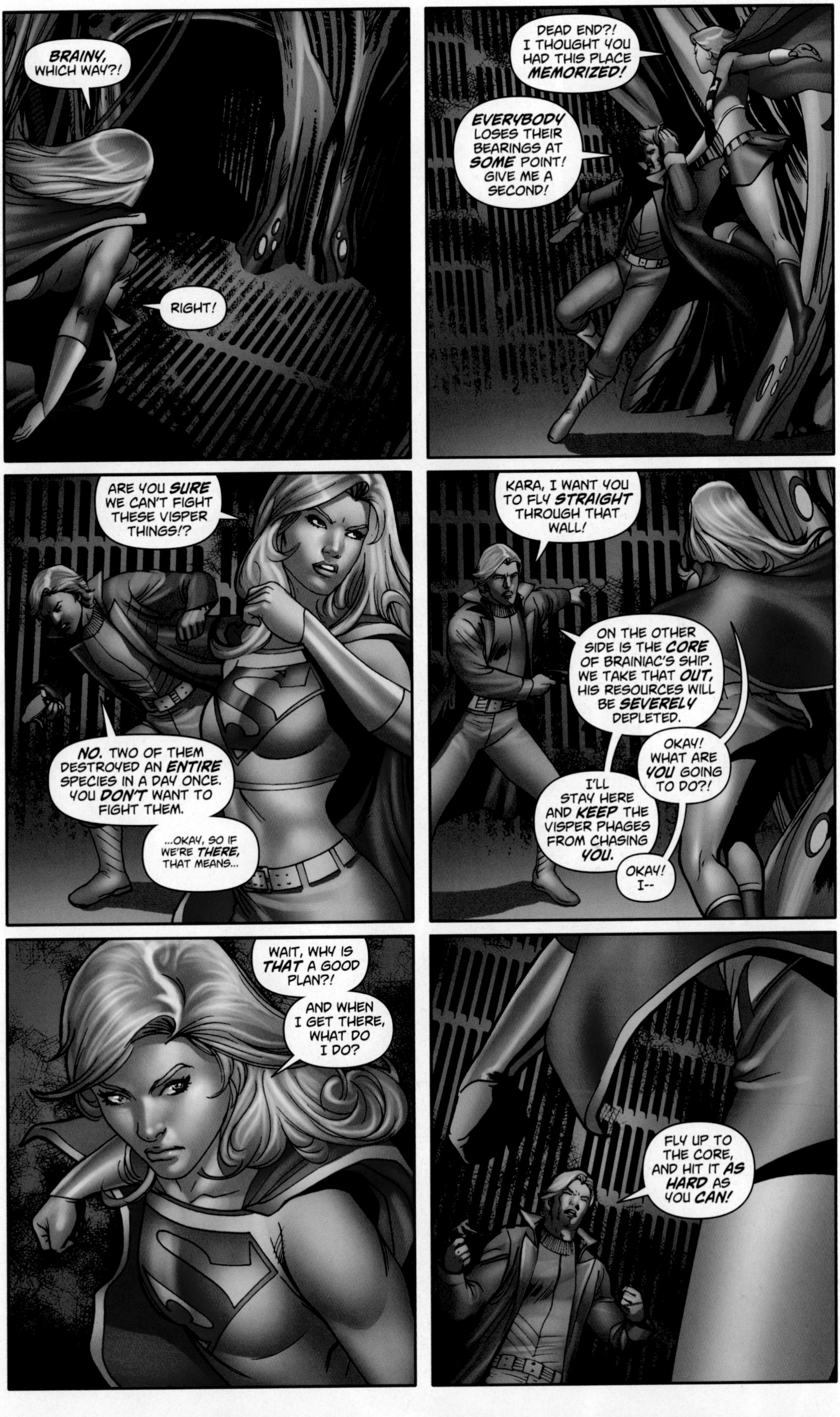
BRAINY, WHICH WAY?!
RIGHT!
DEAD END?! I THOUGHT YOU HAD THIS PLACE MEMORIZED!
EVERYBODY LOSES THEIR BEARINGS AT SOME POINT! GIVE ME A SECOND!
ARE YOU SURE WE CAN'T FIGHT THESE VISPER THINGS!?
NO. TWO OF THEM DESTROYED AN ENTIRE SPECIES IN A DAY ONCE. YOU DON'T WANT TO FIGHT THEM.
...OKAY, SO IF WE'RE THERE, THAT MEANS...
KARA, I WANT YOU TO FLY STRAIGHT THROUGH THAT WALL!
ON THE OTHER SIDE IS THE CORE OF BRAINIAC'S SHIP. WE TAKE THAT OUT, HIS RESOURCES WILL BE SEVERELY DEPLETED.
OKAY! WHAT ARE YOU GOING TO DO?!
I'LL STAY HERE AND KEEP THE VISPER PHAGES FROM CHASING YOU.
OKAY! I--
WAIT, WHY IS THAT A GOOD PLAN?!
AND WHEN I GET THERE, WHAT DO I DO?
FLY UP TO THE CORE, AND HIT IT AS HARD AS YOU CAN!

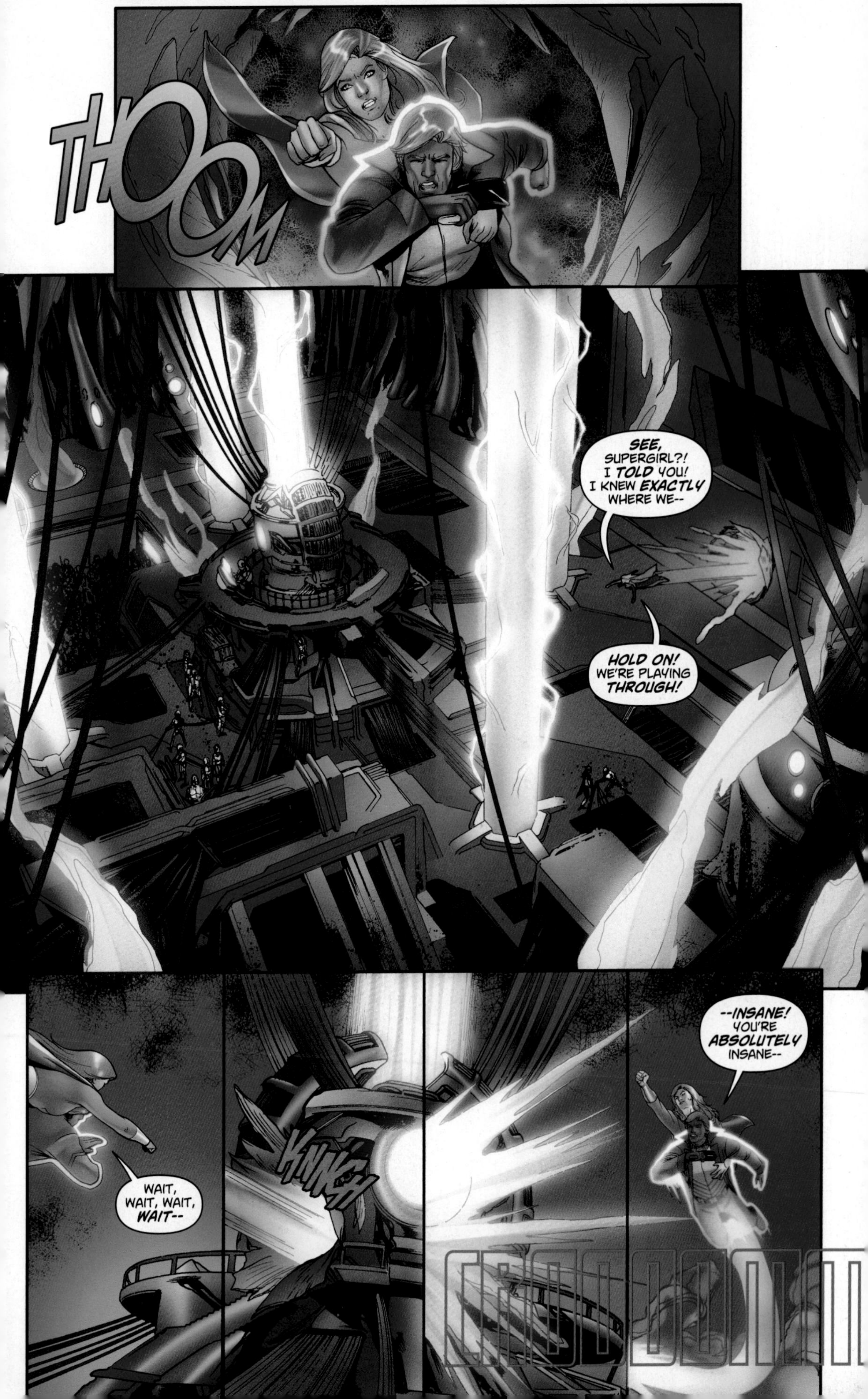
THOOM
SEE, SUPERGIRL?! I TOLD YOU! I KNEW EXACTLY WHERE WE--
HOLD ON! WE'RE PLAYING THROUGH!
WAIT, WAIT, WAIT, WAIT--
KNNCH
--INSANE! YOU'RE ABSOLUTELY INSANE--

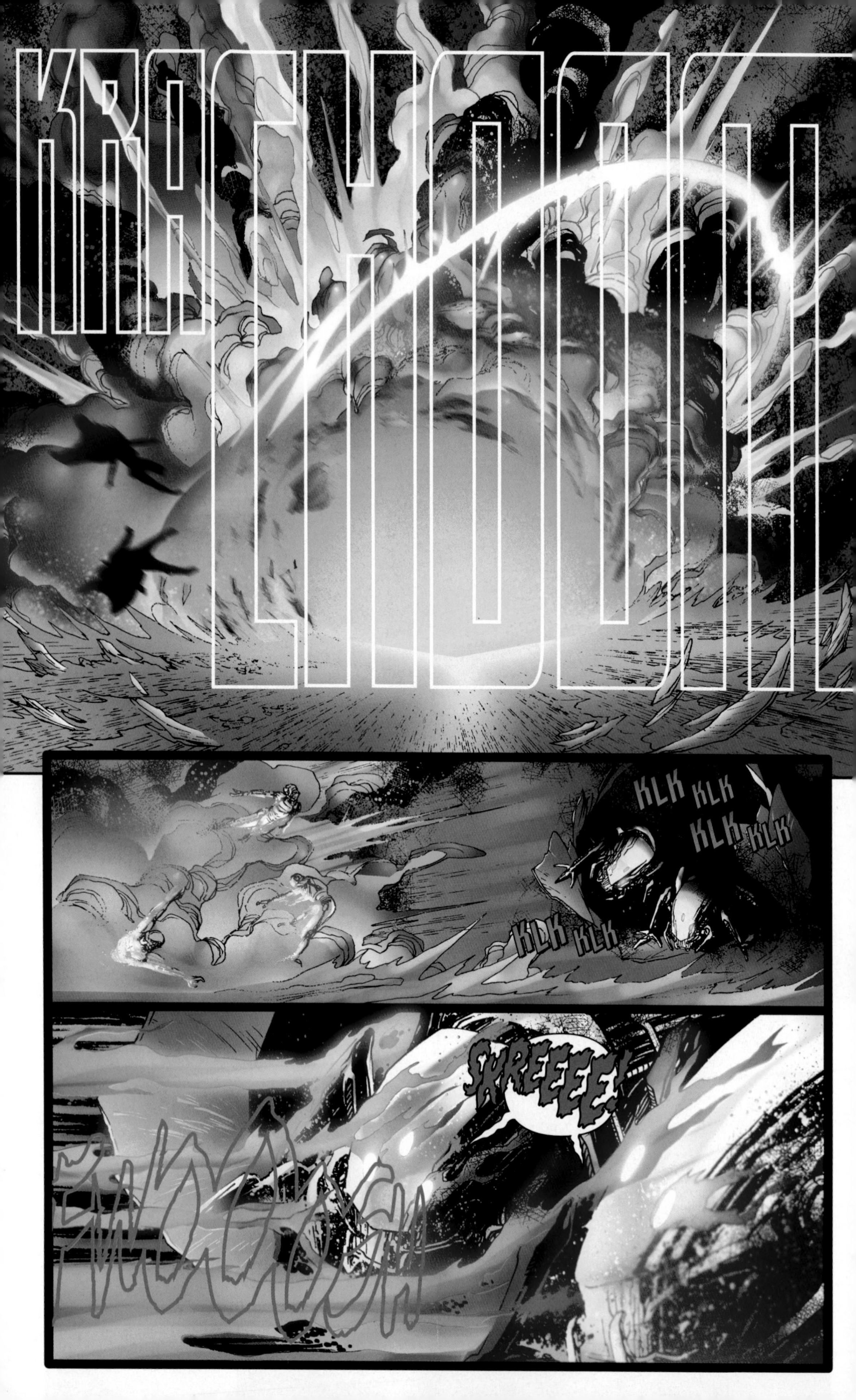
KLK KLK
KLK KLK
KLK KLK
SKREEEEE!

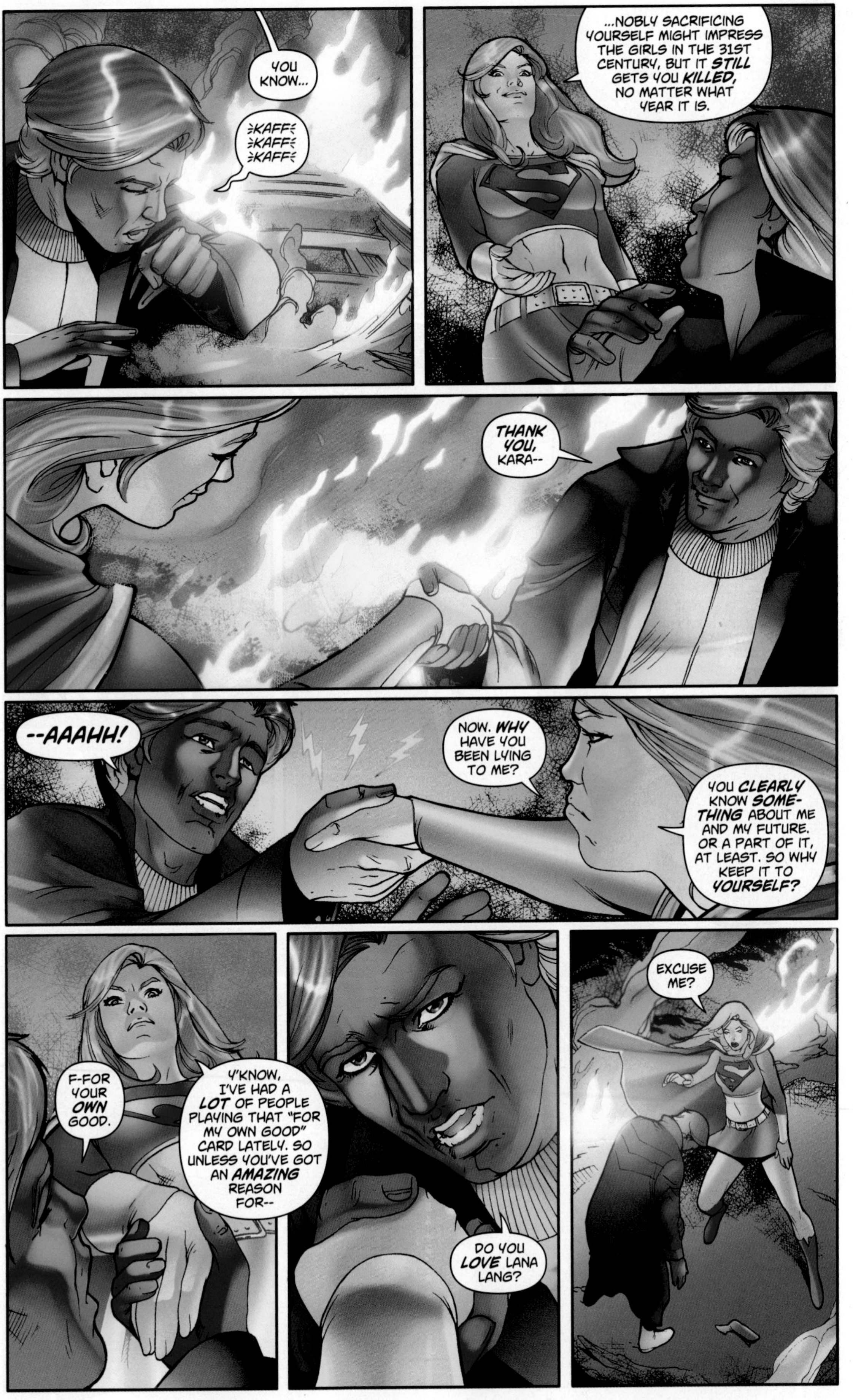
YOU KNOW...
KAFF KAFF KAFF
...NOBLY SACRIFICING YOURSELF MIGHT IMPRESS THE GIRLS IN THE 31ST CENTURY, BUT IT STILL GETS YOU KILLED, NO MATTER WHAT YEAR IT IS.
THANK YOU, KARA--
--AAAHH!
NOW. WHY HAVE YOU BEEN LYING TO ME?
YOU CLEARLY KNOW SOMETHING ABOUT ME AND MY FUTURE. OR A PART OF IT, AT LEAST. SO WHY KEEP IT TO YOURSELF?
F-FOR YOUR OWN GOOD.
Y'KNOW, I'VE HAD A LOT OF PEOPLE PLAYING THAT "FOR MY OWN GOOD" CARD LATELY. SO UNLESS YOU'VE GOT AN AMAZING REASON FOR--
DO YOU LOVE LANA LANG?
EXCUSE ME?

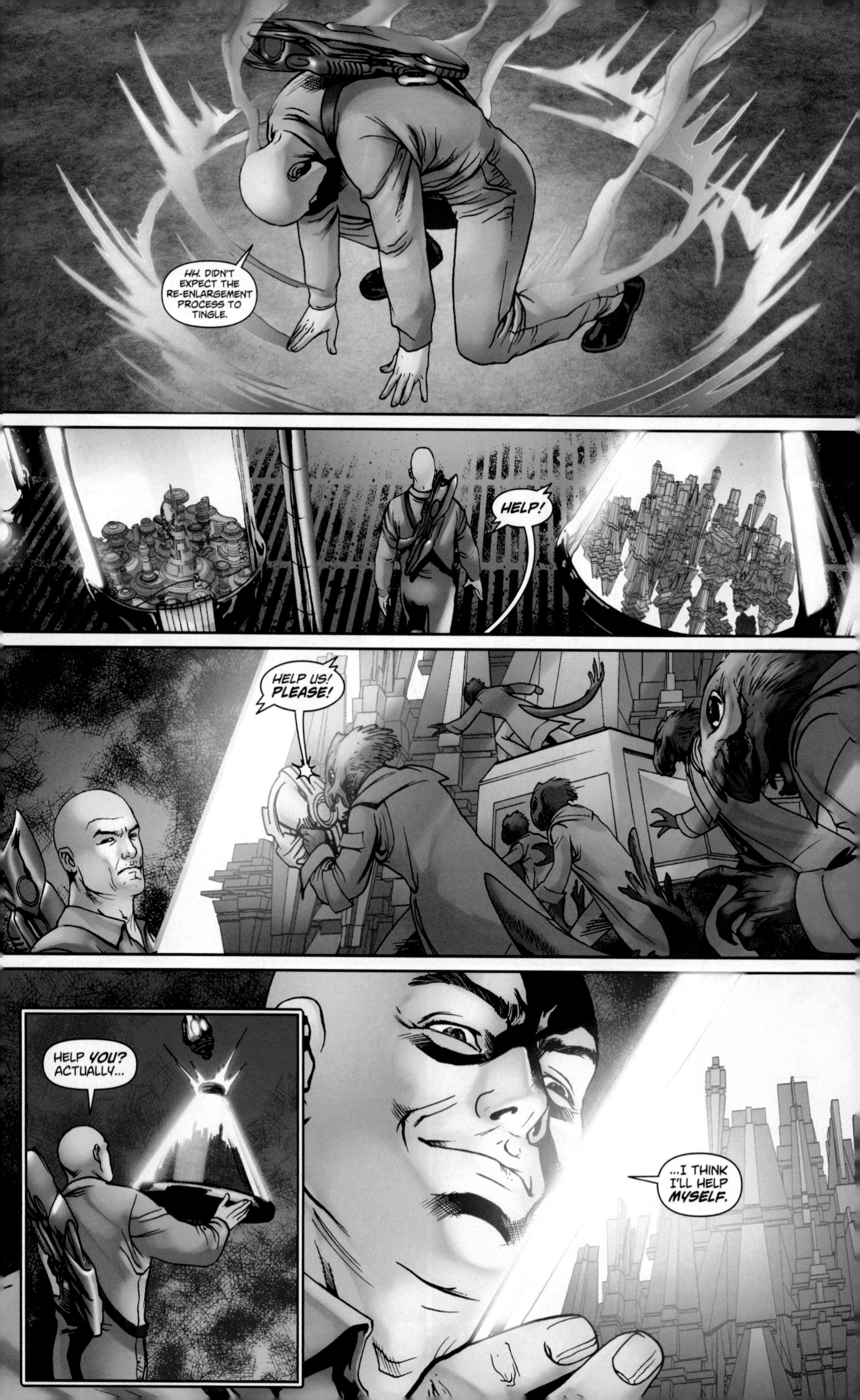
HH. DIDN'T EXPECT THE RE-ENLARGEMENT PROCESS TO TINGLE.
HELP!
HELP US! PLEASE!
HELP YOU? ACTUALLY...
...I THINK I'LL HELP MYSELF.

cover by **AARON LOPRESTI & PETE PANTAZIS**

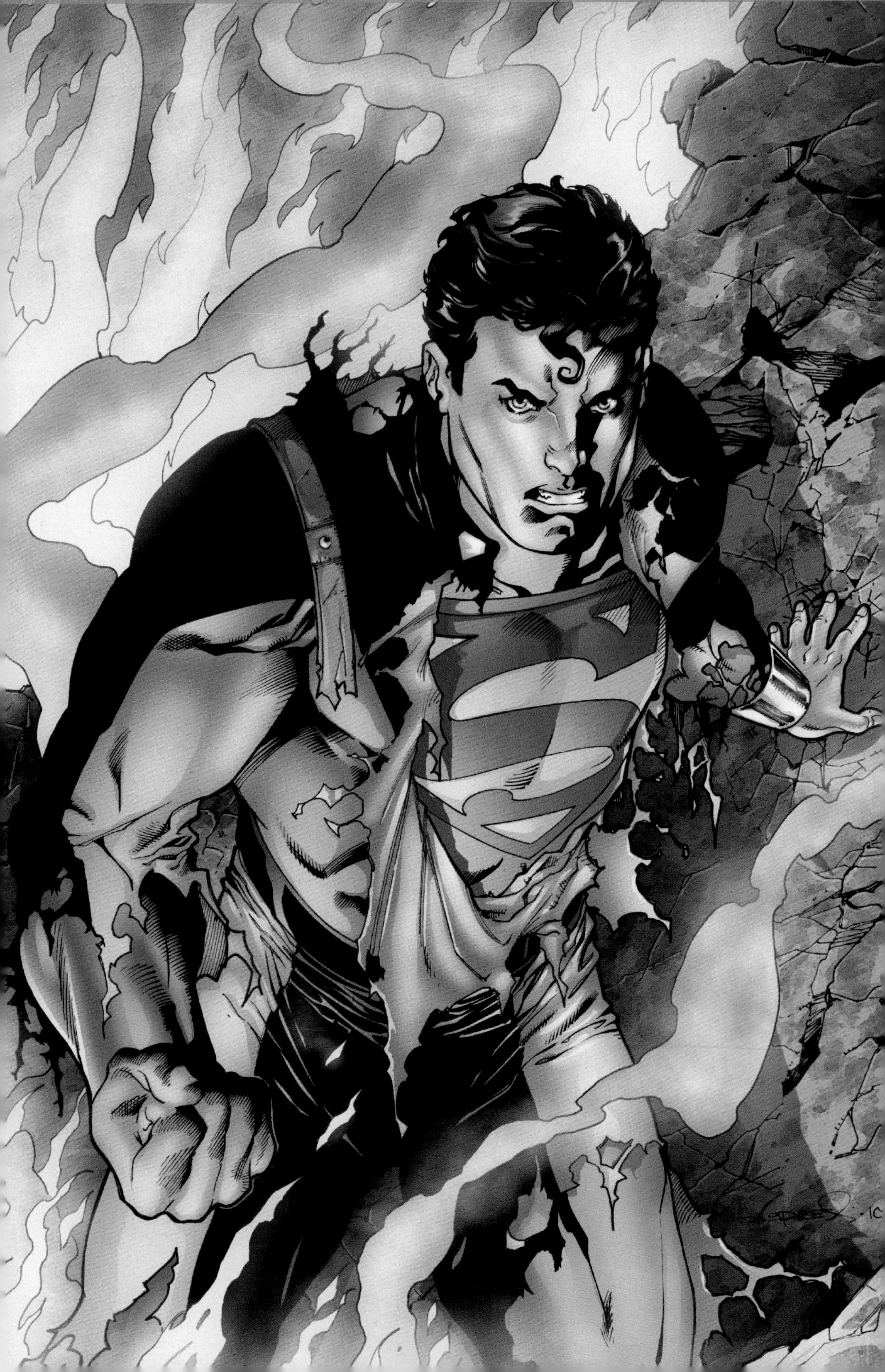

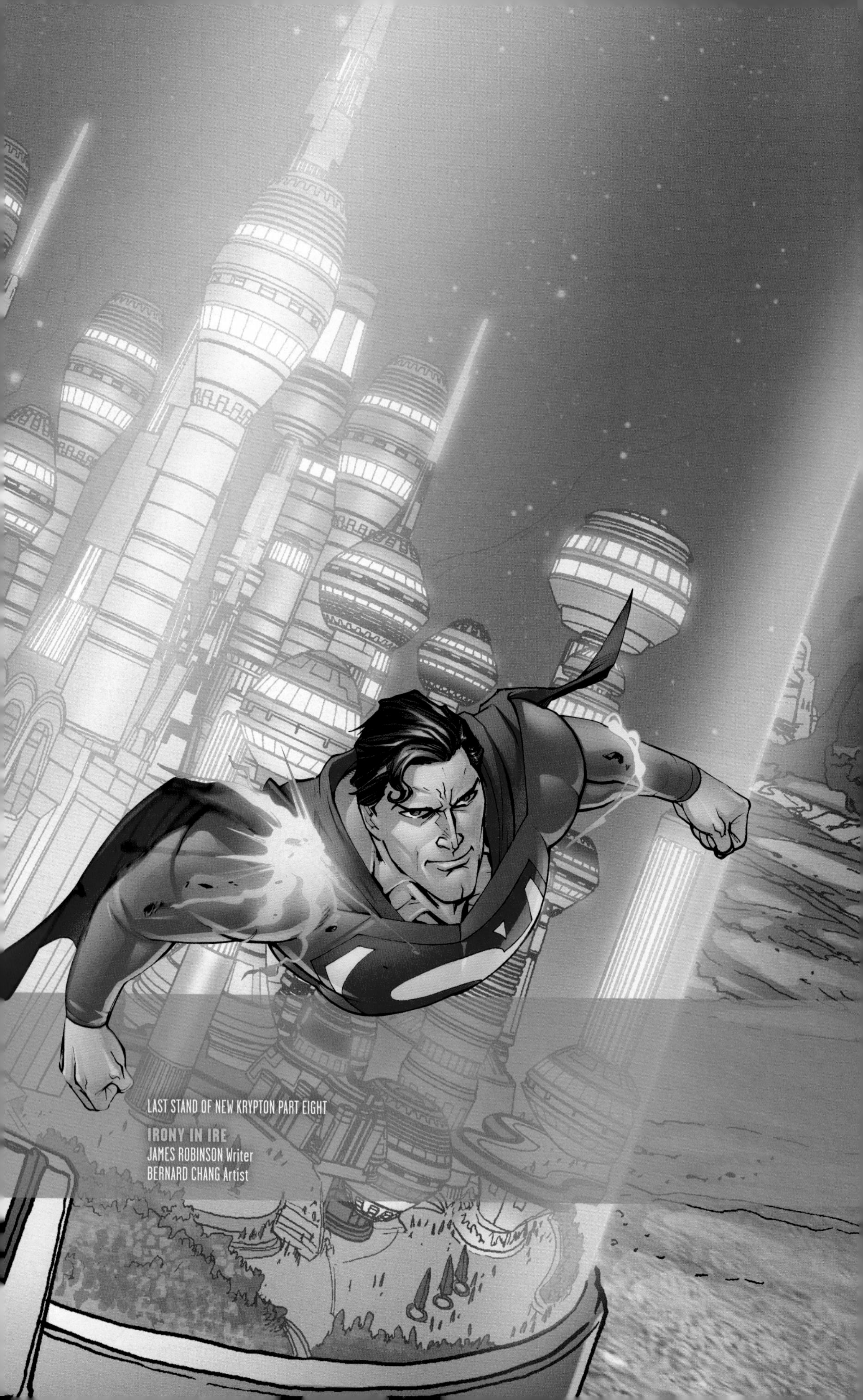
LAST STAND OF NEW KRYPTON PART EIGHT
IRONY IN IRE
JAMES ROBINSON Writer
BERNARD CHANG Artist

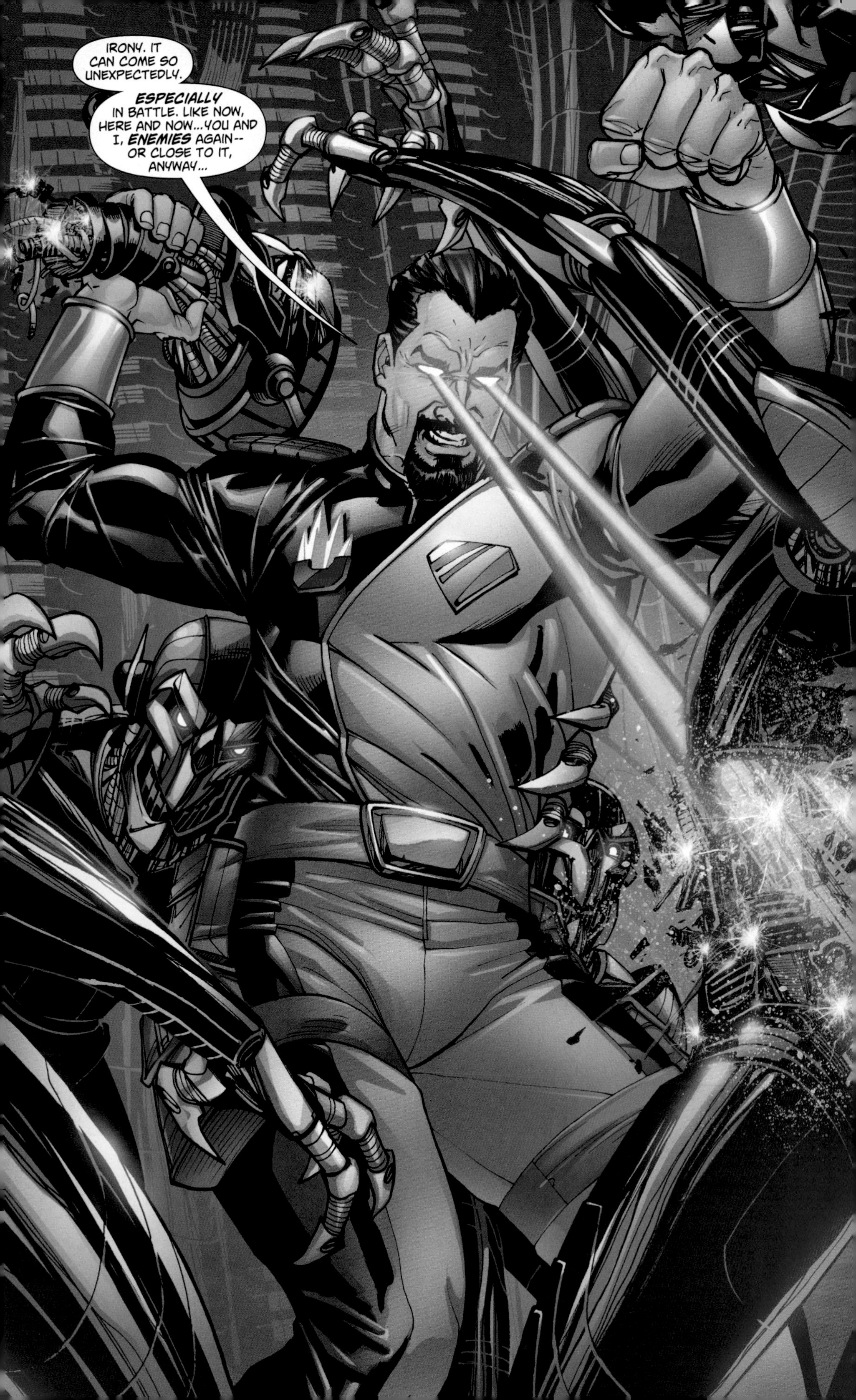
IRONY. IT CAN COME SO UNEXPECTEDLY.
ESPECIALLY IN BATTLE. LIKE NOW, HERE AND NOW...YOU AND I, *ENEMIES* AGAIN-- OR CLOSE TO IT, ANYWAY...

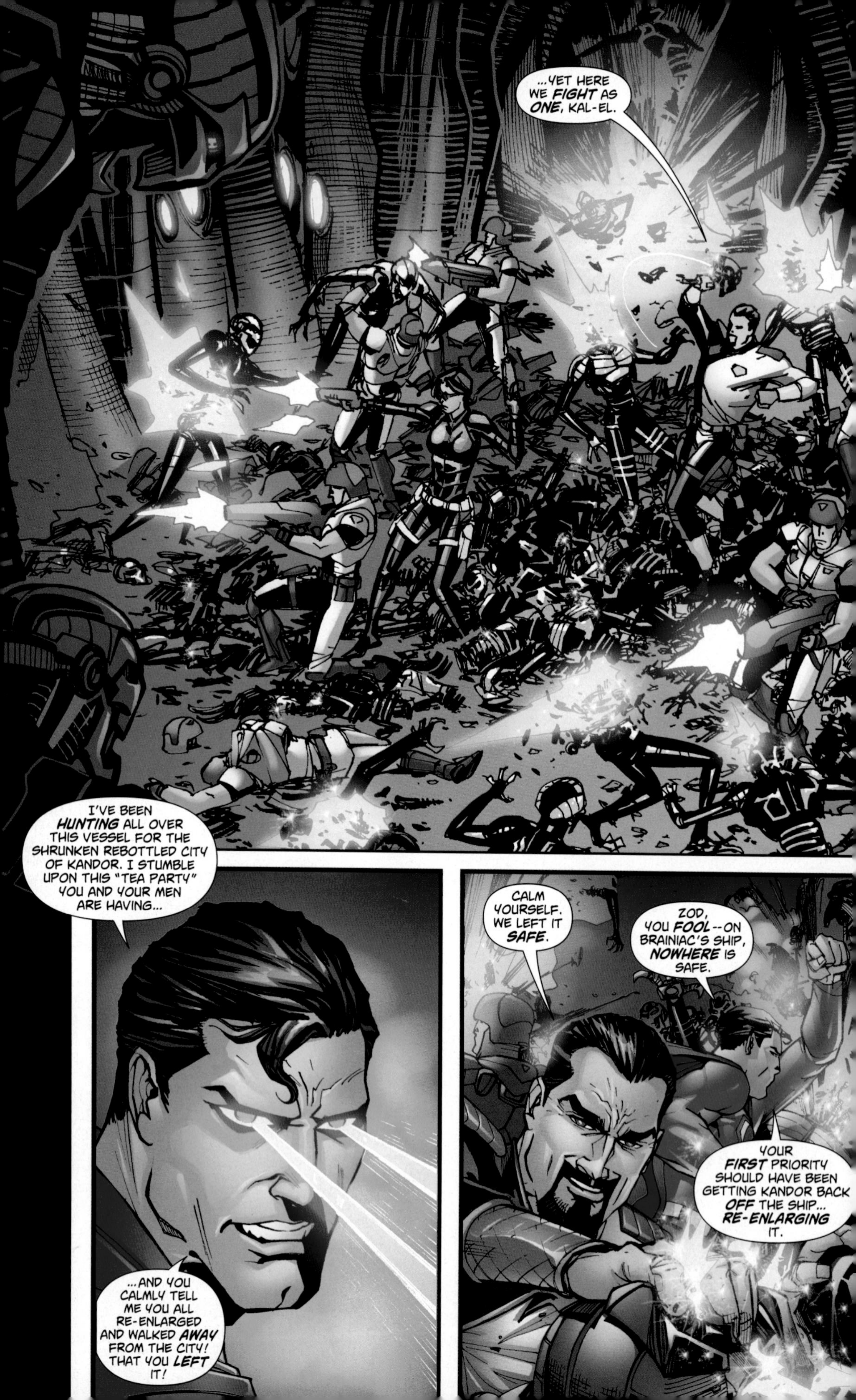

...YET HERE WE FIGHT AS ONE, KAL-EL.
I'VE BEEN HUNTING ALL OVER THIS VESSEL FOR THE SHRUNKEN REBOTTLED CITY OF KANDOR. I STUMBLE UPON THIS "TEA PARTY" YOU AND YOUR MEN ARE HAVING...
...AND YOU CALMLY TELL ME YOU ALL RE-ENLARGED AND WALKED AWAY FROM THE CITY! THAT YOU LEFT IT!
CALM YOURSELF. WE LEFT IT SAFE.
ZOD, YOU FOOL--ON BRAINIAC'S SHIP, NOWHERE IS SAFE.
YOUR FIRST PRIORITY SHOULD HAVE BEEN GETTING KANDOR BACK OFF THE SHIP... RE-ENLARGING IT.

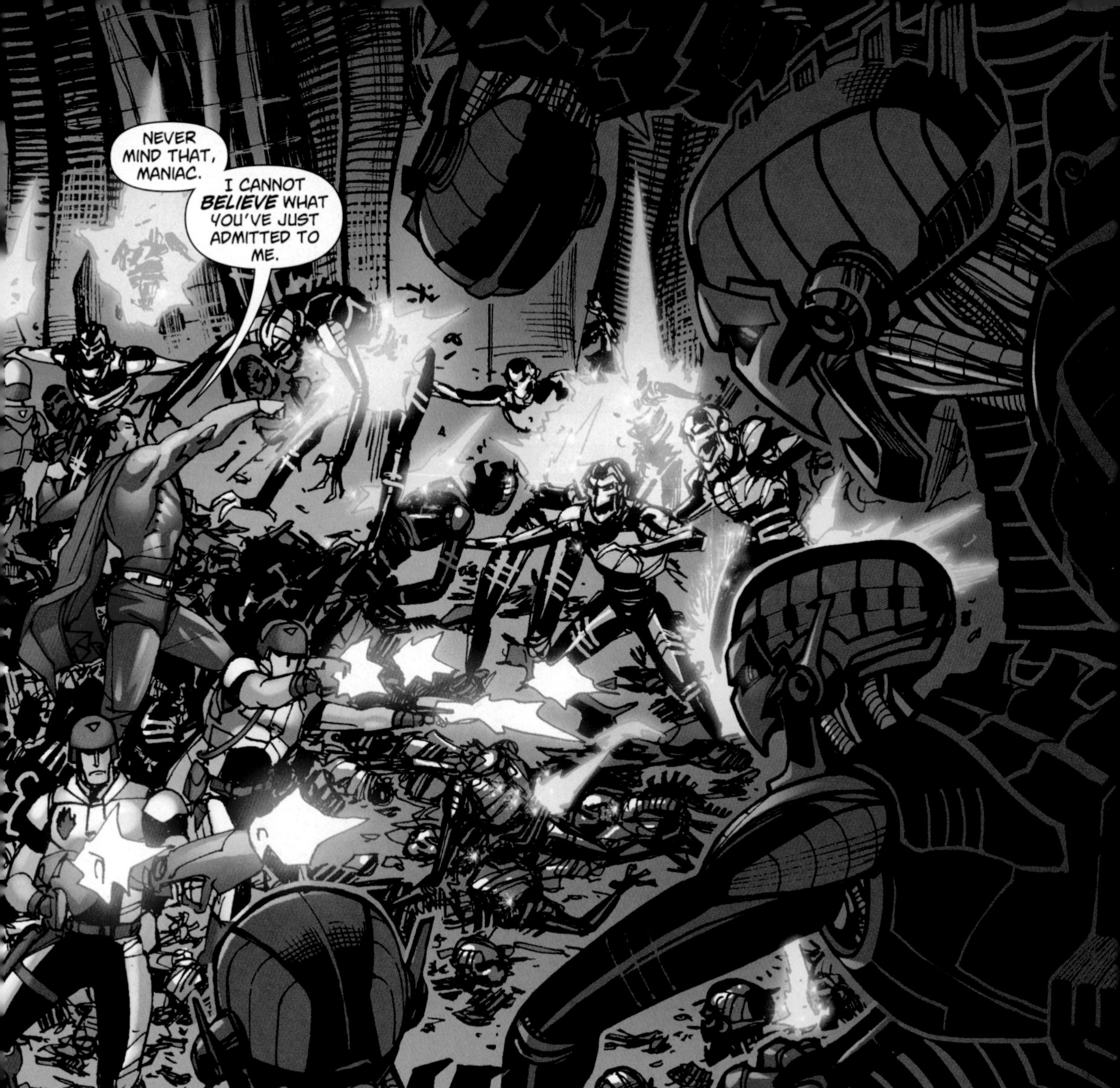
NEVER MIND THAT, MANIAC.
I CANNOT BELIEVE WHAT YOU'VE JUST ADMITTED TO ME.

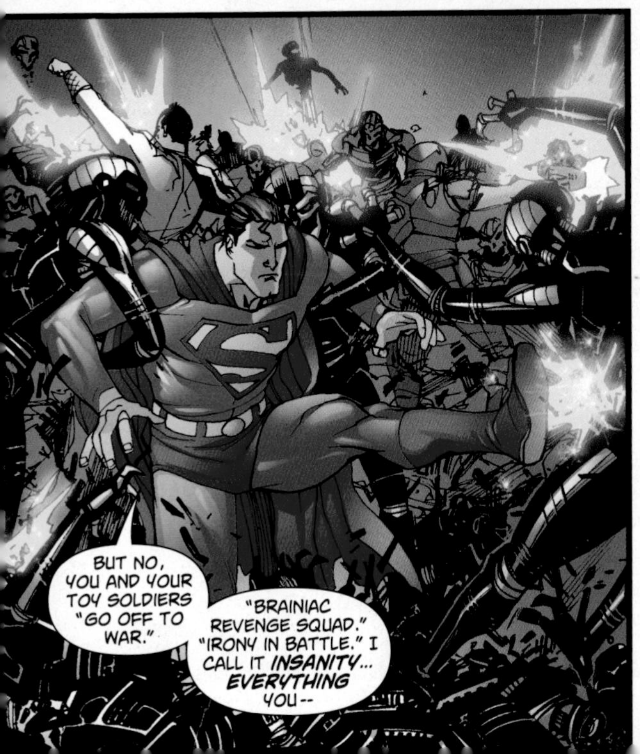
BUT NO, YOU AND YOUR TOY SOLDIERS "GO OFF TO WAR."
"BRAINIAC REVENGE SQUAD." "IRONY IN BATTLE." I CALL IT INSANITY... EVERYTHING YOU--

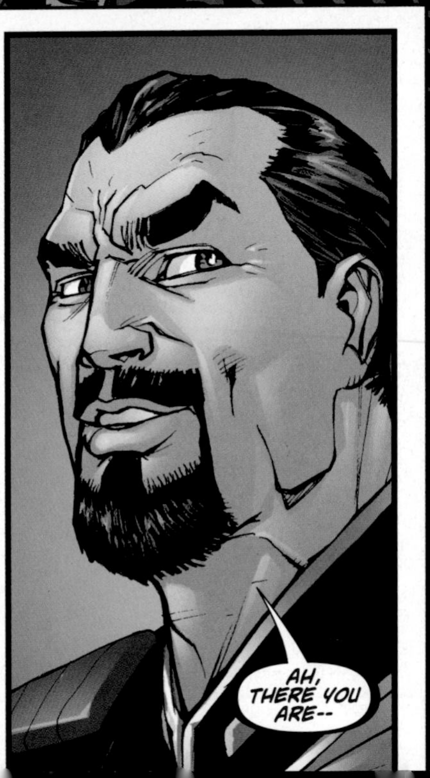
AH, THERE YOU ARE--

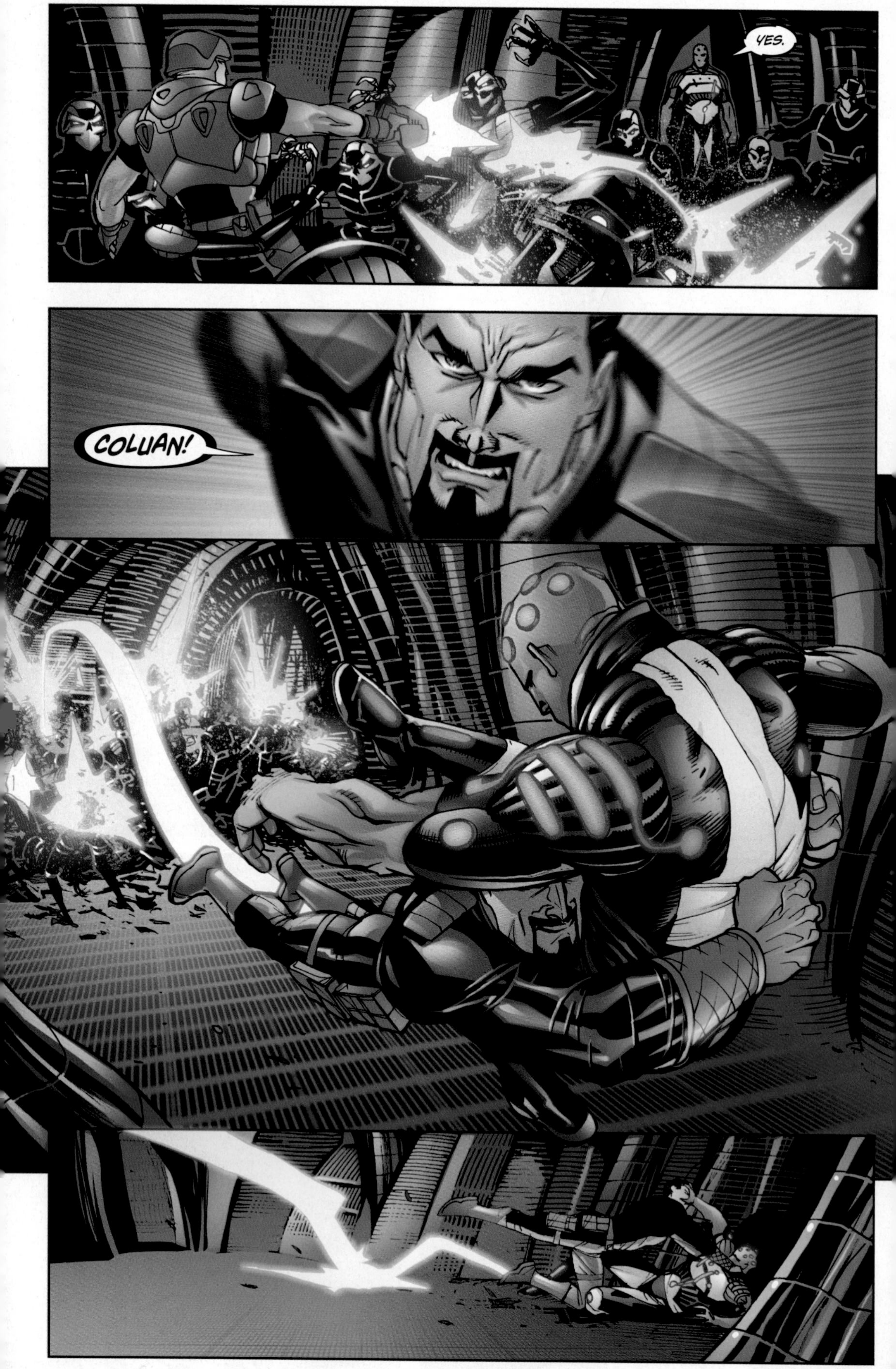
YES.
COLUAN!

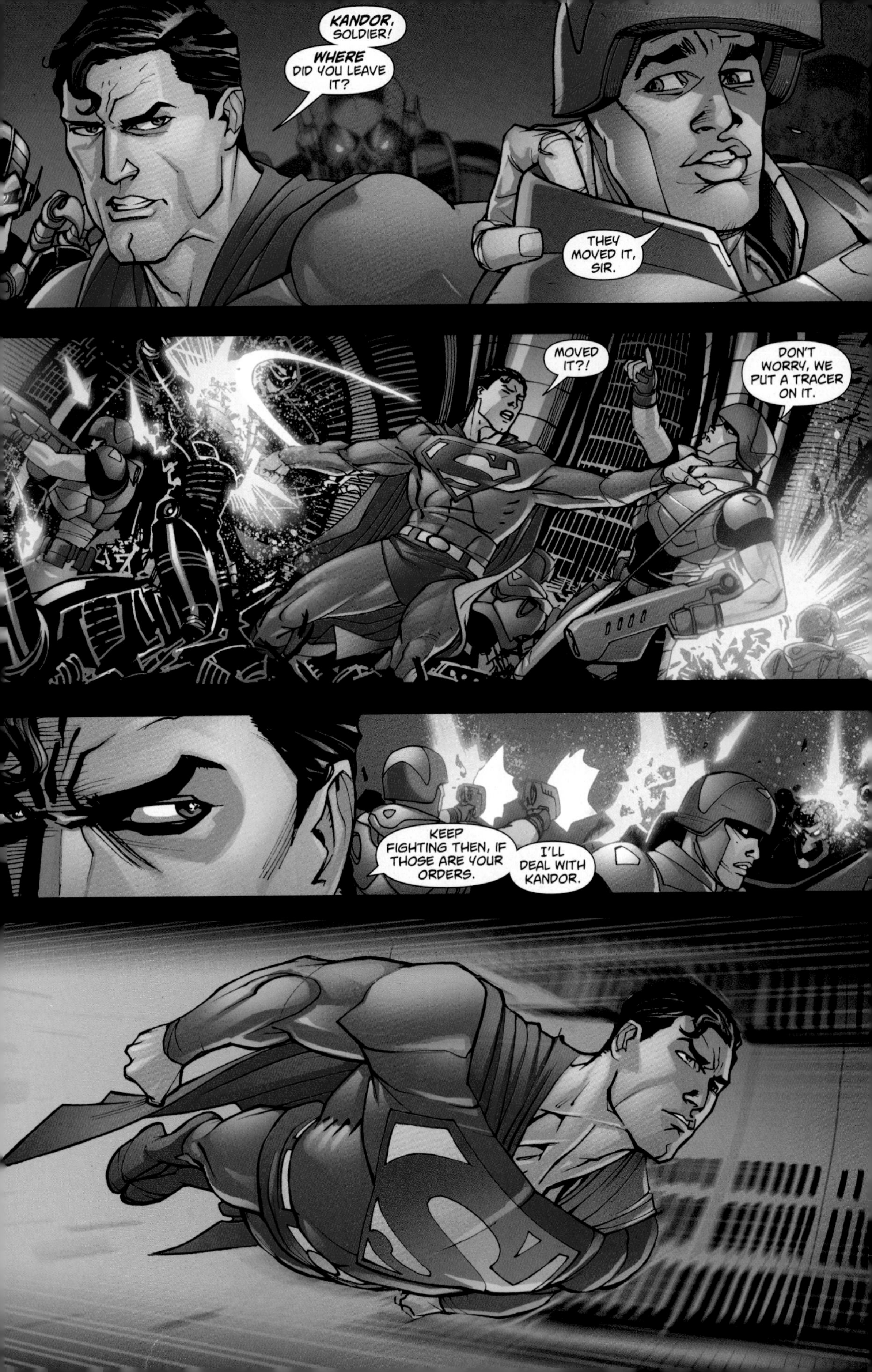
KANDOR, SOLDIER!
WHERE DID YOU LEAVE IT?
THEY MOVED IT, SIR.
MOVED IT?!
DON'T WORRY, WE PUT A TRACER ON IT.
KEEP FIGHTING THEN, IF THOSE ARE YOUR ORDERS.
I'LL DEAL WITH KANDOR.

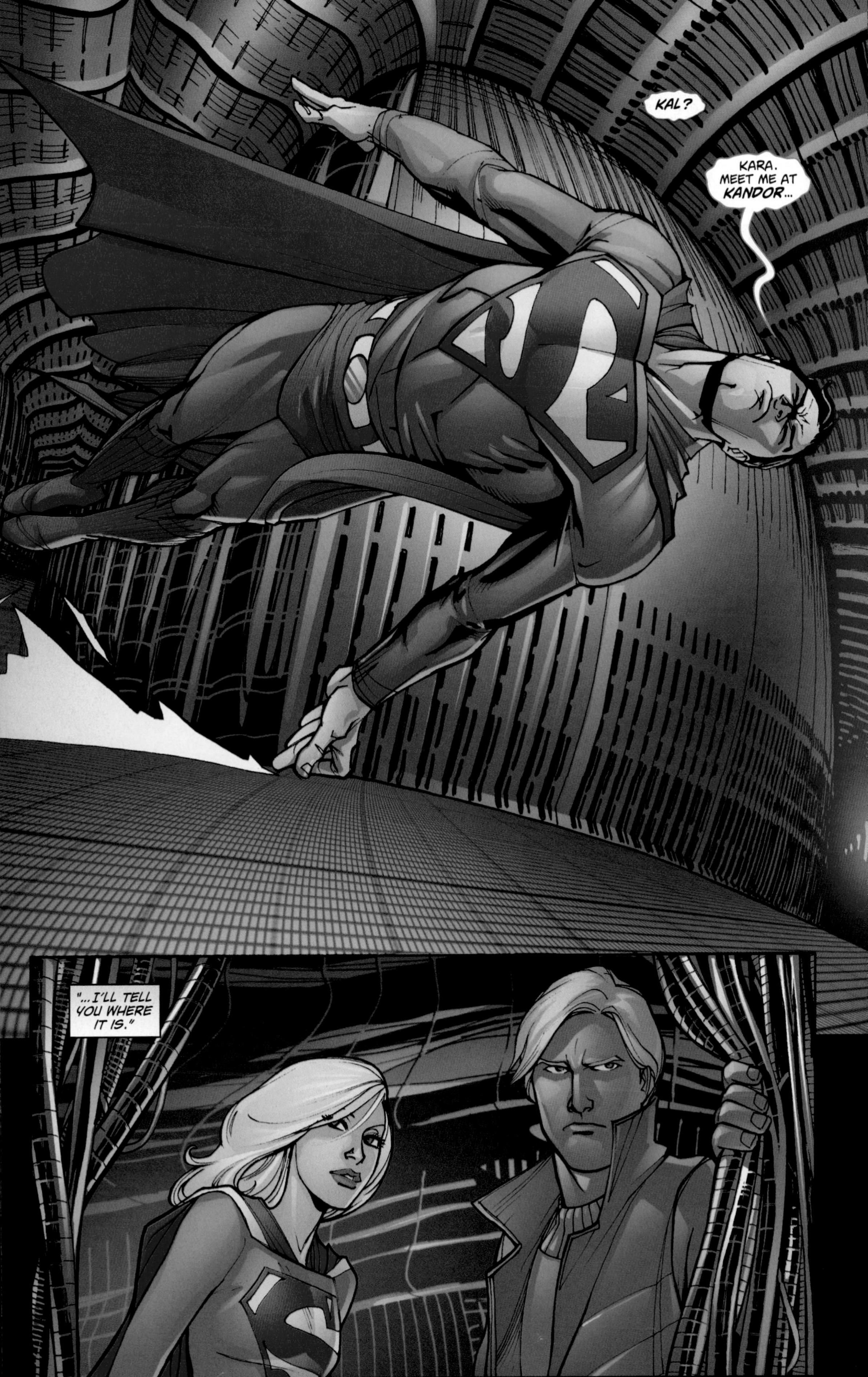
KAL?
KARA. MEET ME AT KANDOR...
"...I'LL TELL YOU WHERE IT IS."

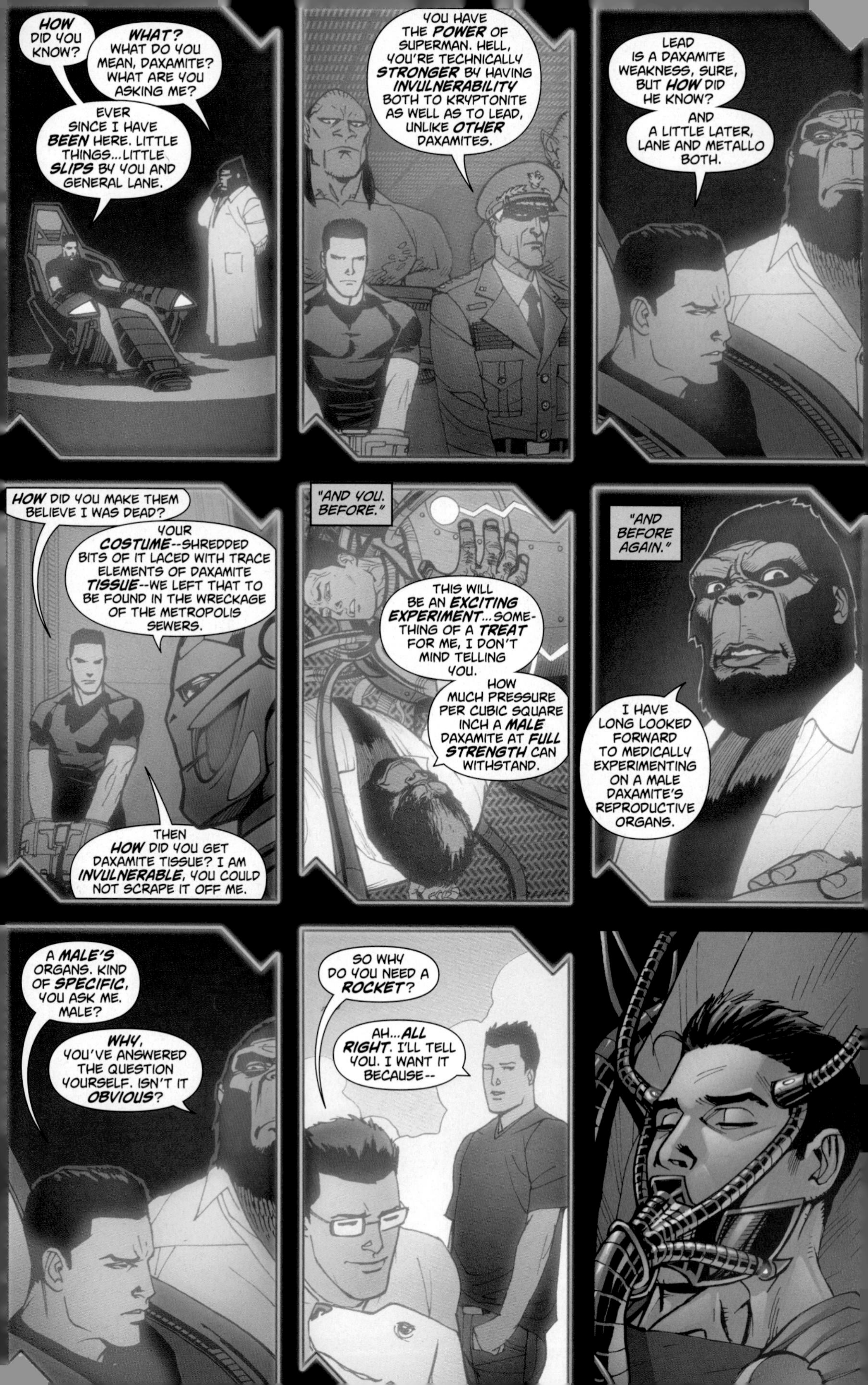
HOW DID YOU KNOW?
WHAT? WHAT DO YOU MEAN, DAXAMITE? WHAT ARE YOU ASKING ME?
EVER SINCE I HAVE BEEN HERE. LITTLE THINGS...LITTLE SLIPS BY YOU AND GENERAL LANE.
YOU HAVE THE POWER OF SUPERMAN. HELL, YOU'RE TECHNICALLY STRONGER BY HAVING INVULNERABILITY BOTH TO KRYPTONITE AS WELL AS TO LEAD, UNLIKE OTHER DAXAMITES.
LEAD IS A DAXAMITE WEAKNESS, SURE, BUT HOW DID HE KNOW?
AND A LITTLE LATER, LANE AND METALLO BOTH.
HOW DID YOU MAKE THEM BELIEVE I WAS DEAD?
YOUR COSTUME--SHREDDED BITS OF IT LACED WITH TRACE ELEMENTS OF DAXAMITE TISSUE--WE LEFT THAT TO BE FOUND IN THE WRECKAGE OF THE METROPOLIS SEWERS.
THEN HOW DID YOU GET DAXAMITE TISSUE? I AM INVULNERABLE, YOU COULD NOT SCRAPE IT OFF ME.
"AND YOU. BEFORE."
THIS WILL BE AN EXCITING EXPERIMENT...SOMETHING OF A TREAT FOR ME, I DON'T MIND TELLING YOU.
HOW MUCH PRESSURE PER CUBIC SQUARE INCH A MALE DAXAMITE AT FULL STRENGTH CAN WITHSTAND.
"AND BEFORE AGAIN."
I HAVE LONG LOOKED FORWARD TO MEDICALLY EXPERIMENTING ON A MALE DAXAMITE'S REPRODUCTIVE ORGANS.
A MALE'S ORGANS. KIND OF SPECIFIC, YOU ASK ME. MALE?
WHY, YOU'VE ANSWERED THE QUESTION YOURSELF. ISN'T IT OBVIOUS?
SO WHY DO YOU NEED A ROCKET?
AH...ALL RIGHT. I'LL TELL YOU. I WANT IT BECAUSE--

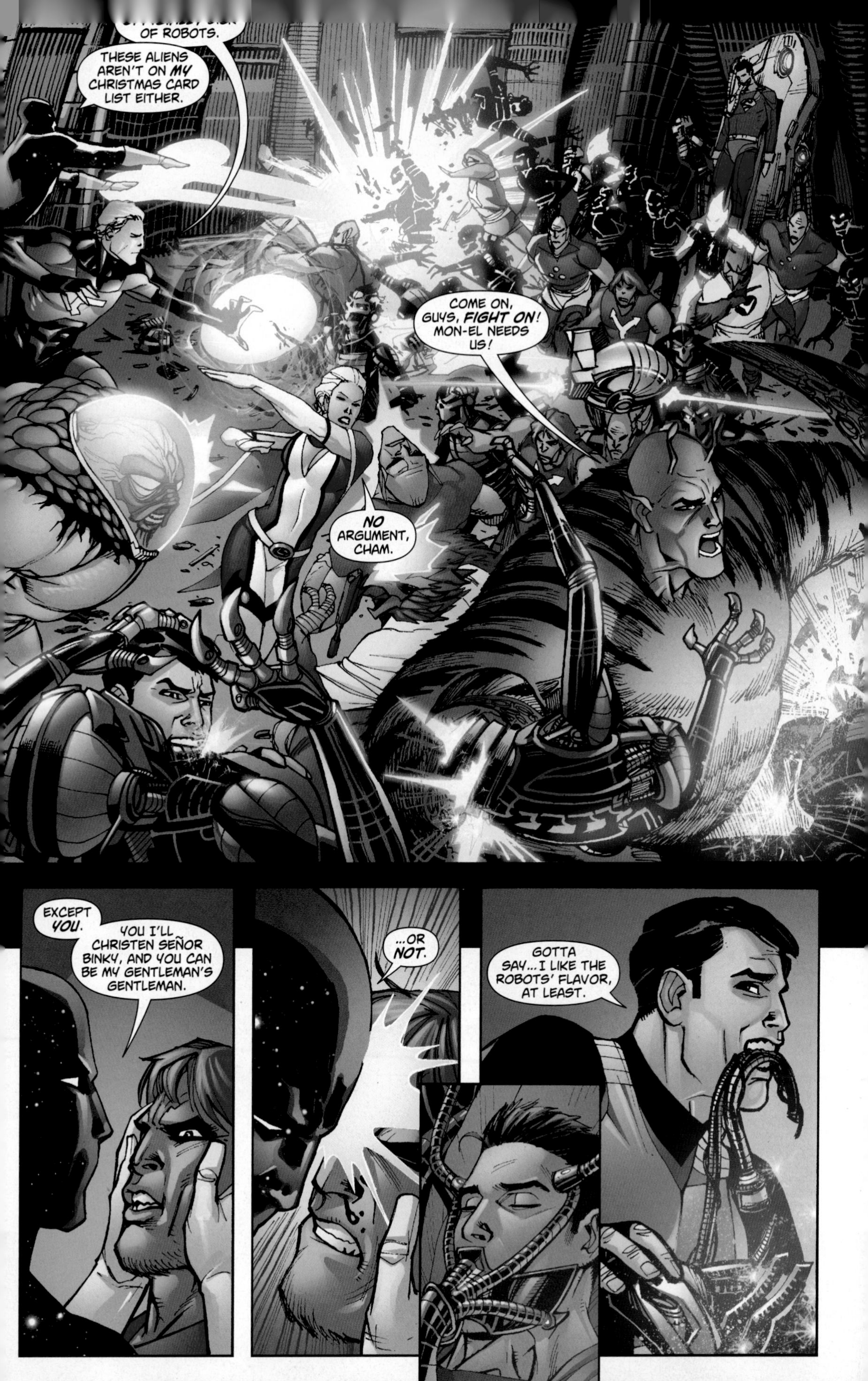

OF ROBOTS.
THESE ALIENS AREN'T ON MY CHRISTMAS CARD LIST EITHER.
COME ON, GUYS, FIGHT ON! MON-EL NEEDS US!
NO ARGUMENT, CHAM.
EXCEPT YOU.
YOU I'LL CHRISTEN SEÑOR BINKY, AND YOU CAN BE MY GENTLEMAN'S GENTLEMAN.
...OR NOT.
GOTTA SAY... I LIKE THE ROBOTS' FLAVOR, AT LEAST.

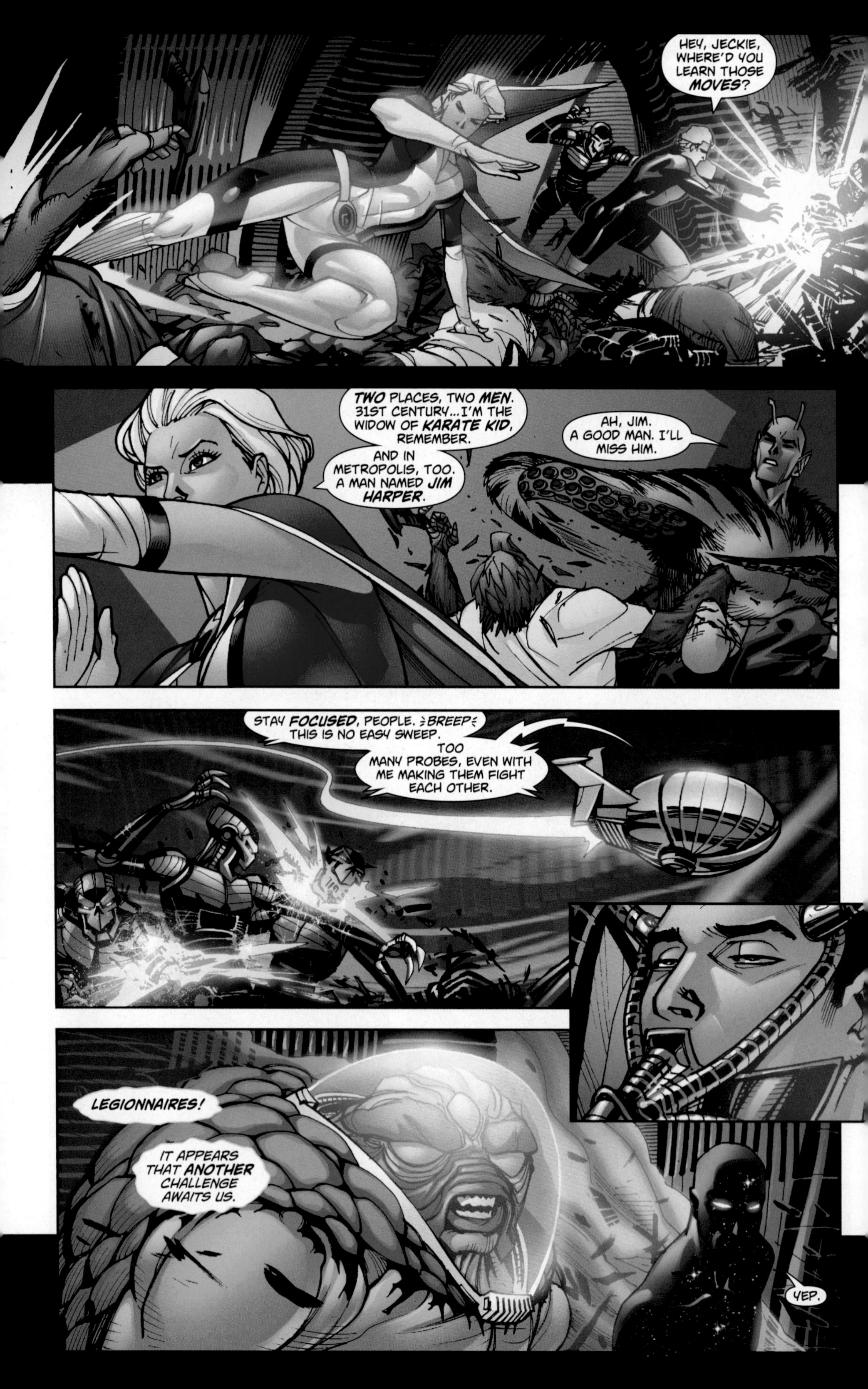
HEY, JECKIE, WHERE'D YOU LEARN THOSE MOVES?
TWO PLACES, TWO MEN. 31ST CENTURY... I'M THE WIDOW OF KARATE KID, REMEMBER.
AND IN METROPOLIS, TOO. A MAN NAMED JIM HARPER.
AH, JIM. A GOOD MAN. I'LL MISS HIM.
STAY FOCUSED, PEOPLE. BREEP THIS IS NO EASY SWEEP.
TOO MANY PROBES, EVEN WITH ME MAKING THEM FIGHT EACH OTHER.
LEGIONNAIRES!
IT APPEARS THAT ANOTHER CHALLENGE AWAITS US.
YEP.

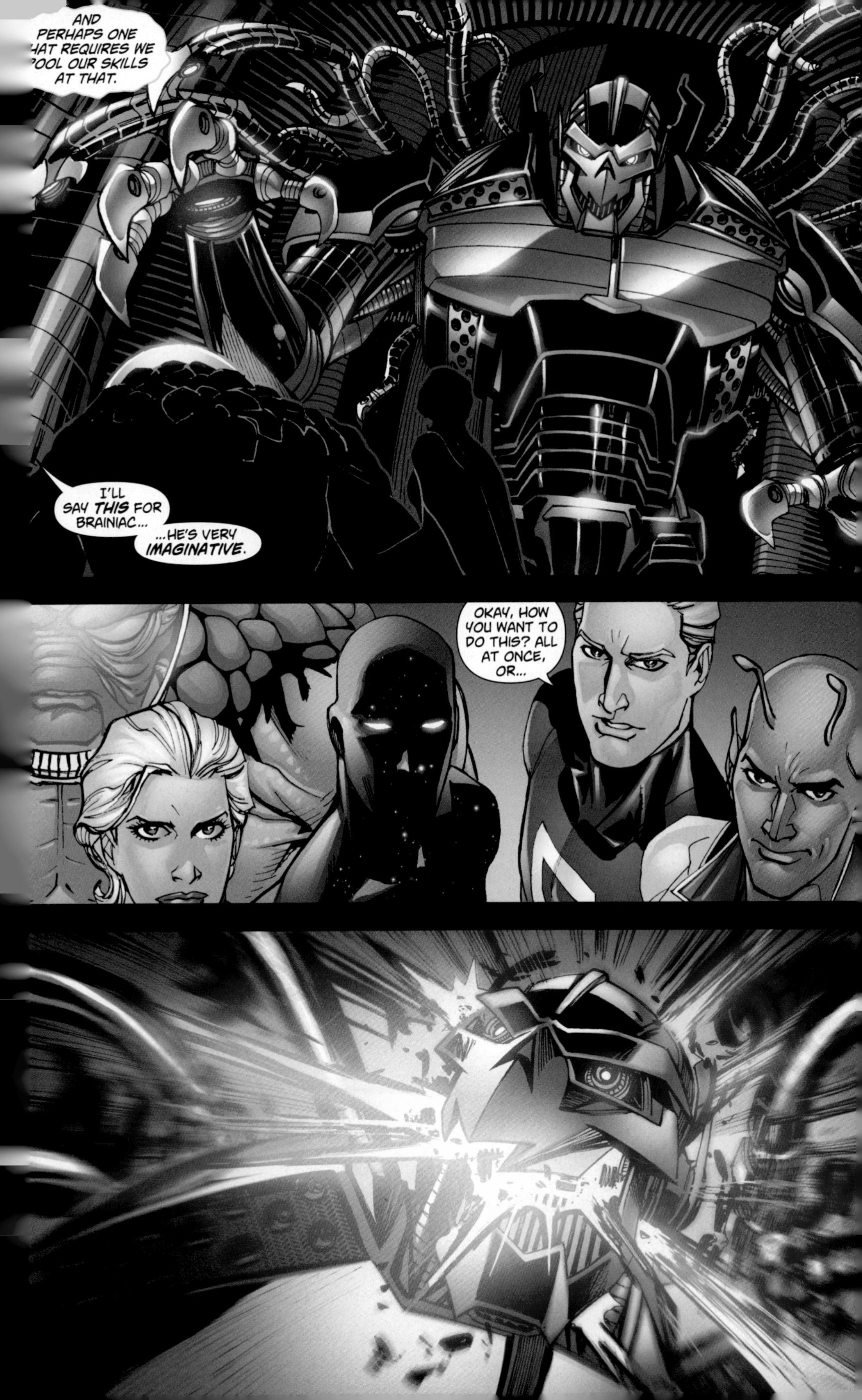
AND PERHAPS ONE THAT REQUIRES WE POOL OUR SKILLS AT THAT.
I'LL SAY THIS FOR BRAINIAC...
...HE'S VERY IMAGINATIVE.
OKAY, HOW YOU WANT TO DO THIS? ALL AT ONCE, OR...

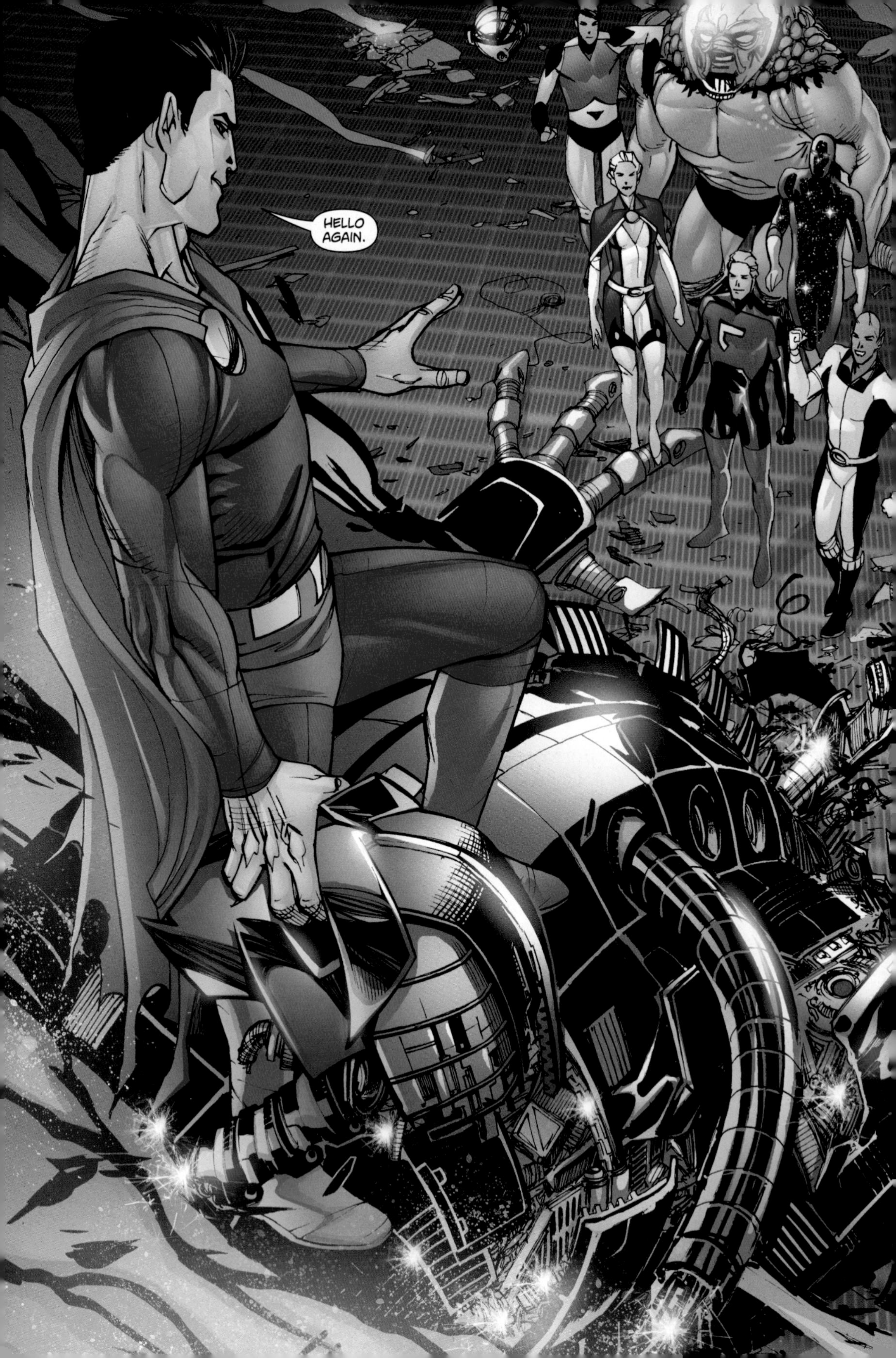
HELLO AGAIN.

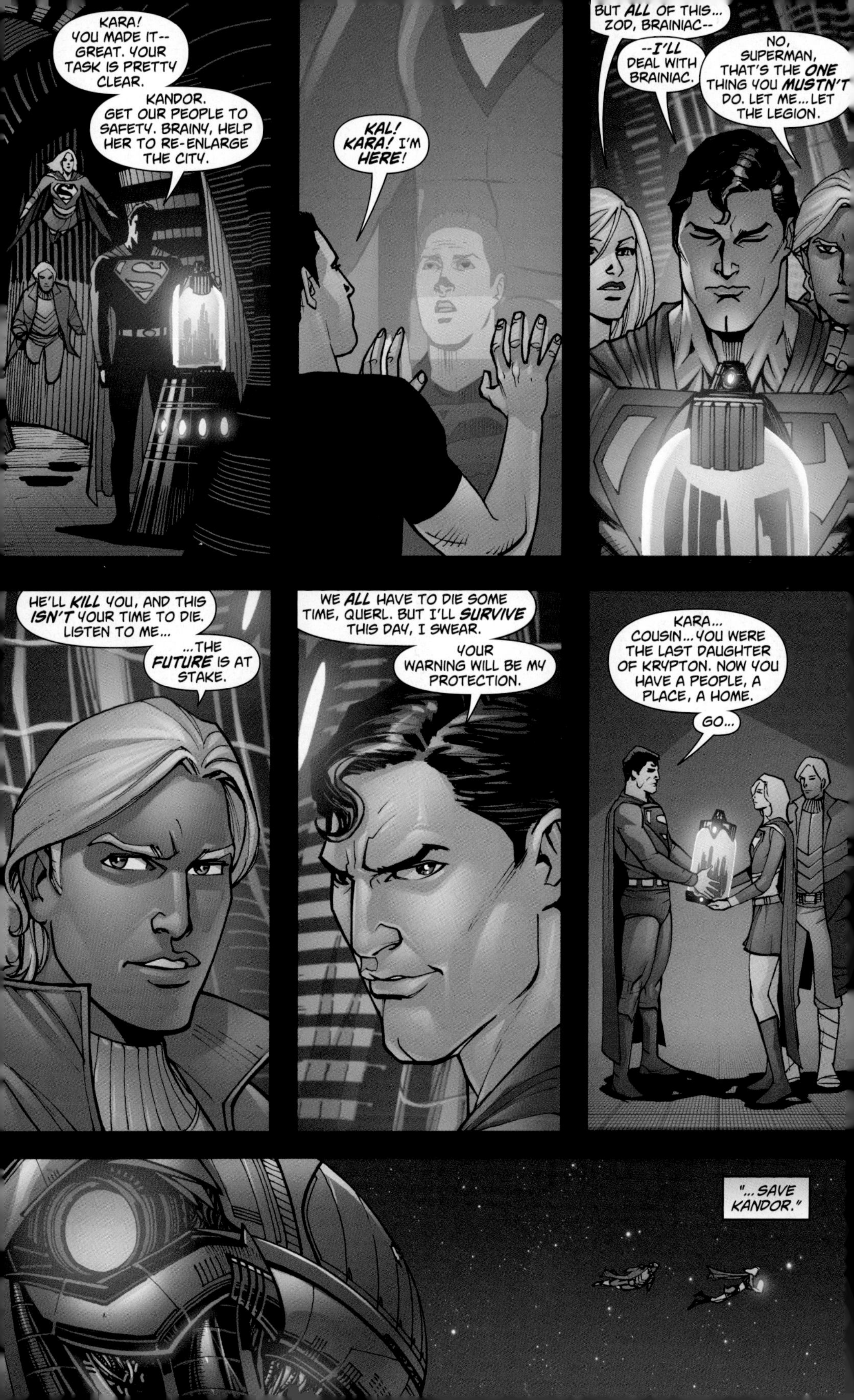
KARA! YOU MADE IT-- GREAT. YOUR TASK IS PRETTY CLEAR.
KANDOR. GET OUR PEOPLE TO SAFETY. BRAINY, HELP HER TO RE-ENLARGE THE CITY.
KAL! KARA! I'M HERE!
BUT ALL OF THIS... ZOD, BRAINIAC--
--I'LL DEAL WITH BRAINIAC.
NO, SUPERMAN, THAT'S THE ONE THING YOU MUSTN'T DO. LET ME...LET THE LEGION.
HE'LL KILL YOU, AND THIS ISN'T YOUR TIME TO DIE. LISTEN TO ME...
...THE FUTURE IS AT STAKE.
WE ALL HAVE TO DIE SOME TIME, QUERL. BUT I'LL SURVIVE THIS DAY, I SWEAR.
YOUR WARNING WILL BE MY PROTECTION.
KARA... COUSIN...YOU WERE THE LAST DAUGHTER OF KRYPTON. NOW YOU HAVE A PEOPLE, A PLACE, A HOME.
GO...
"...SAVE KANDOR."

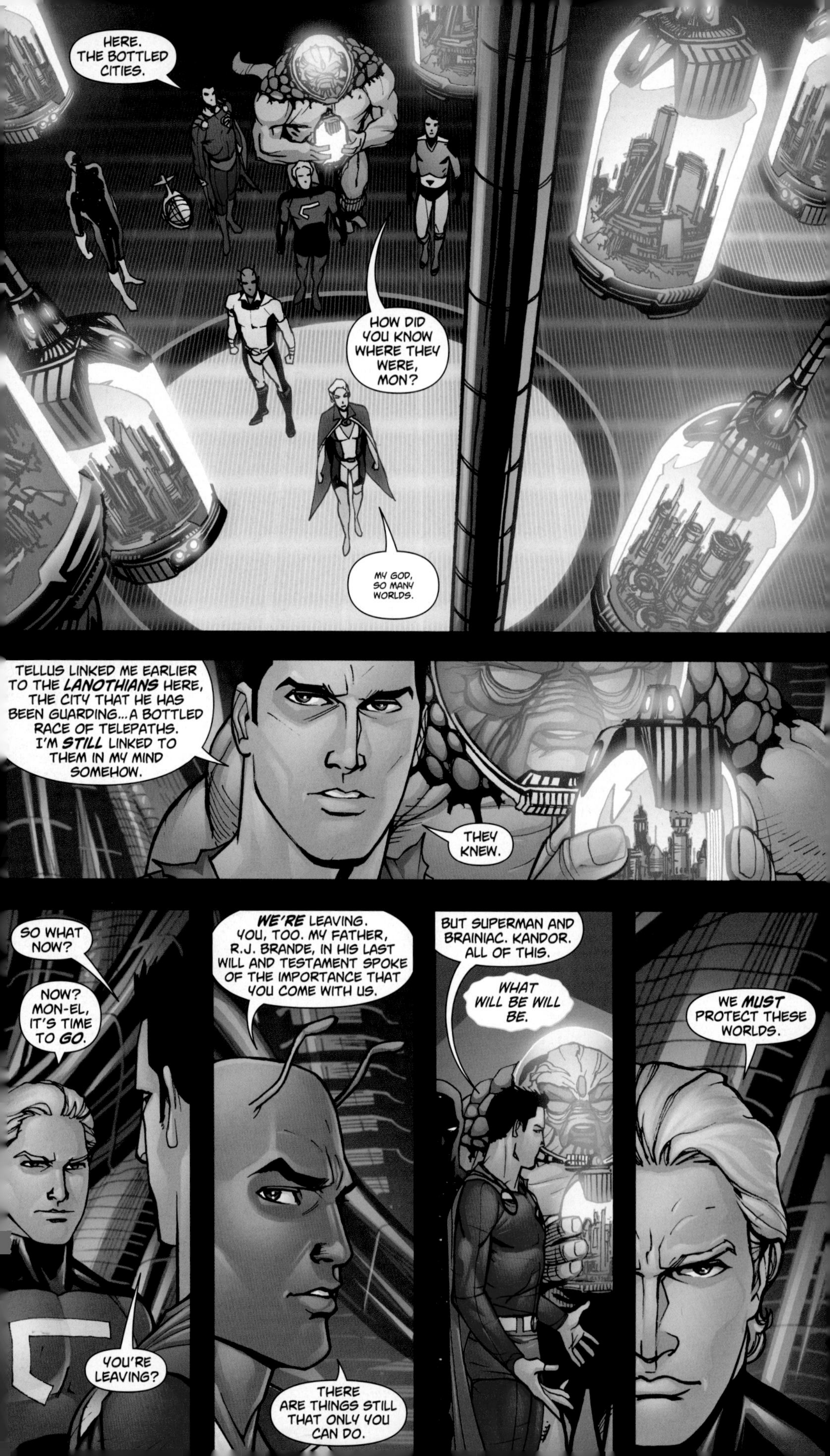
HERE. THE BOTTLED CITIES.
HOW DID YOU KNOW WHERE THEY WERE, MON?
MY GOD, SO MANY WORLDS.
TELLUS LINKED ME EARLIER TO THE LANOTHIANS HERE, THE CITY THAT HE HAS BEEN GUARDING...A BOTTLED RACE OF TELEPATHS. I'M STILL LINKED TO THEM IN MY MIND SOMEHOW.
THEY KNEW.
SO WHAT NOW?
NOW? MON-EL, IT'S TIME TO GO.
YOU'RE LEAVING?
WE'RE LEAVING. YOU, TOO. MY FATHER, R.J. BRANDE, IN HIS LAST WILL AND TESTAMENT SPOKE OF THE IMPORTANCE THAT YOU COME WITH US.
THERE ARE THINGS STILL THAT ONLY YOU CAN DO.
BUT SUPERMAN AND BRAINIAC. KANDOR. ALL OF THIS.
WHAT WILL BE WILL BE.
WE MUST PROTECT THESE WORLDS.

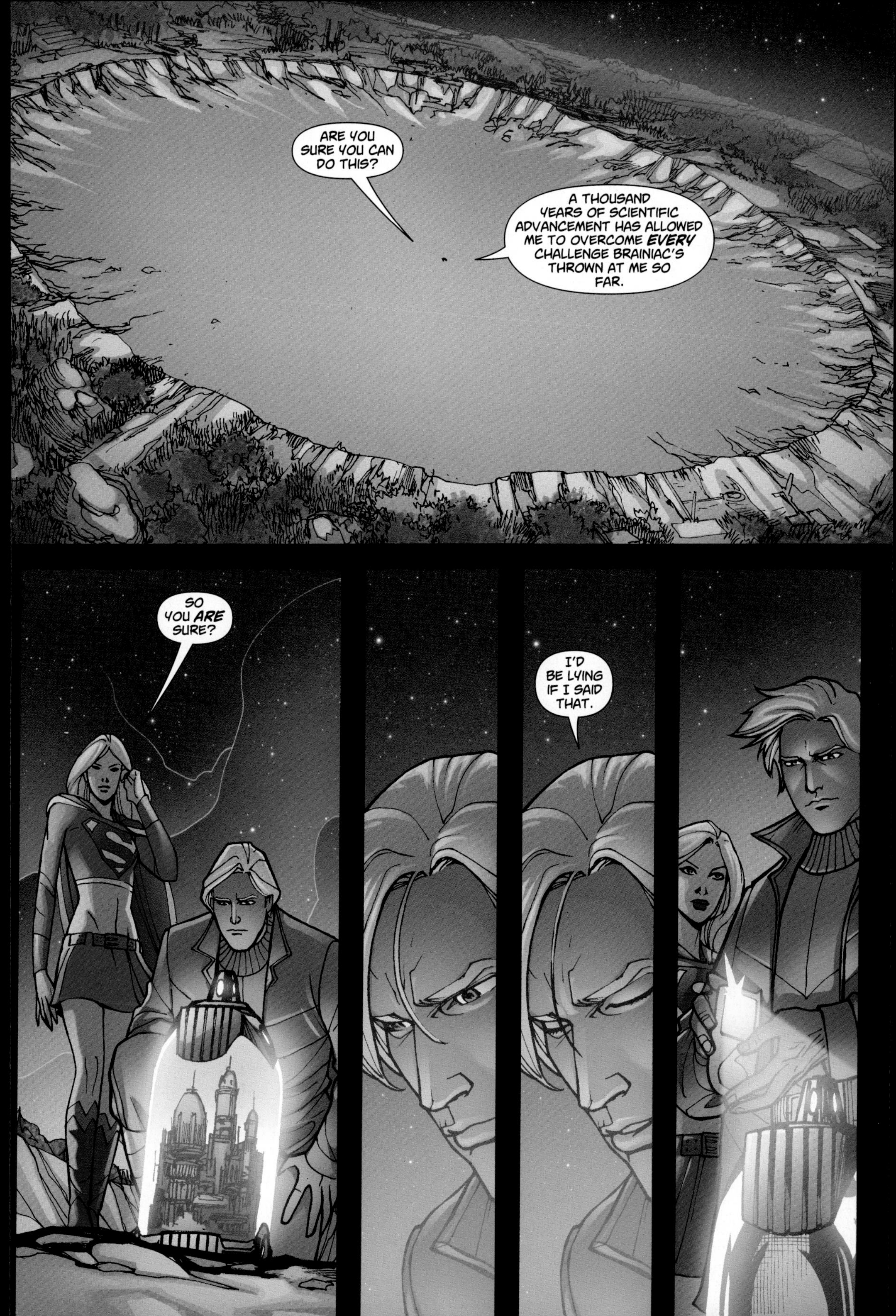

ARE YOU SURE YOU CAN DO THIS?
A THOUSAND YEARS OF SCIENTIFIC ADVANCEMENT HAS ALLOWED ME TO OVERCOME EVERY CHALLENGE BRAINIAC'S THROWN AT ME SO FAR.
SO YOU ARE SURE?
I'D BE LYING IF I SAID THAT.

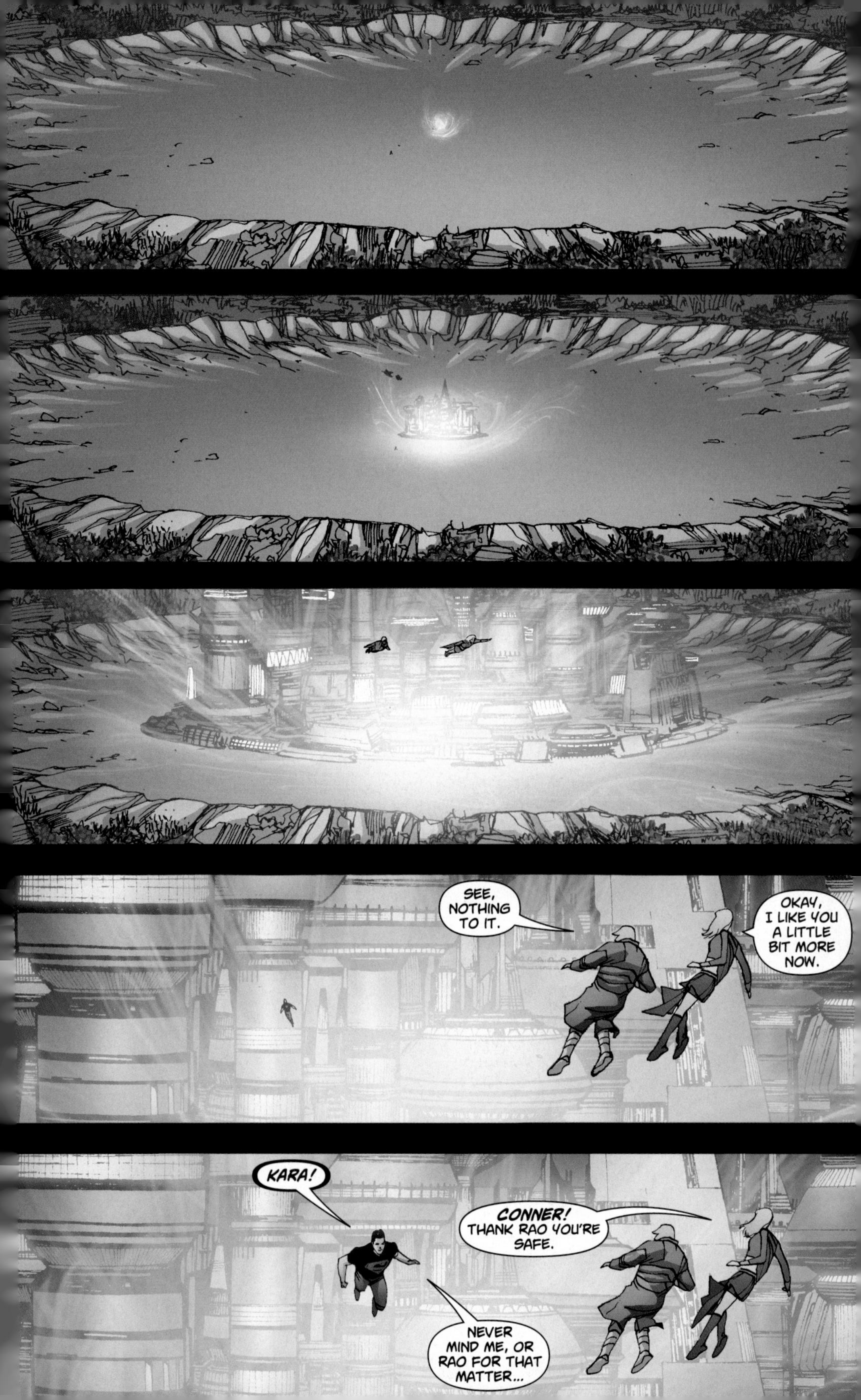
SEE, NOTHING TO IT.
OKAY, I LIKE YOU A LITTLE BIT MORE NOW.
KARA!
CONNER! THANK RAO YOU'RE SAFE.
NEVER MIND ME, OR RAO FOR THAT MATTER...

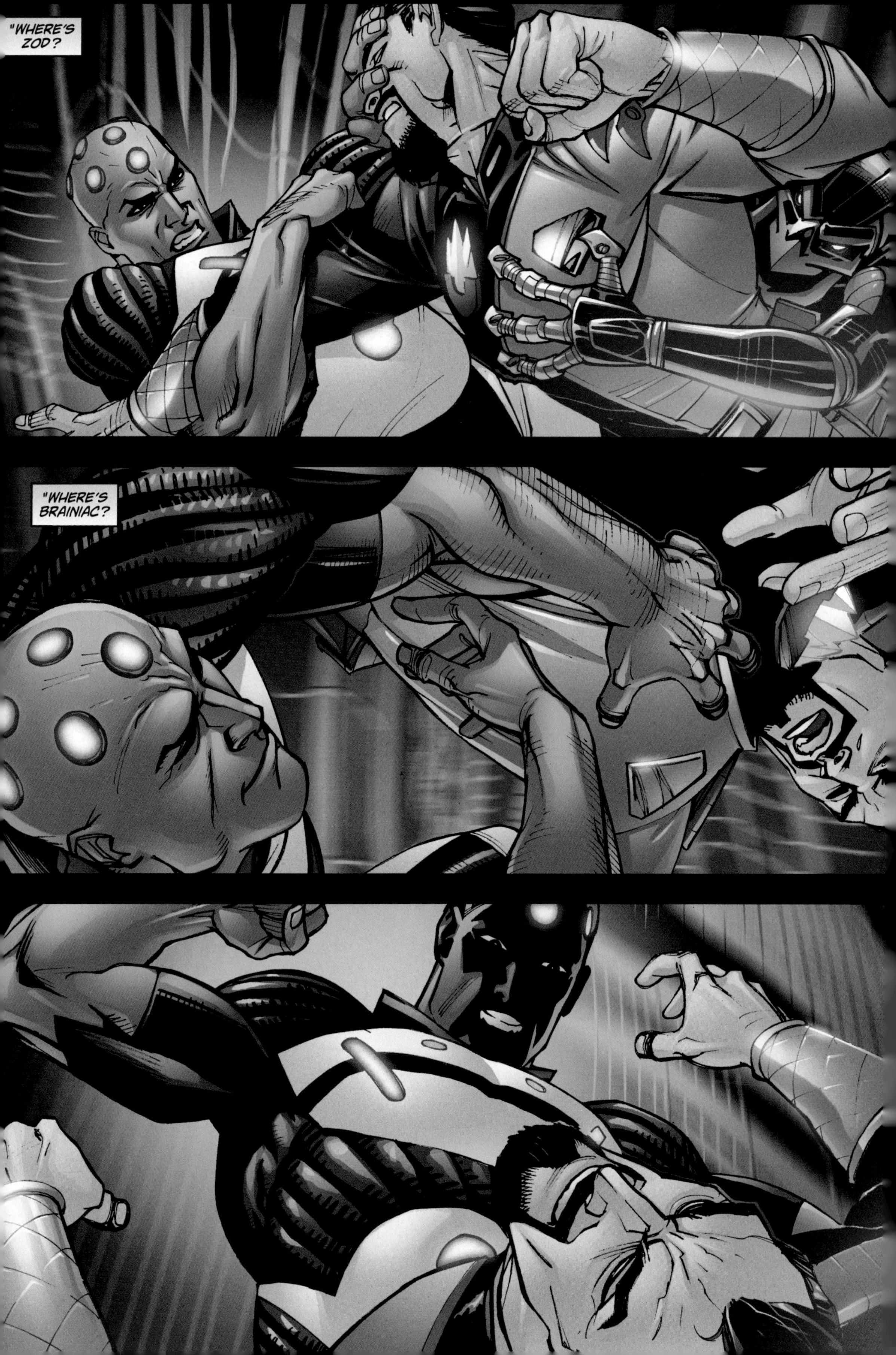
"WHERE'S ZOD?
"WHERE'S BRAINIAC?

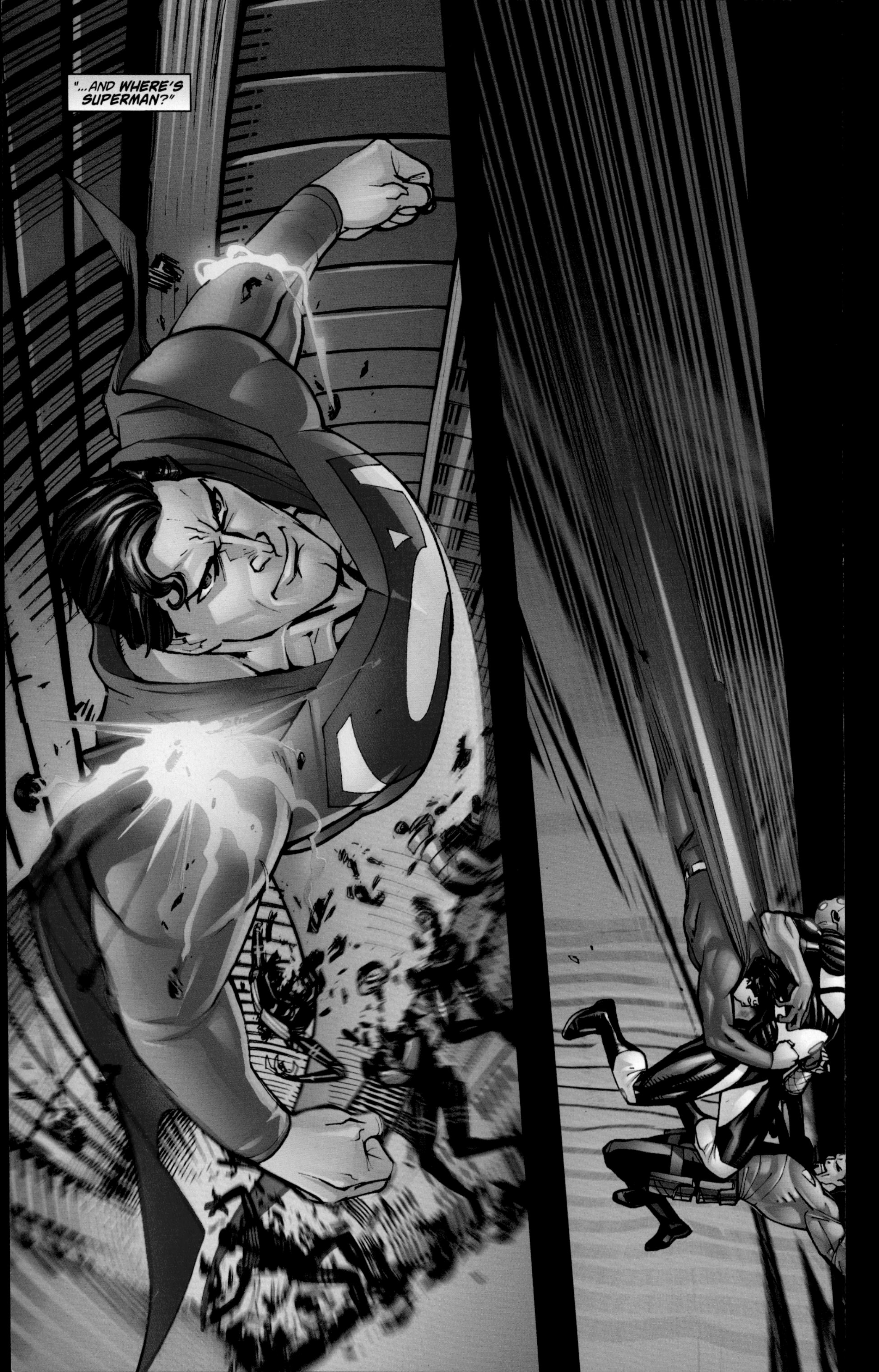
"...AND WHERE'S SUPERMAN?"

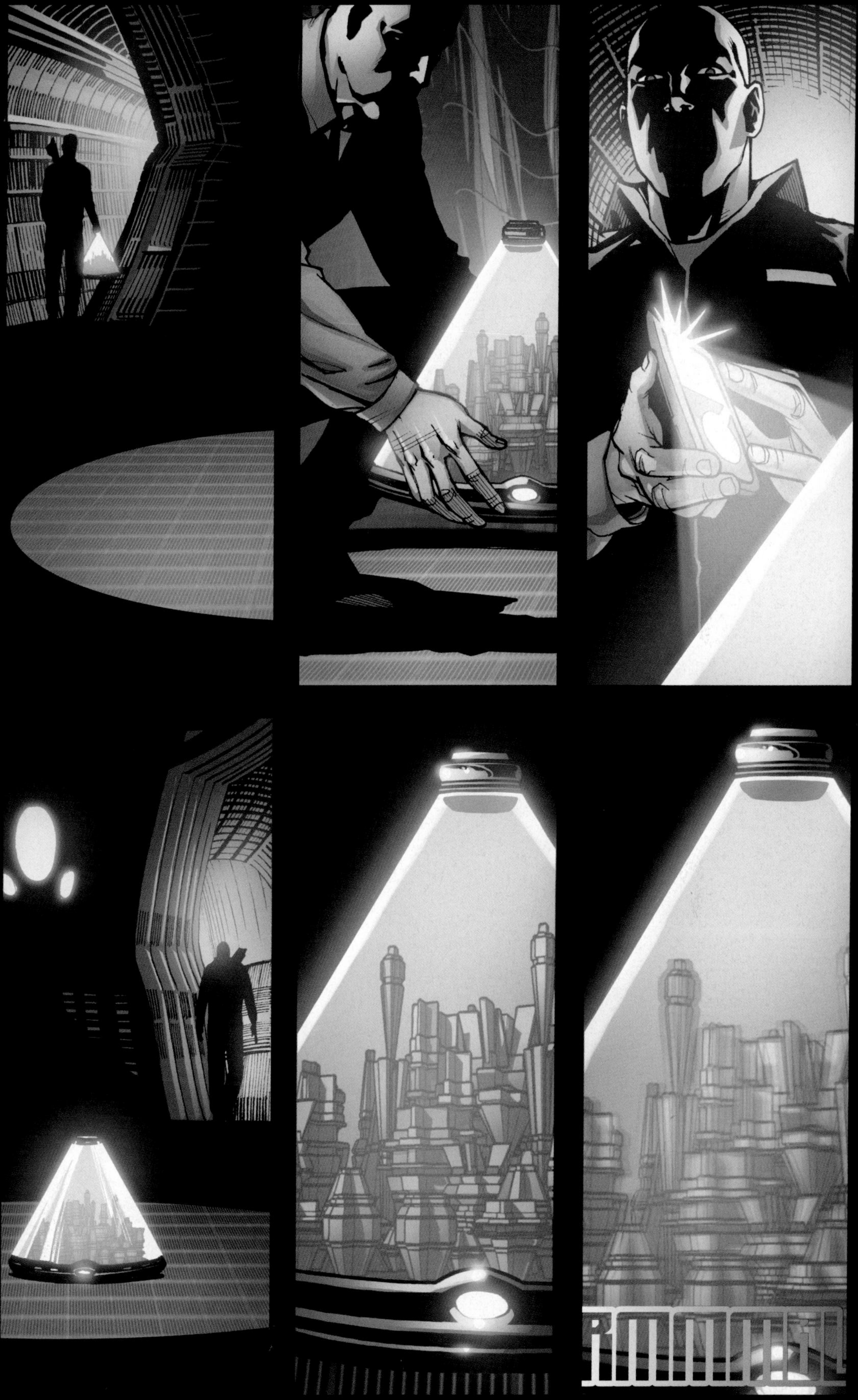

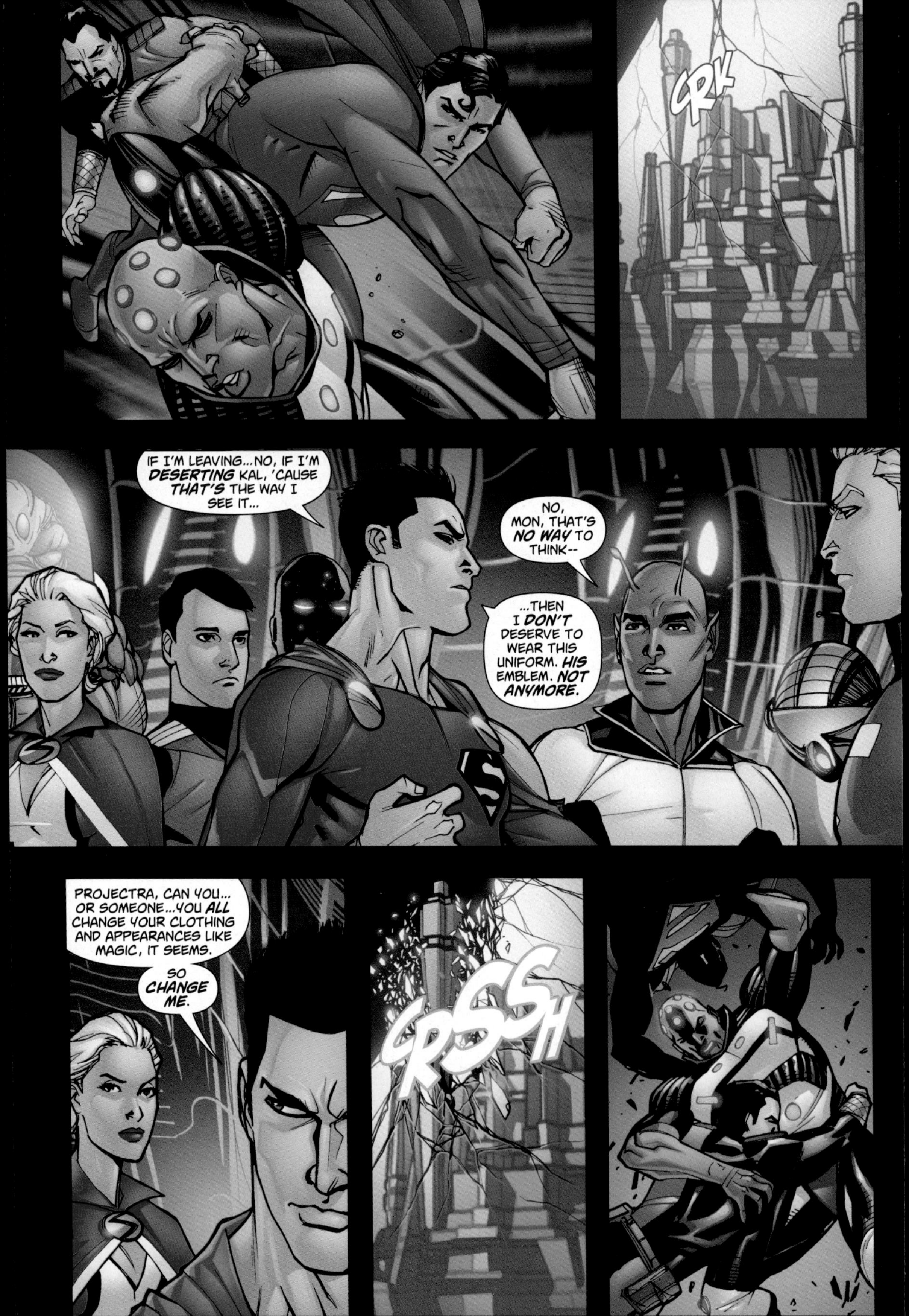
CRK
IF I'M LEAVING...NO, IF I'M DESERTING KAL, 'CAUSE THAT'S THE WAY I SEE IT...
NO, MON, THAT'S NO WAY TO THINK--
...THEN I DON'T DESERVE TO WEAR THIS UNIFORM. HIS EMBLEM. NOT ANYMORE.
PROJECTRA, CAN YOU... OR SOMEONE...YOU ALL CHANGE YOUR CLOTHING AND APPEARANCES LIKE MAGIC, IT SEEMS.
SO CHANGE ME.
CRSSH

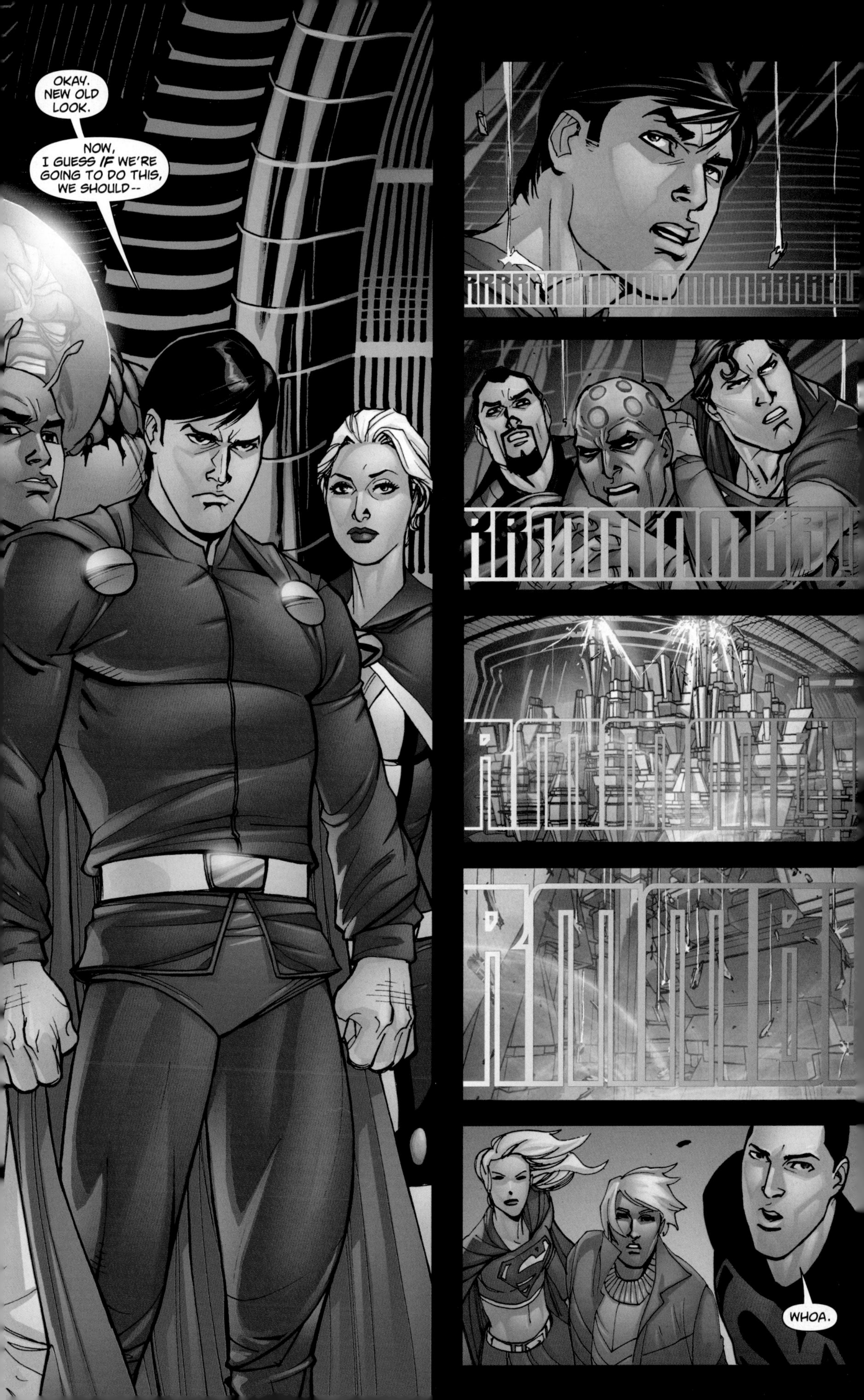
OKAY. NEW OLD LOOK.
NOW, I GUESS IF WE'RE GOING TO DO THIS, WE SHOULD--
WHOA.

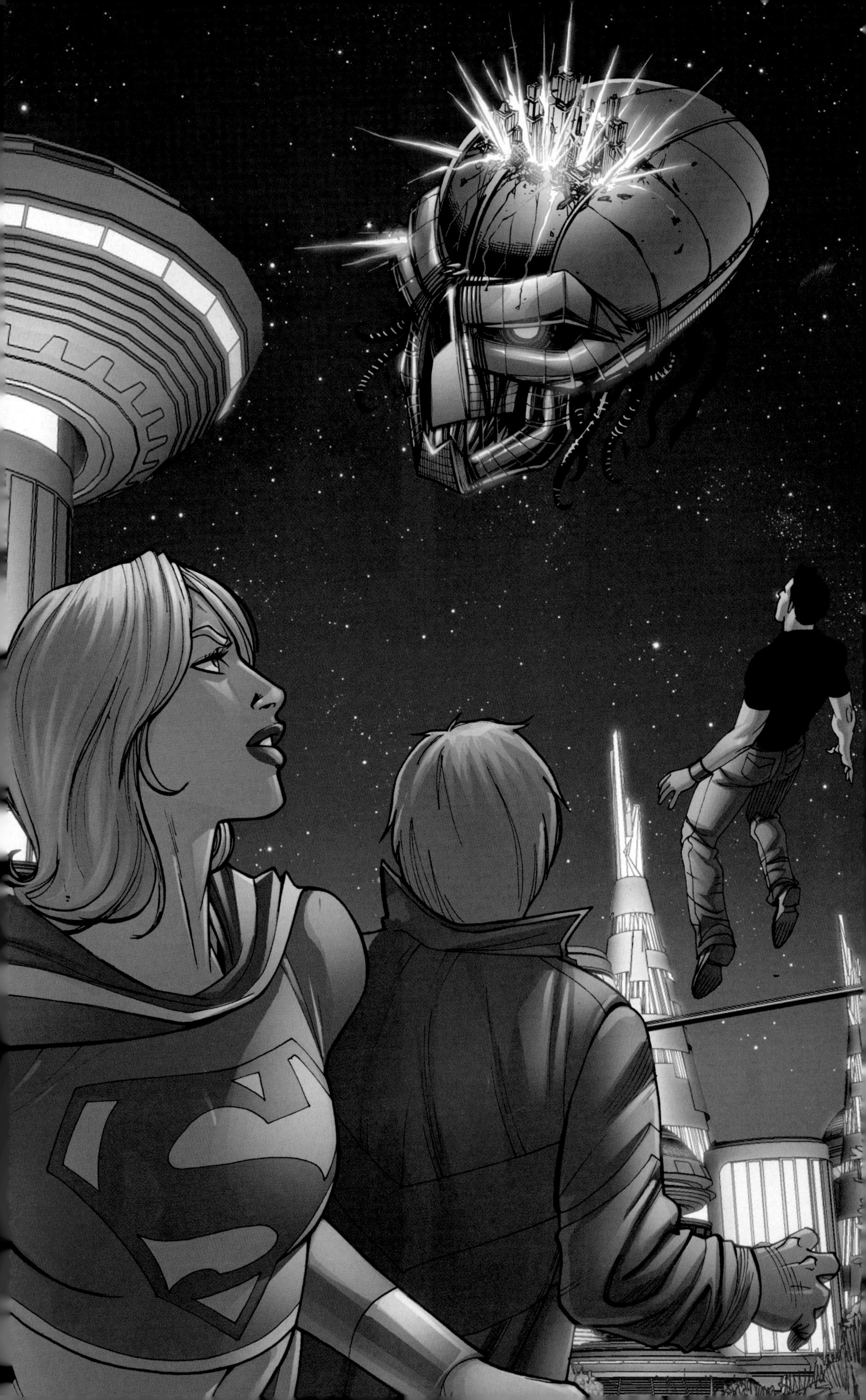

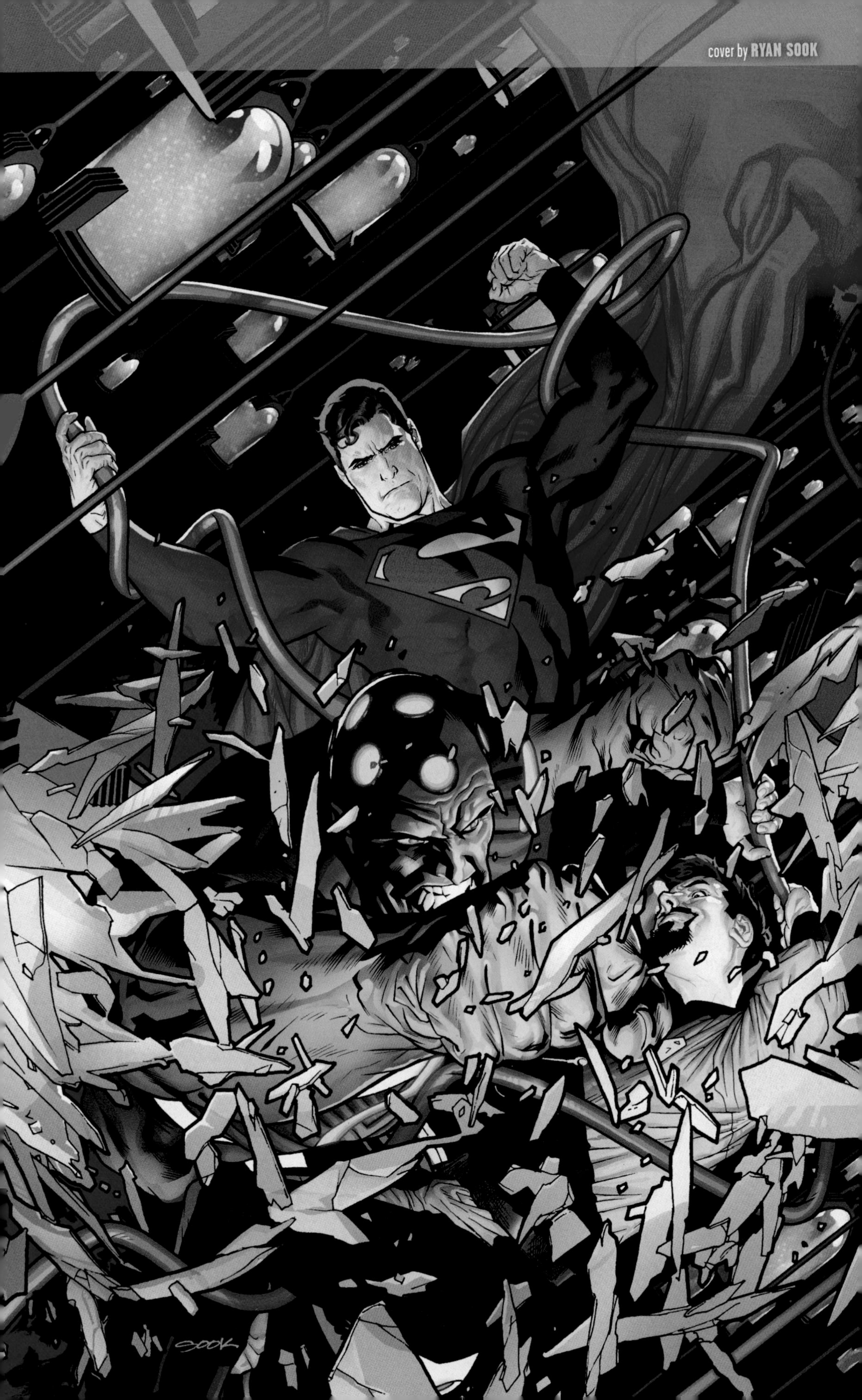
cover by **RYAN SOOK**

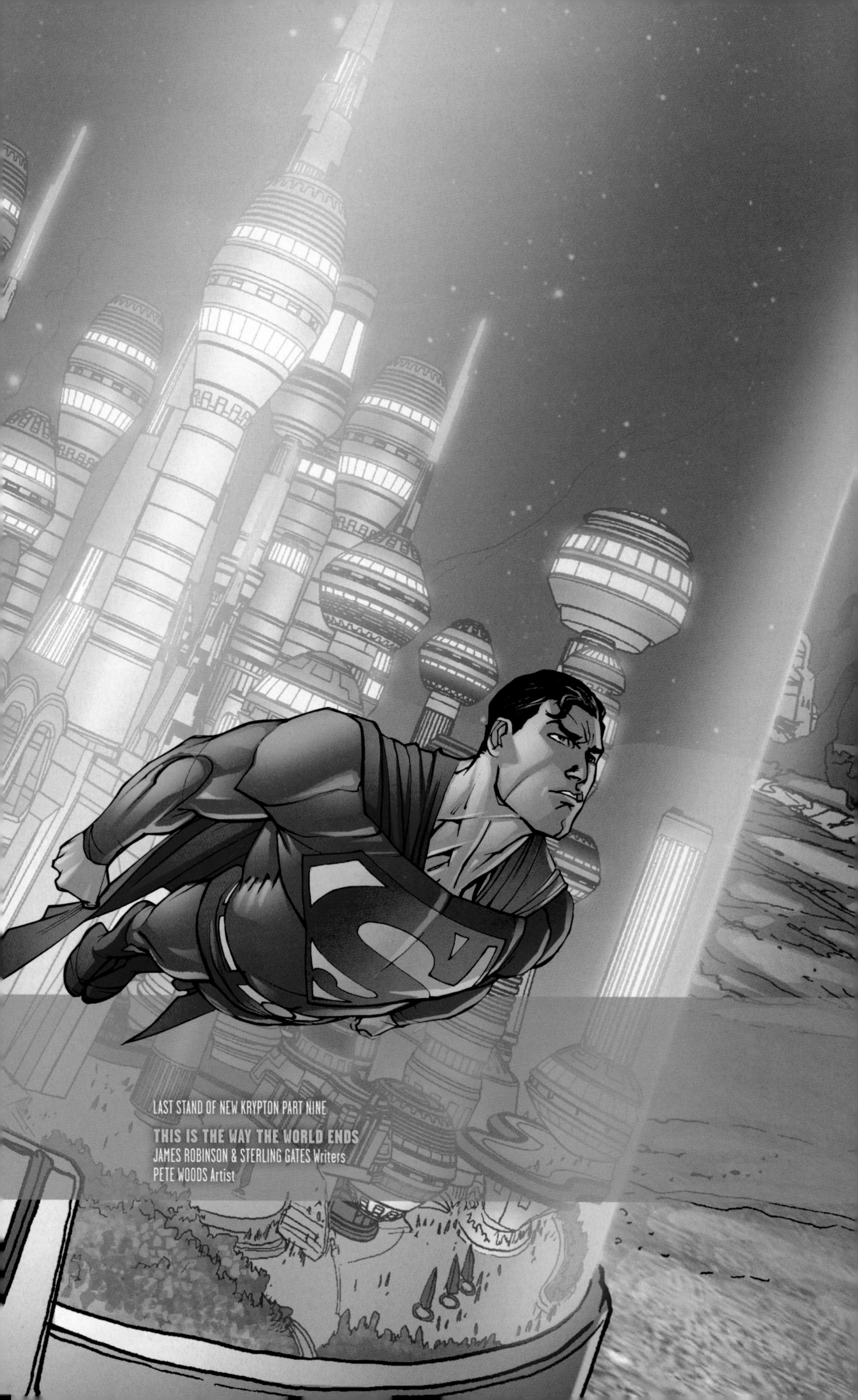
LAST STAND OF NEW KRYPTON PART NINE
THIS IS THE WAY THE WORLD ENDS
JAMES ROBINSON & STERLING GATES Writers
PETE WOODS Artist

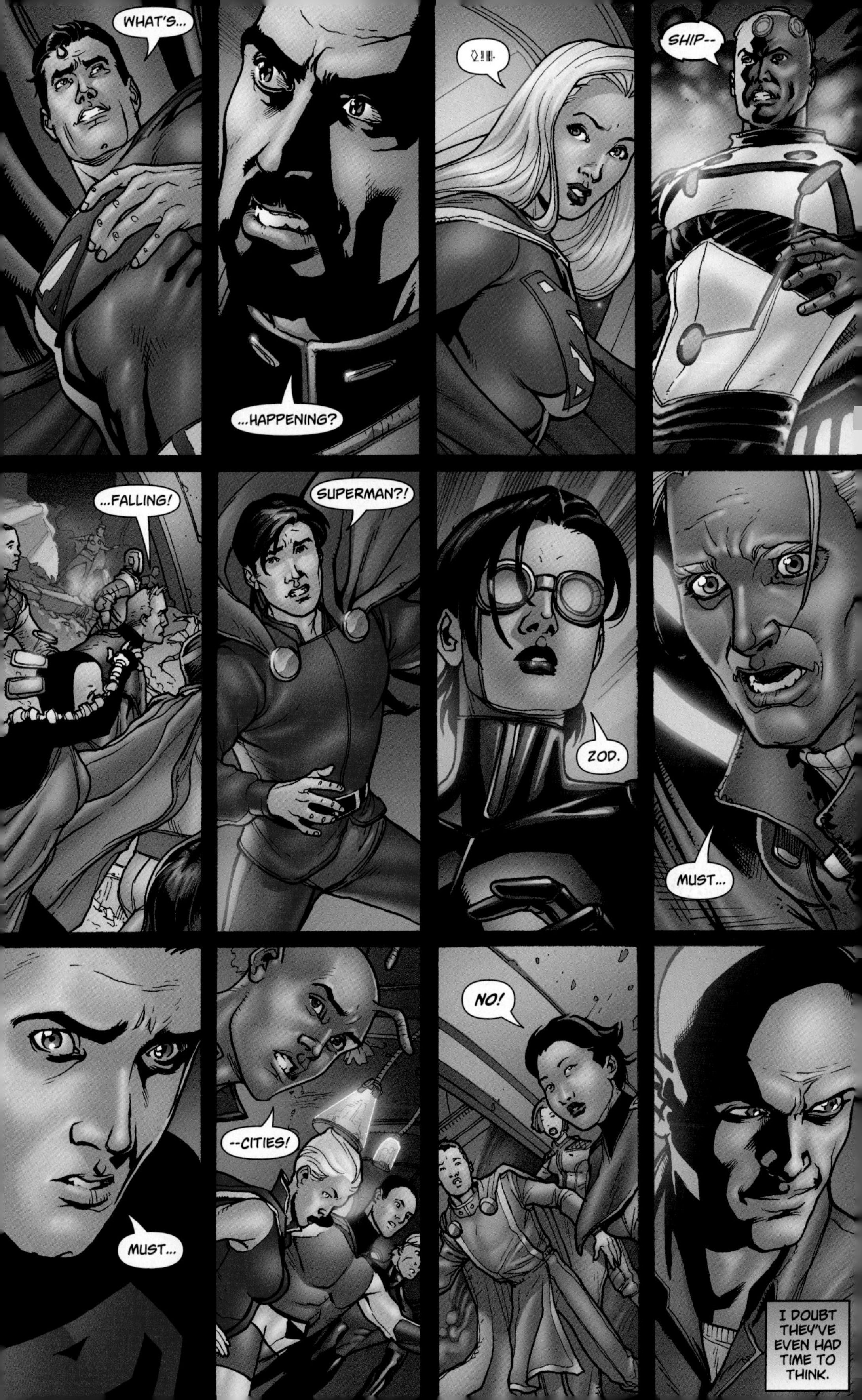
WHAT'S...
...HAPPENING?
SHIP--
...FALLING!
SUPERMAN?!
ZOD.
MUST...
MUST...
--CITIES!
NO!
I DOUBT THEY'VE EVEN HAD TIME TO THINK.

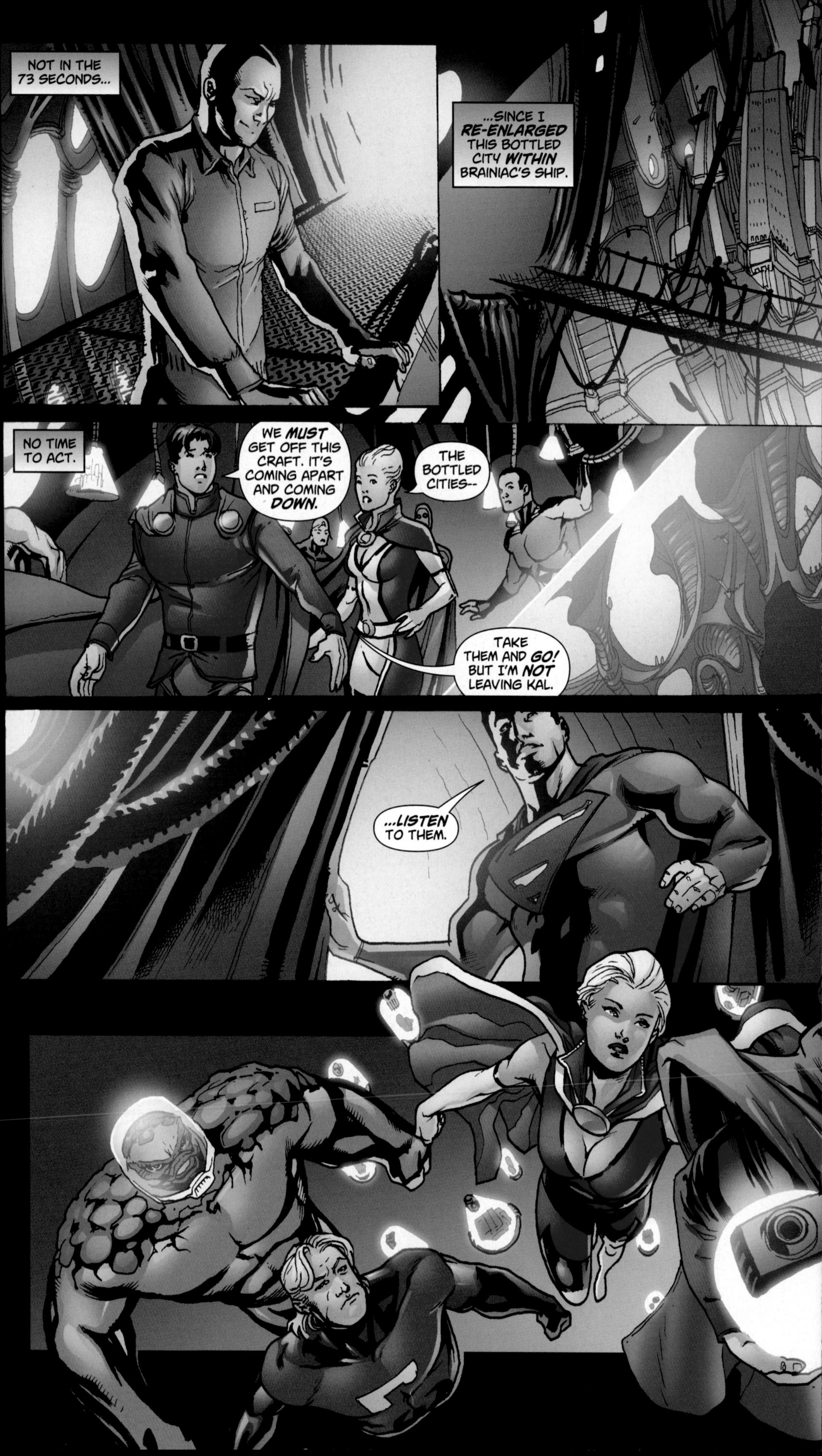
NOT IN THE 73 SECONDS...
...SINCE I RE-ENLARGED THIS BOTTLED CITY WITHIN BRAINIAC'S SHIP.
NO TIME TO ACT.
WE MUST GET OFF THIS CRAFT. IT'S COMING APART AND COMING DOWN.
THE BOTTLED CITIES--
TAKE THEM AND GO! BUT I'M NOT LEAVING KAL.
...LISTEN TO THEM.

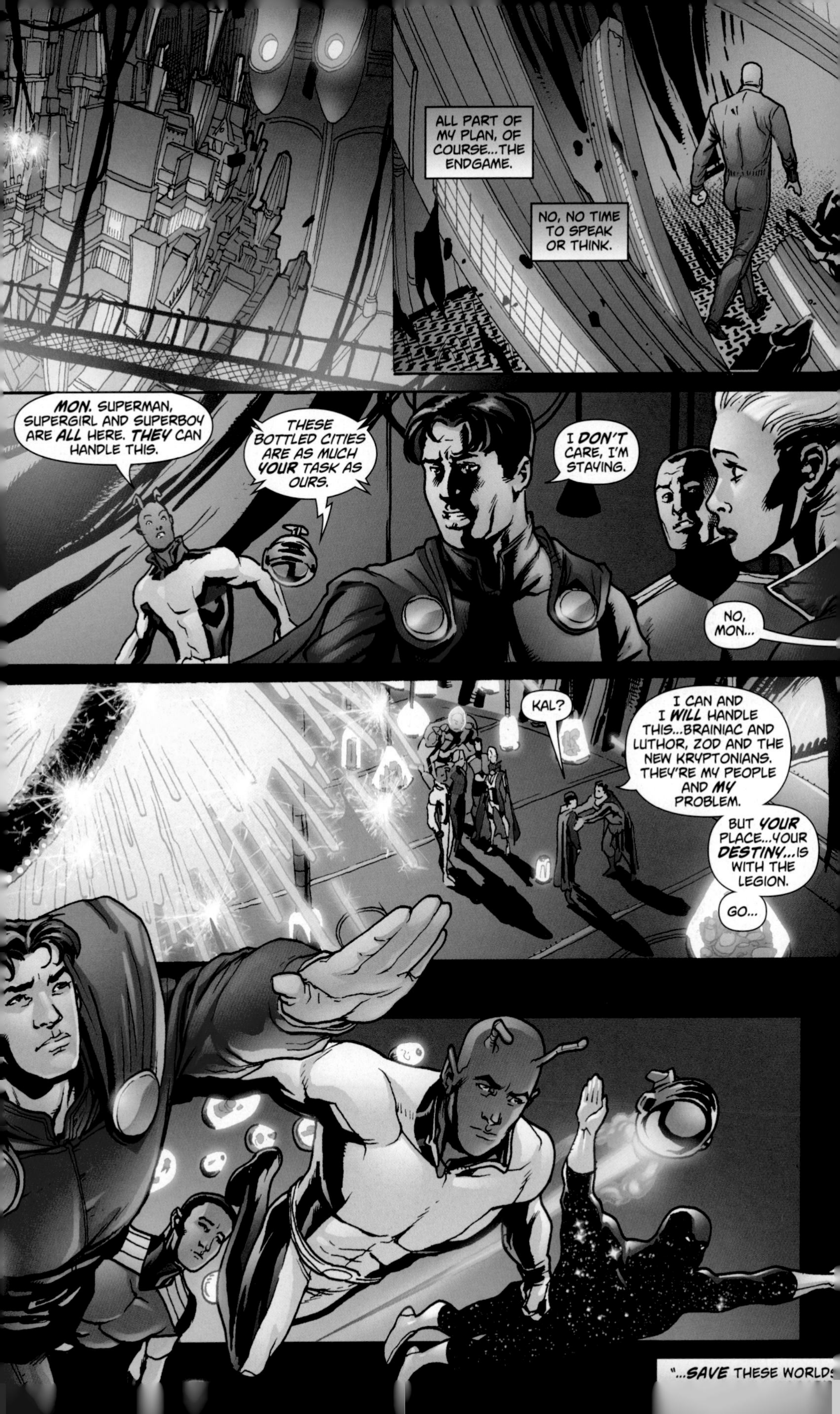
ALL PART OF MY PLAN, OF COURSE...THE ENDGAME.
NO, NO TIME TO SPEAK OR THINK.
MON. SUPERMAN, SUPERGIRL AND SUPERBOY ARE ALL HERE. THEY CAN HANDLE THIS.
THESE BOTTLED CITIES ARE AS MUCH YOUR TASK AS OURS.
I DON'T CARE, I'M STAYING.
NO, MON...
KAL?
I CAN AND I WILL HANDLE THIS...BRAINIAC AND LUTHOR, ZOD AND THE NEW KRYPTONIANS. THEY'RE MY PEOPLE AND MY PROBLEM.
BUT YOUR PLACE...YOUR DESTINY...IS WITH THE LEGION.
GO...
"...SAVE THESE WORLDS

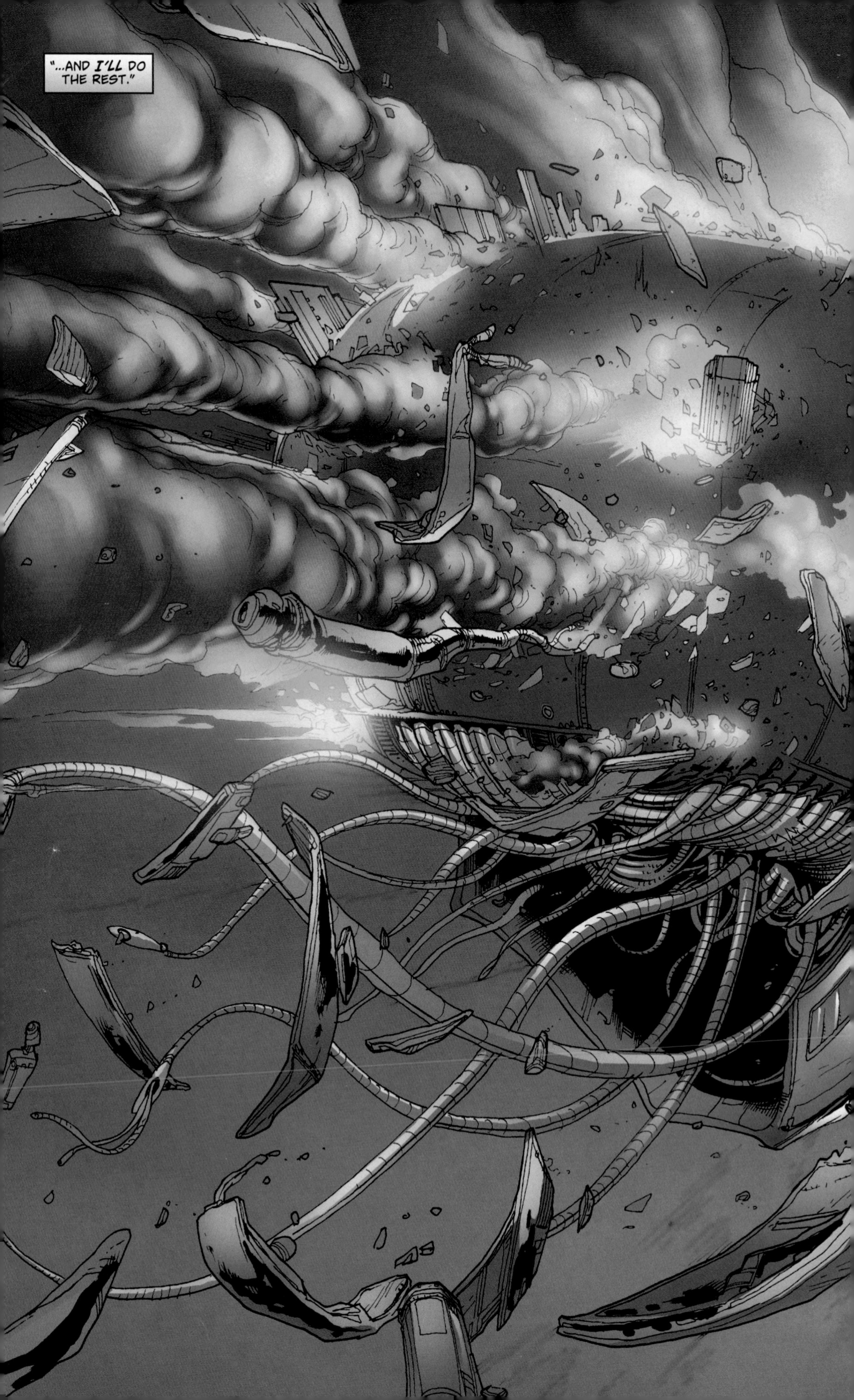
"...AND I'LL DO THE REST."

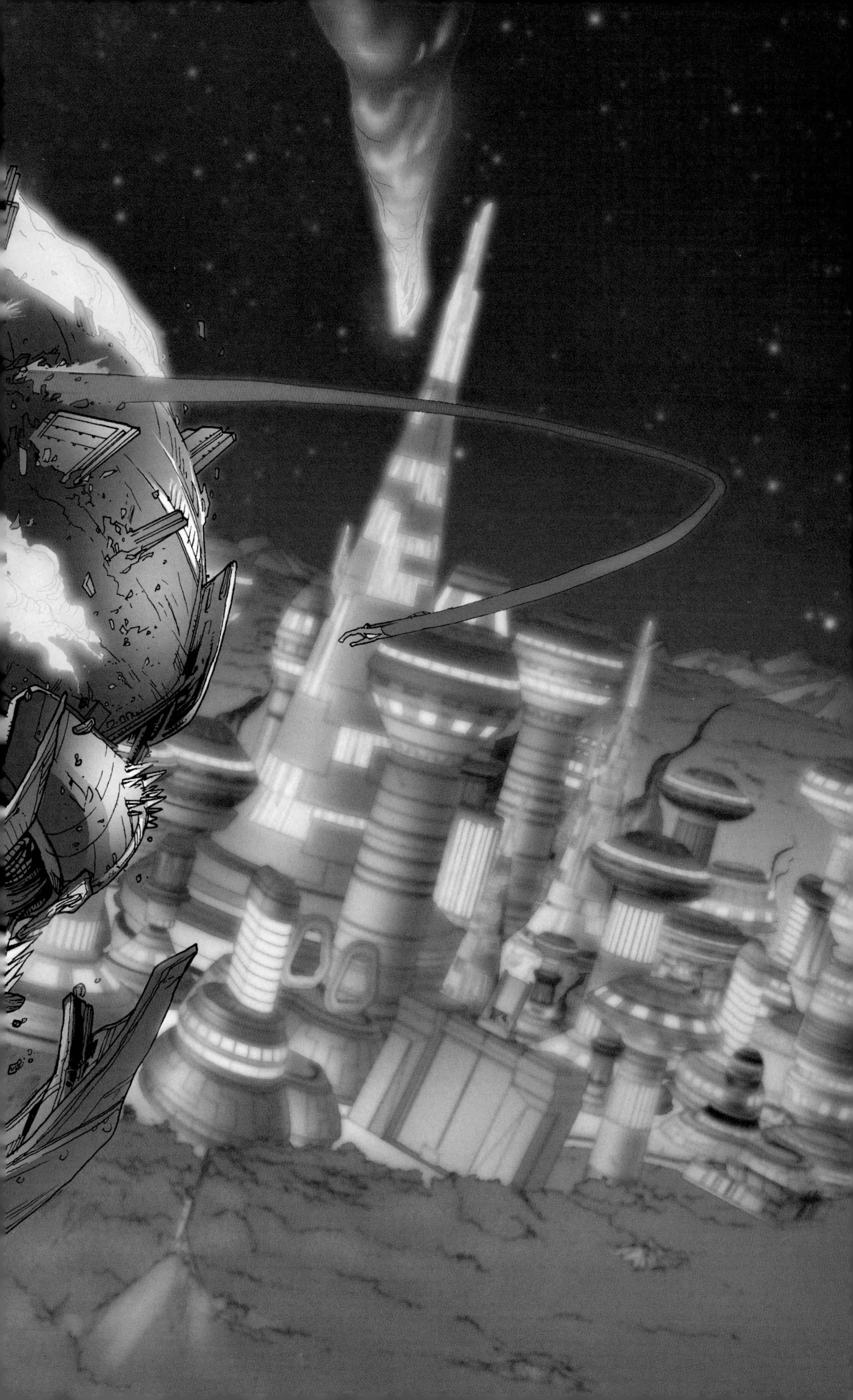

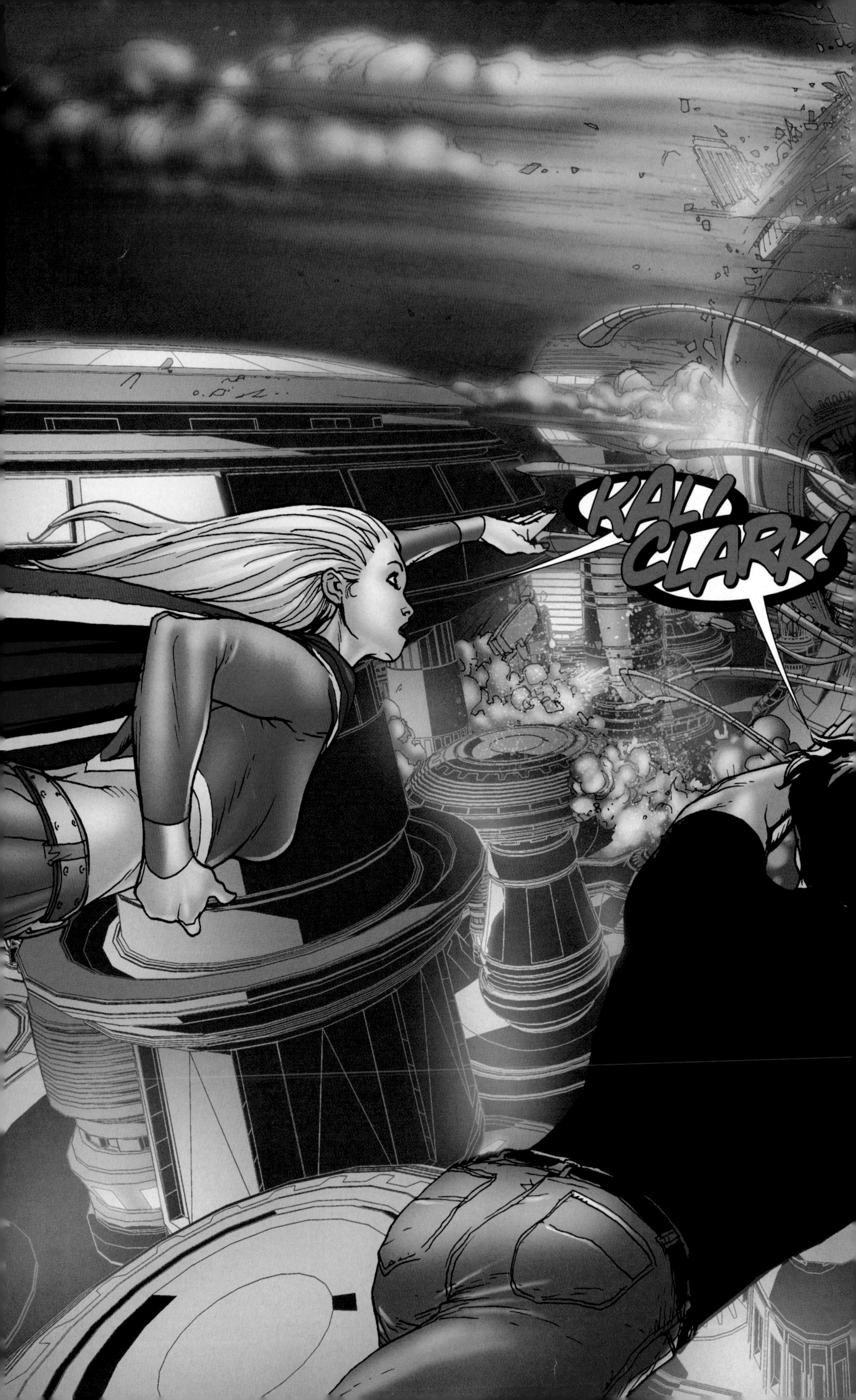
KAL! CLARK!

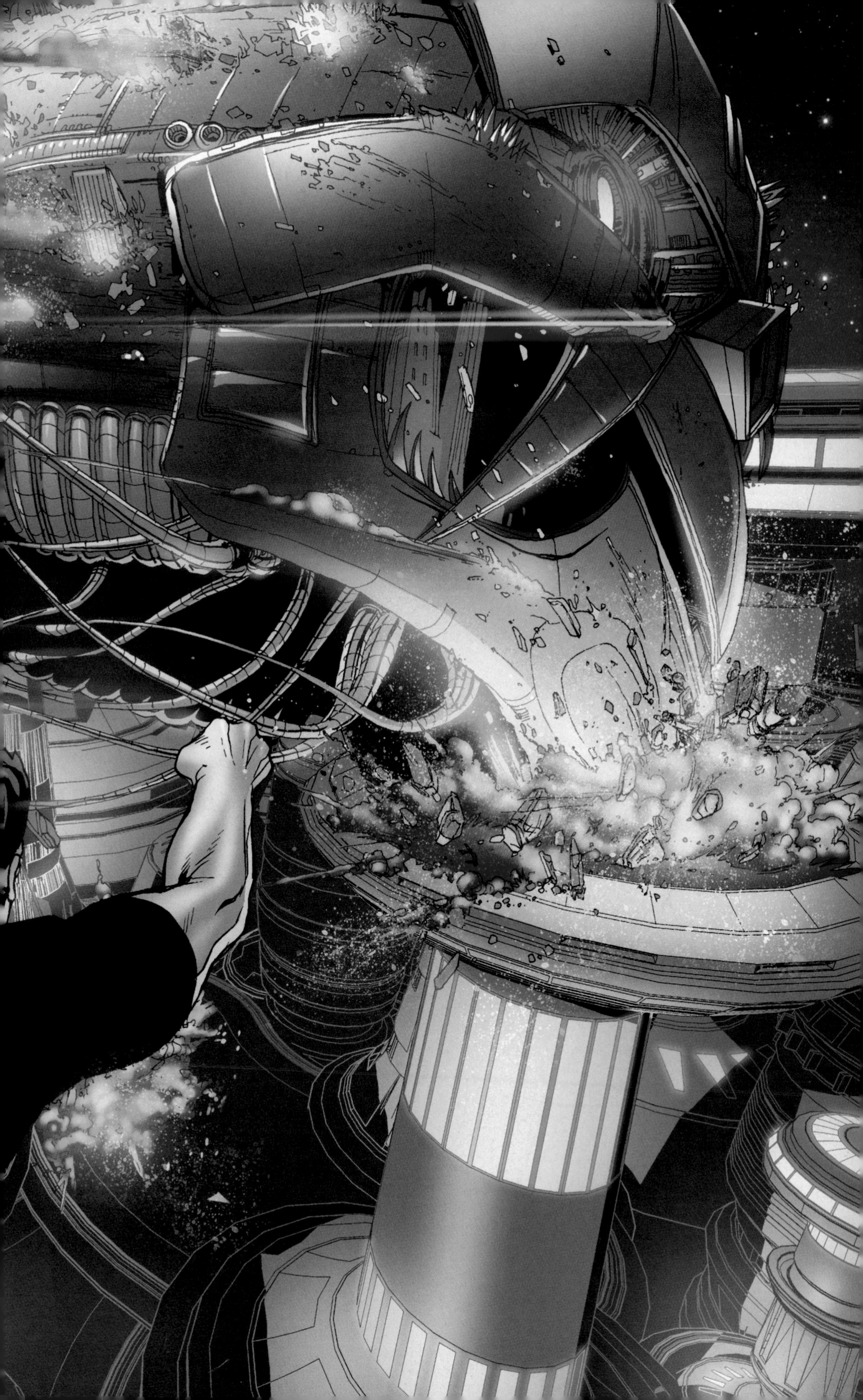

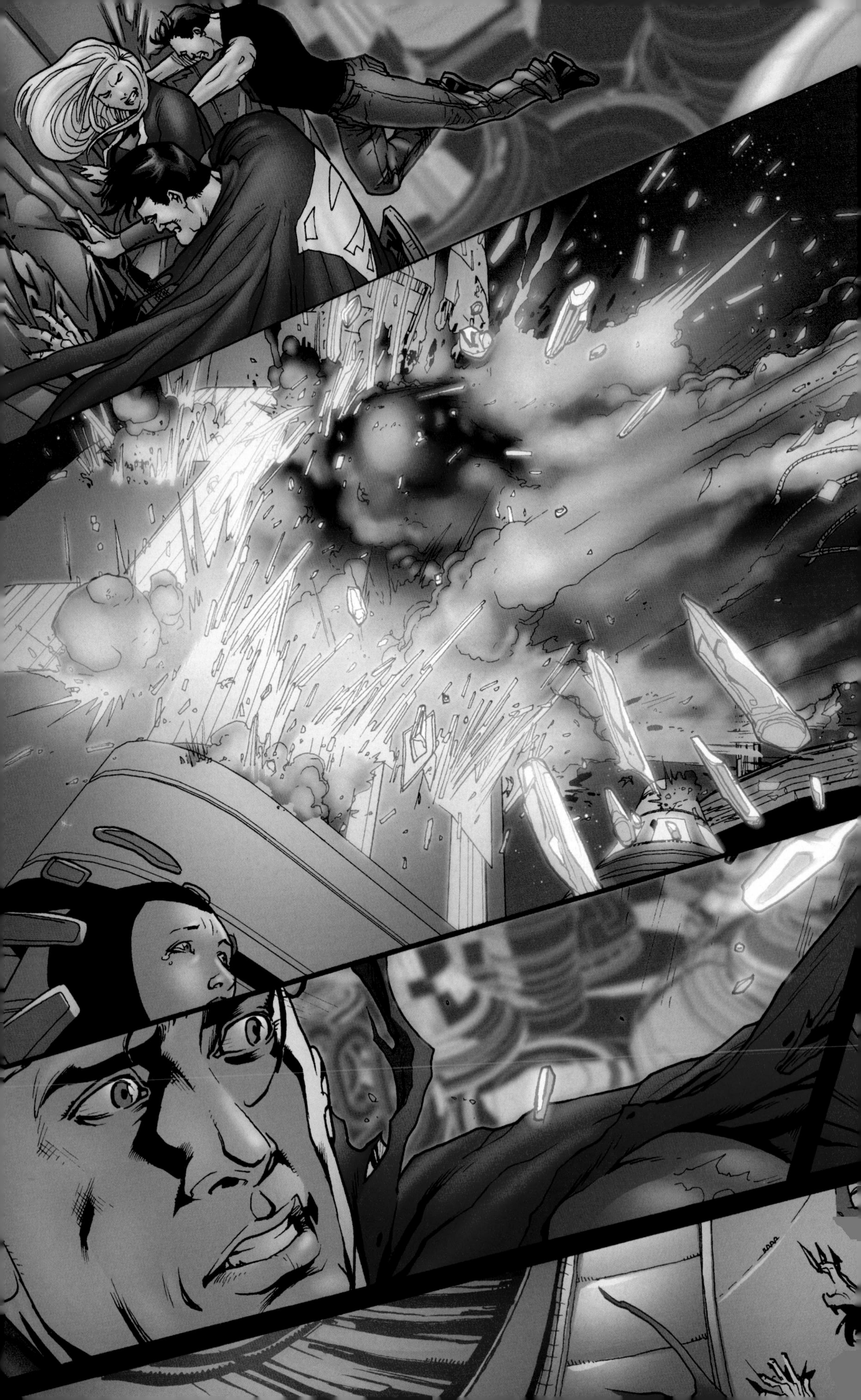

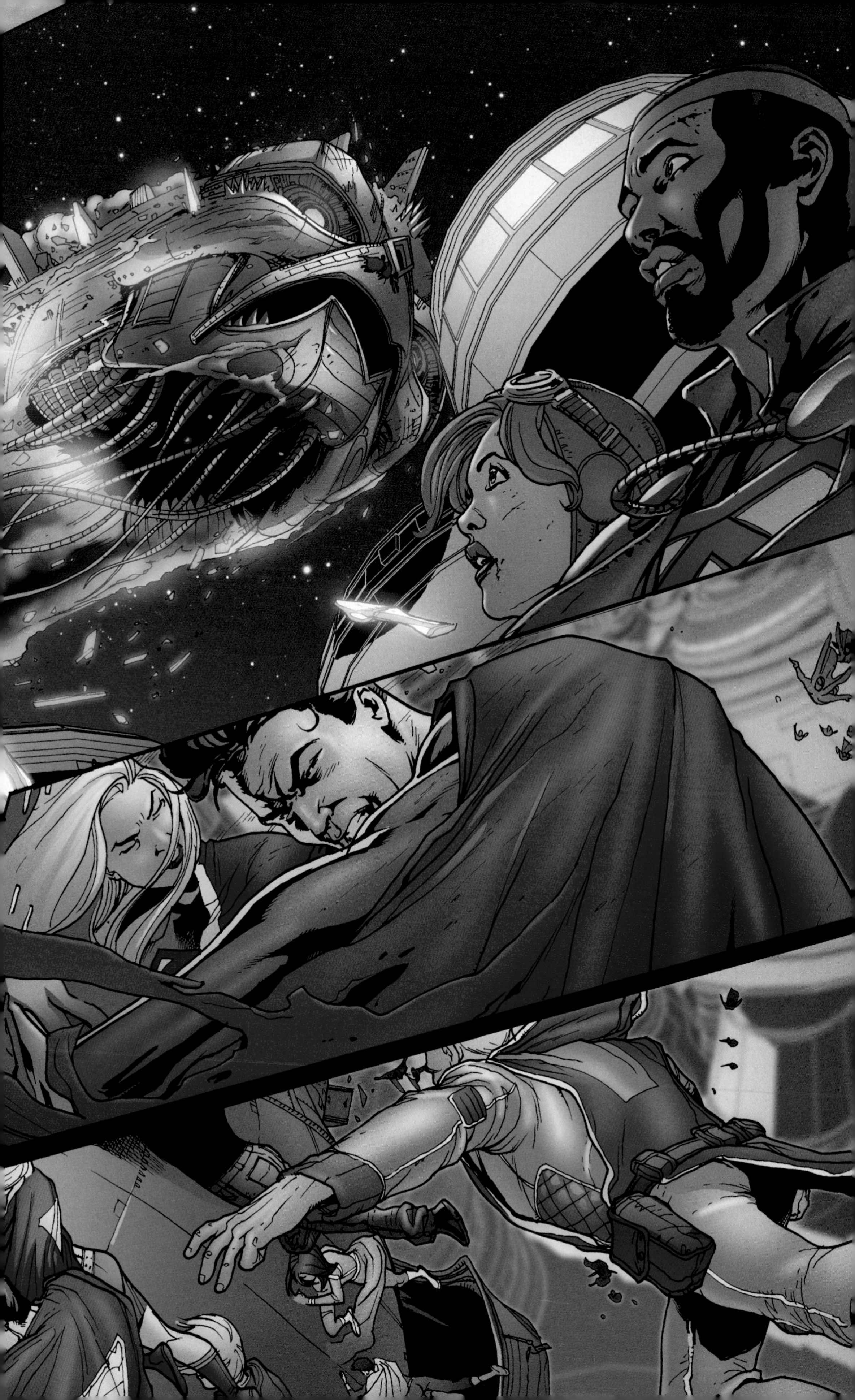

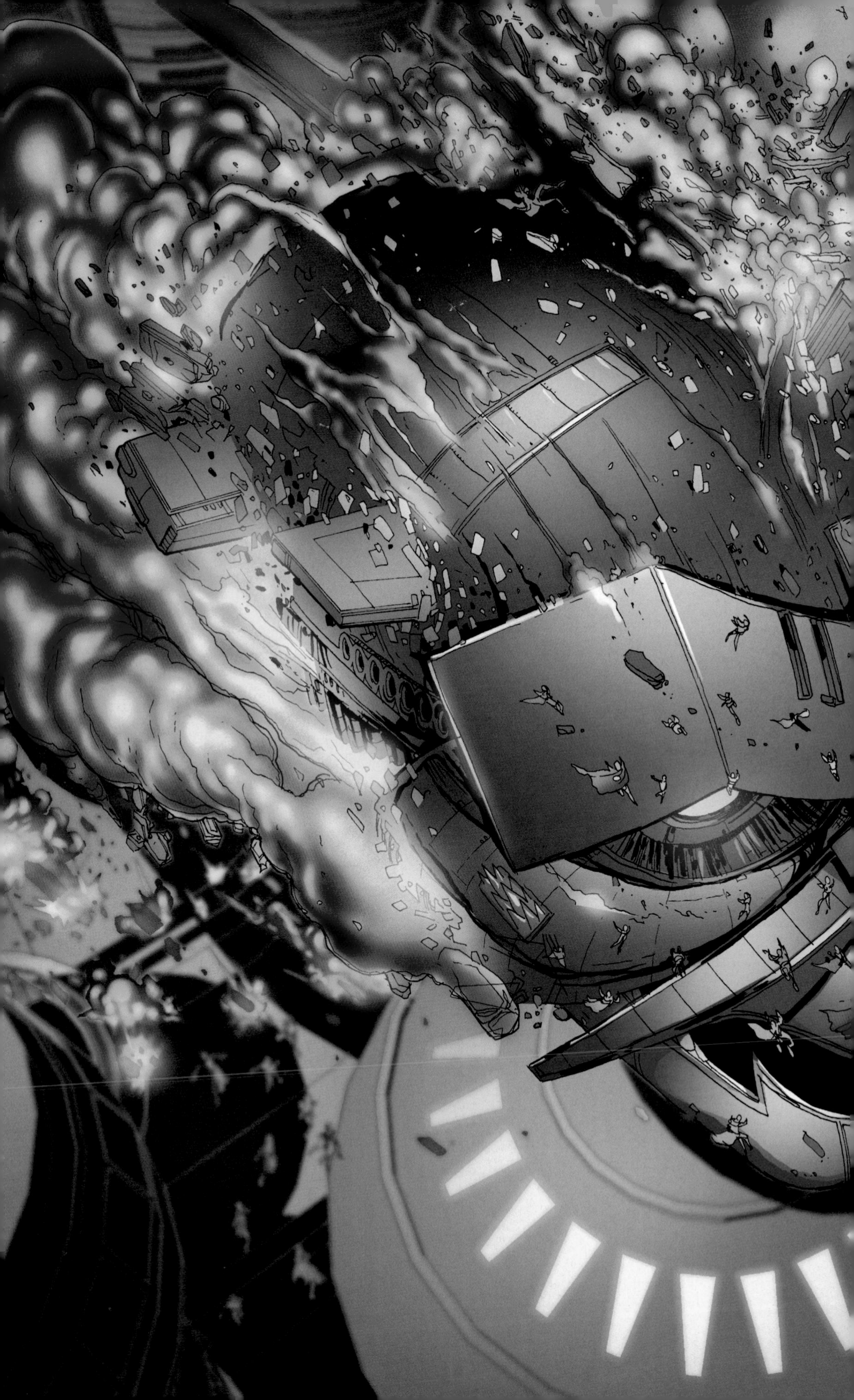

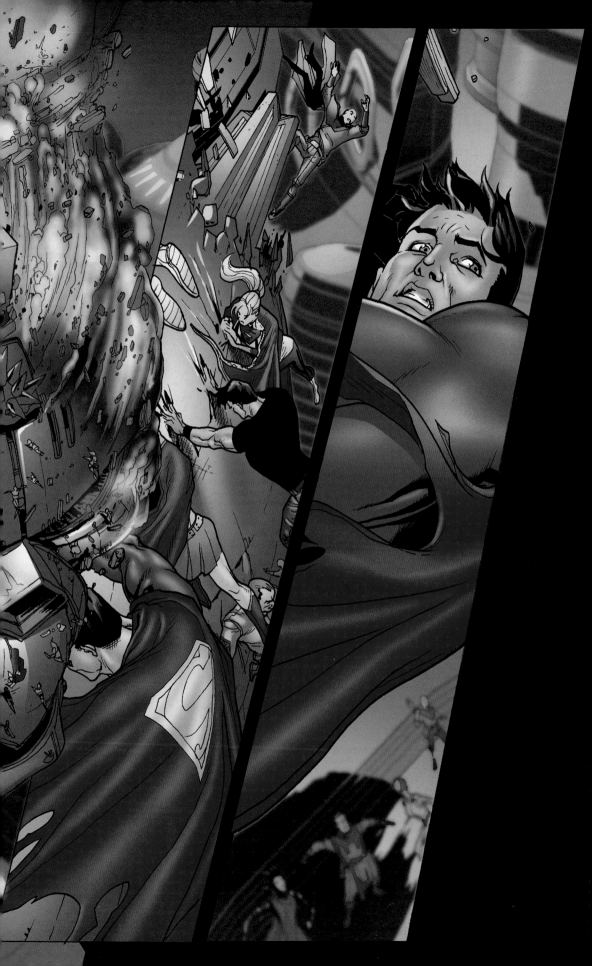

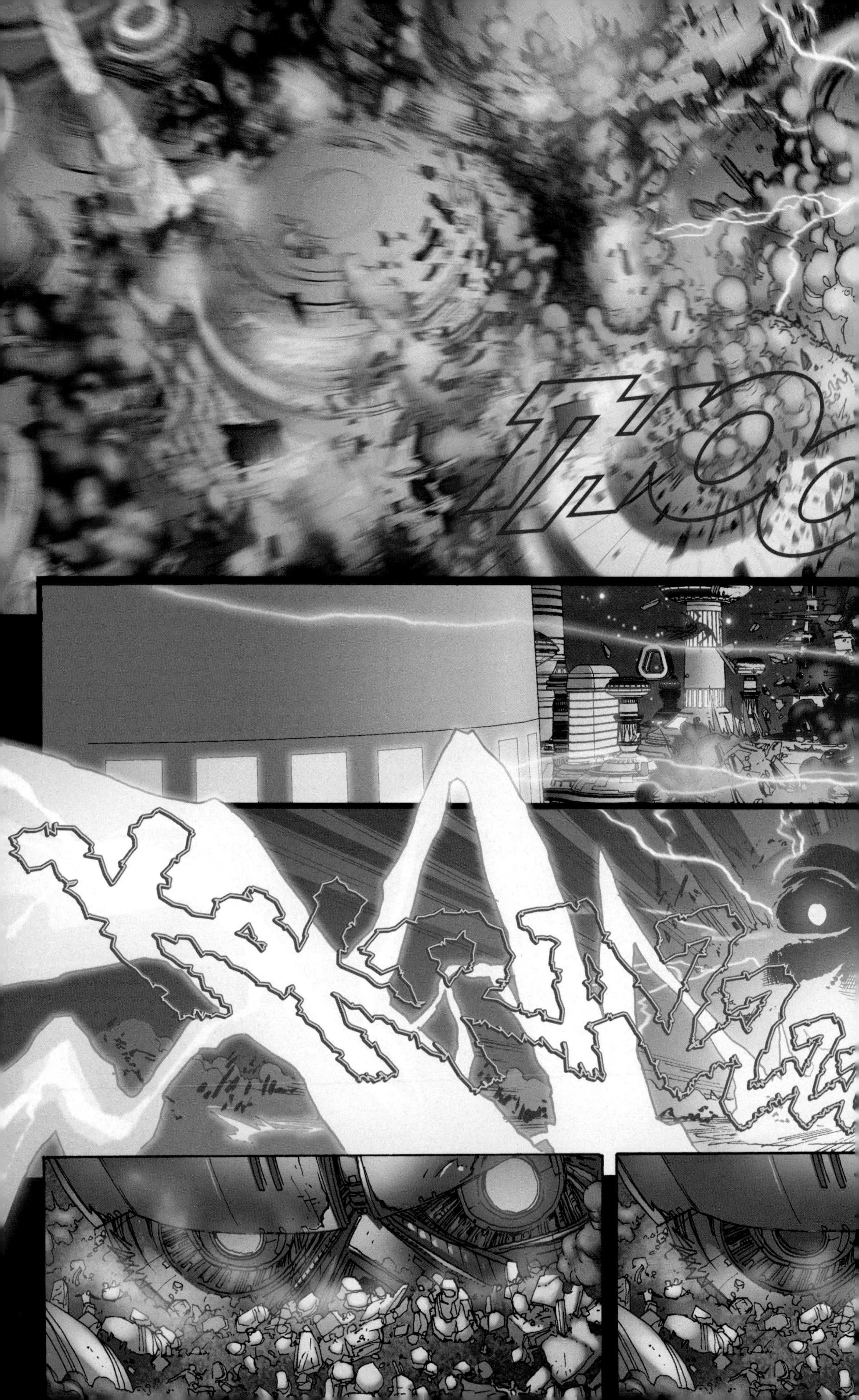

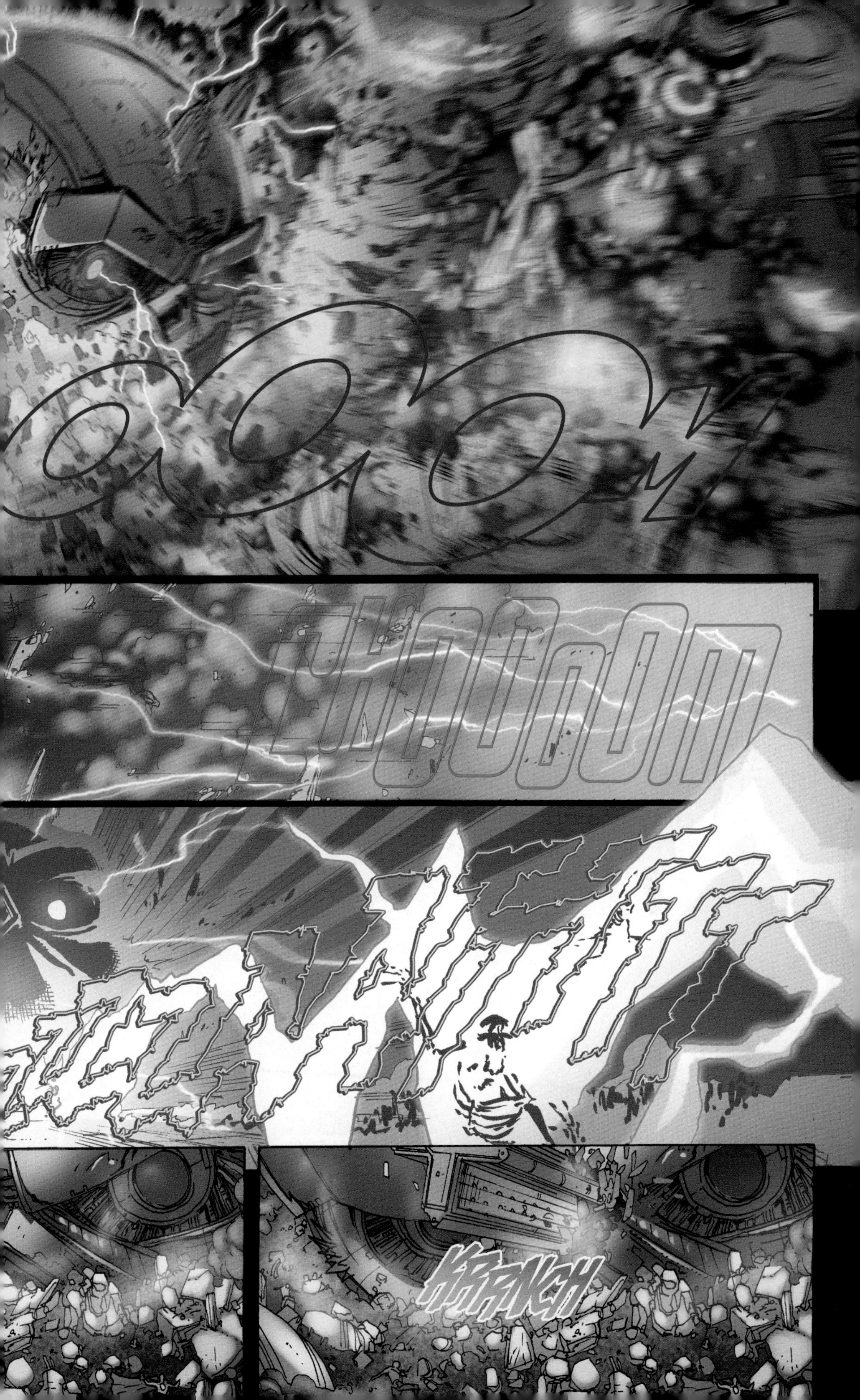
CHOOOOM
KRRNCH

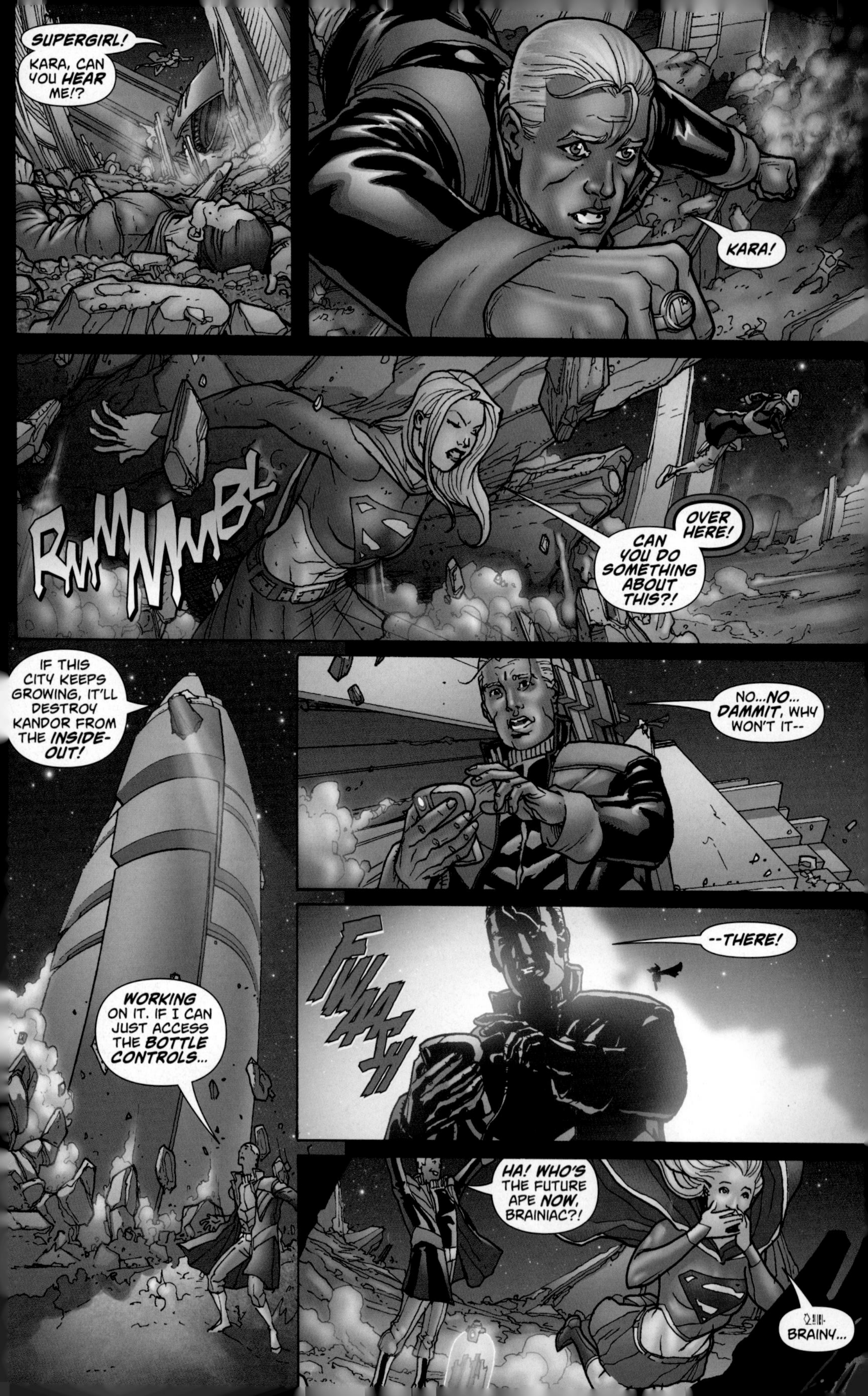
SUPERGIRL! KARA, CAN YOU HEAR ME!?
KARA!
RMMMMBL
OVER HERE!
CAN YOU DO SOMETHING ABOUT THIS?!
IF THIS CITY KEEPS GROWING, IT'LL DESTROY KANDOR FROM THE INSIDE-OUT!
WORKING ON IT. IF I CAN JUST ACCESS THE BOTTLE CONTROLS...
NO...NO... DAMMIT, WHY WON'T IT--
--THERE!
FWAAH
HA! WHO'S THE FUTURE APE NOW, BRAINIAC?!
BRAINY...

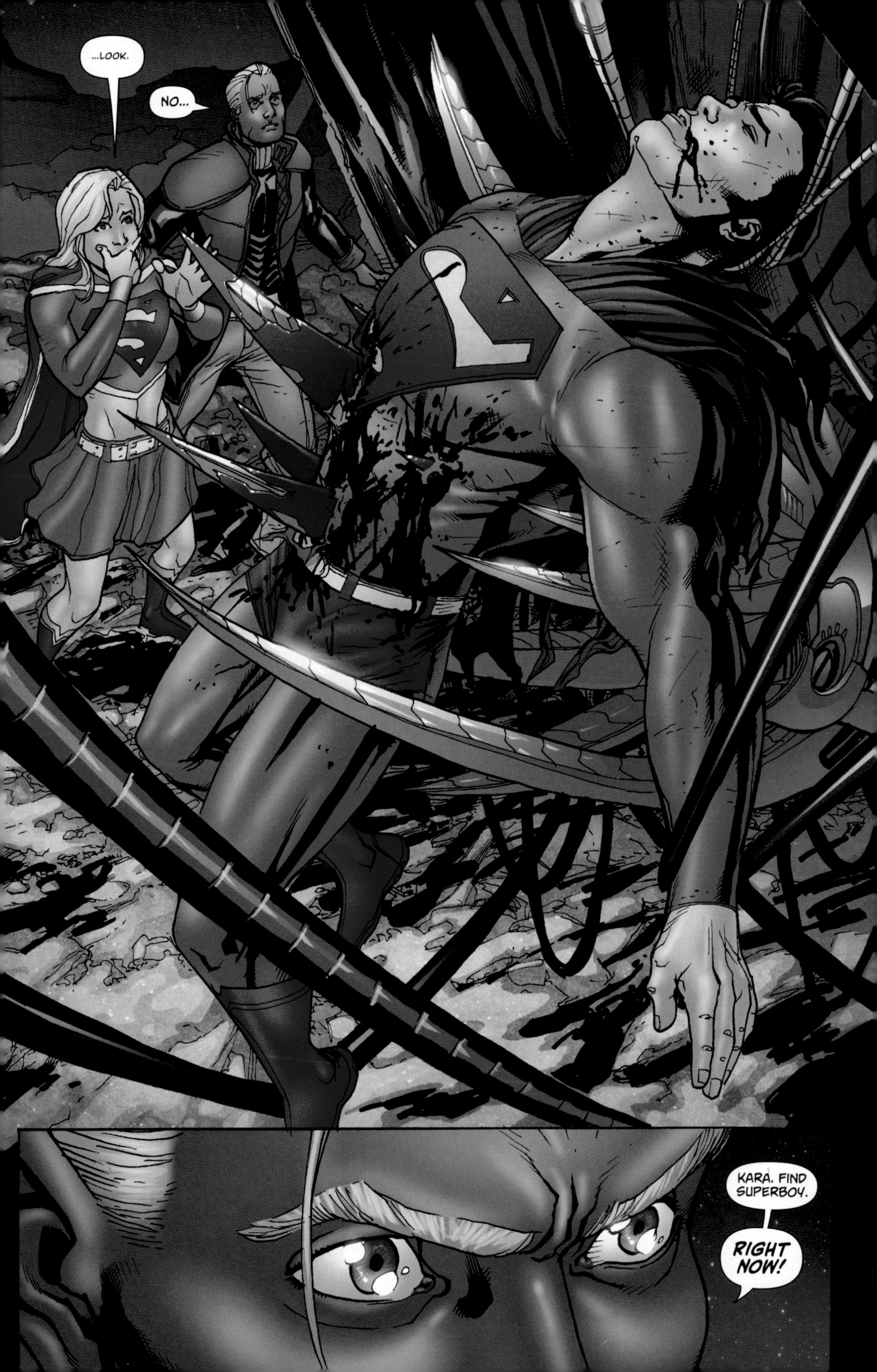
...LOOK.
NO...
KARA. FIND SUPERBOY.
RIGHT NOW!

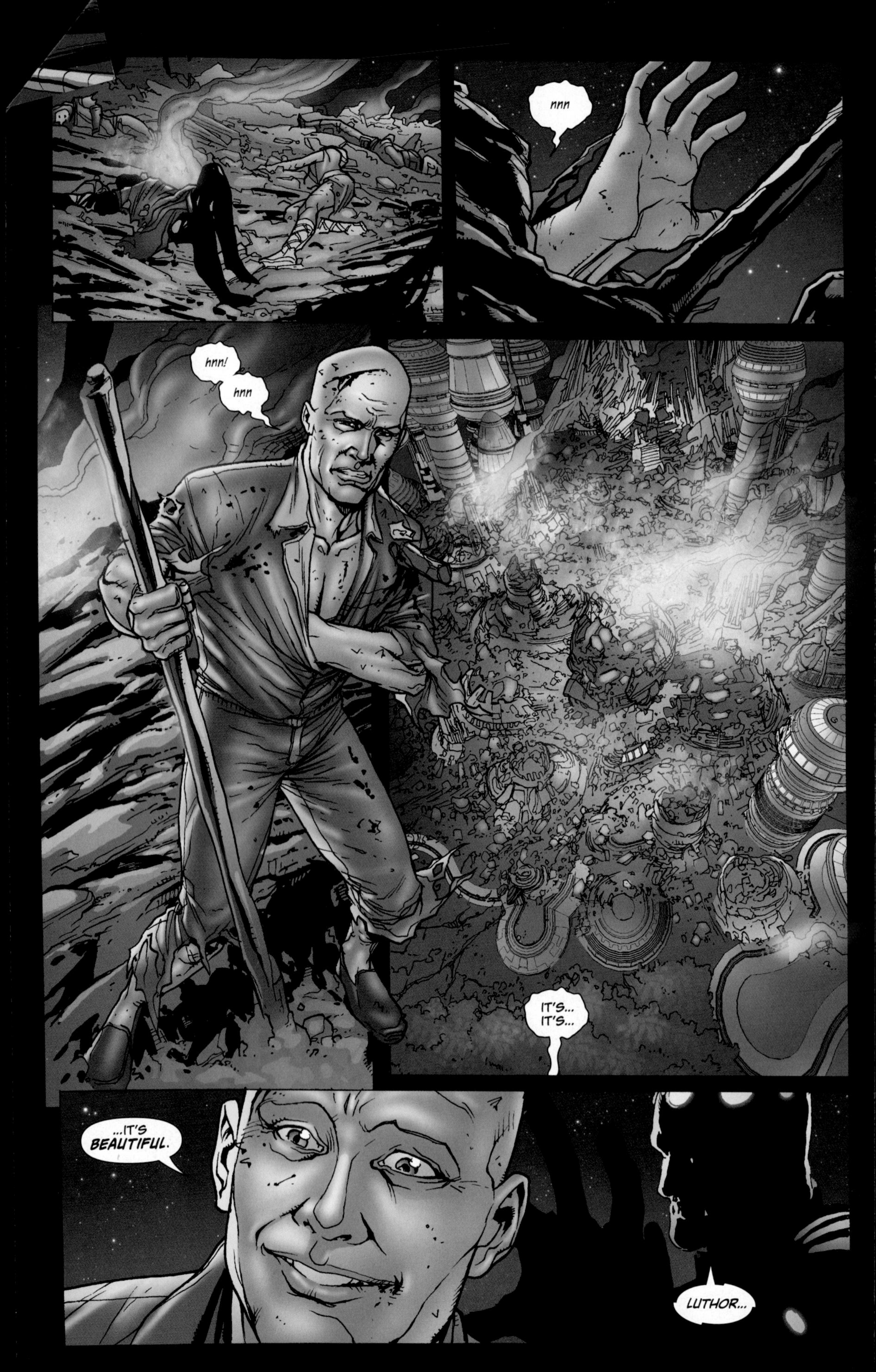
nnn
hnn!
hnn
IT'S...
IT'S...
...IT'S
BEAUTIFUL.
LUTHOR...

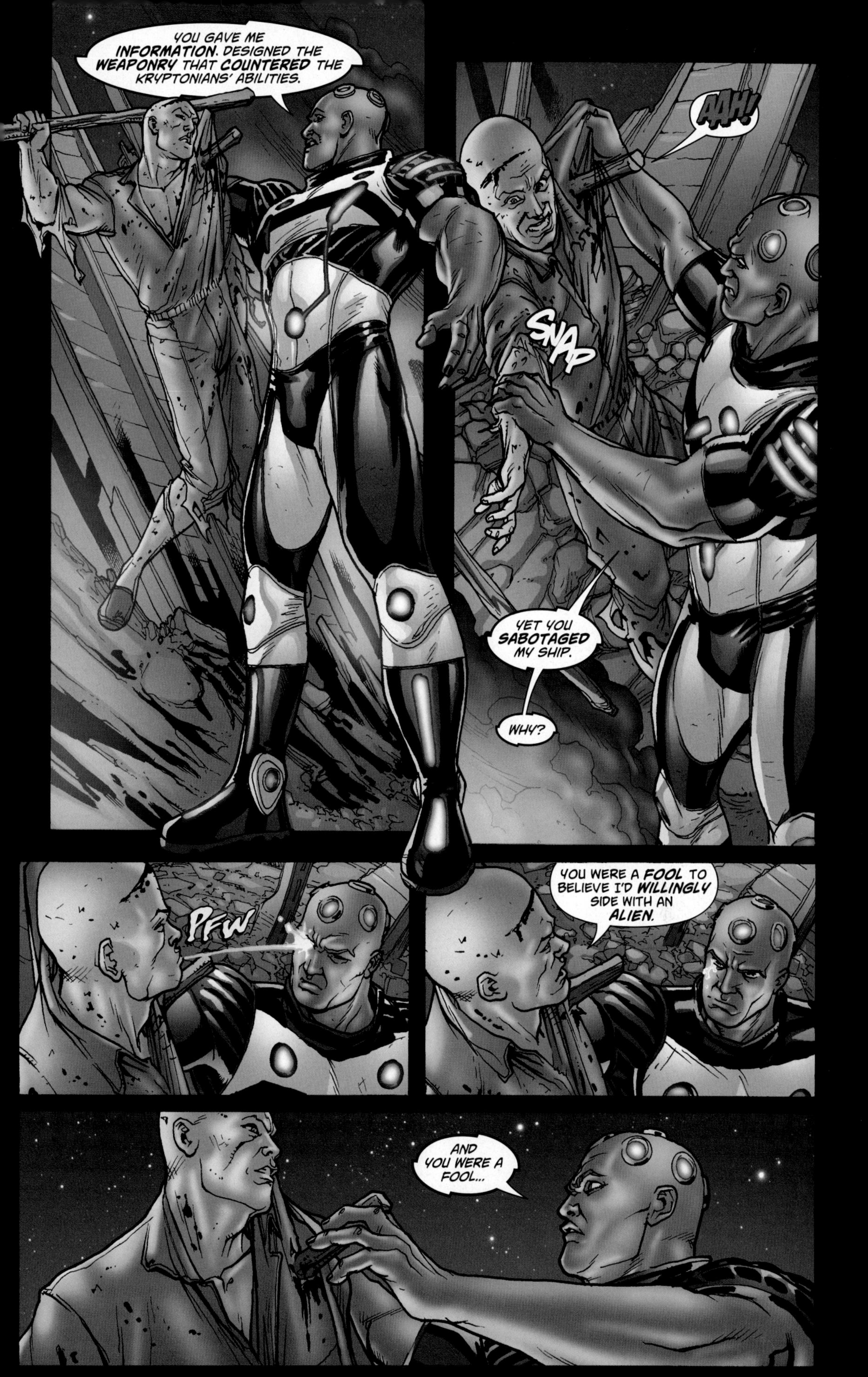

YOU GAVE ME INFORMATION. DESIGNED THE WEAPONRY THAT COUNTERED THE KRYPTONIANS' ABILITIES.
AAH!
SNAP
YET YOU SABOTAGED MY SHIP.
WHY?
PFW
YOU WERE A FOOL TO BELIEVE I'D WILLINGLY SIDE WITH AN ALIEN.
AND YOU WERE A FOOL...

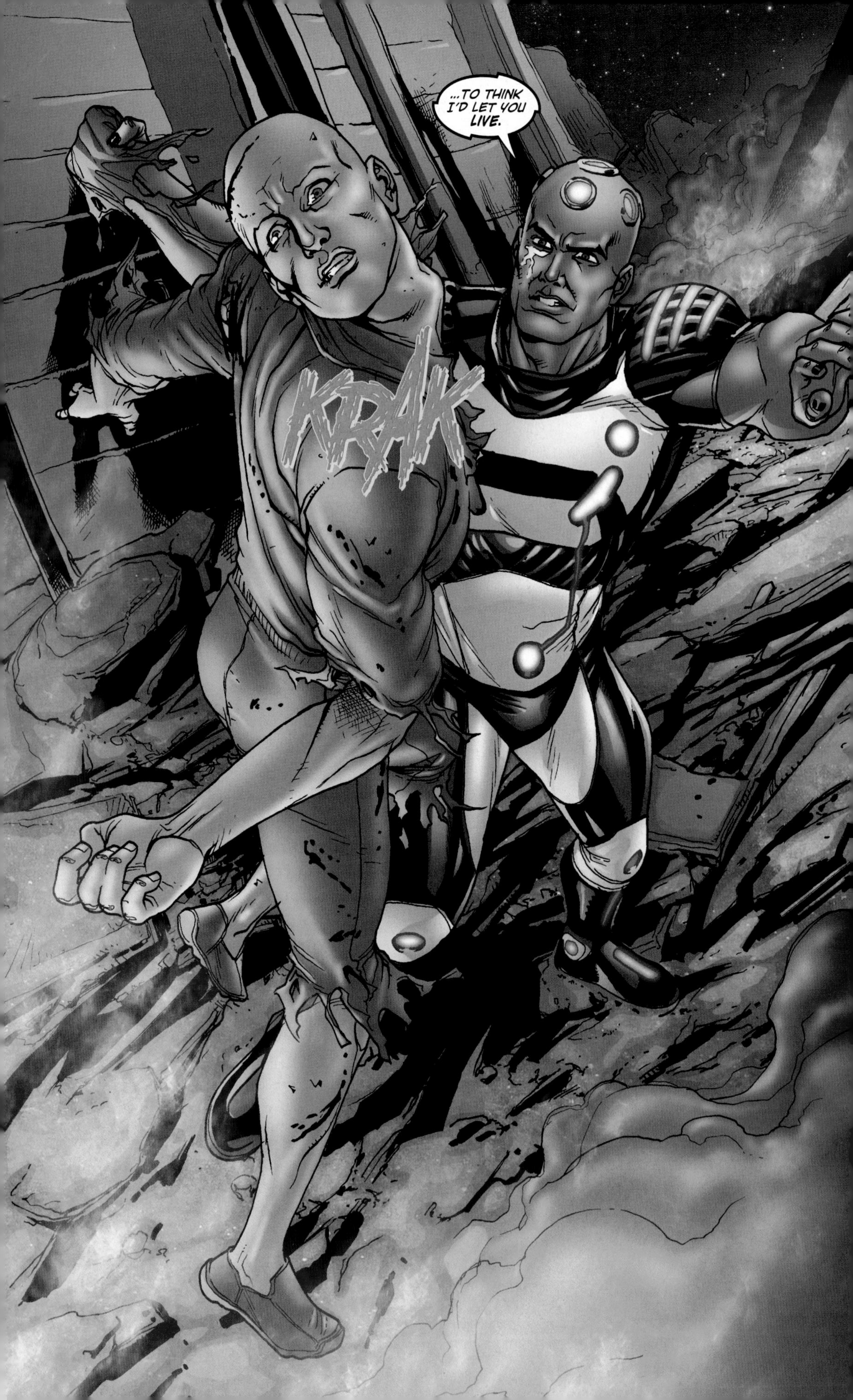
...TO THINK I'D LET YOU LIVE.
KRAK

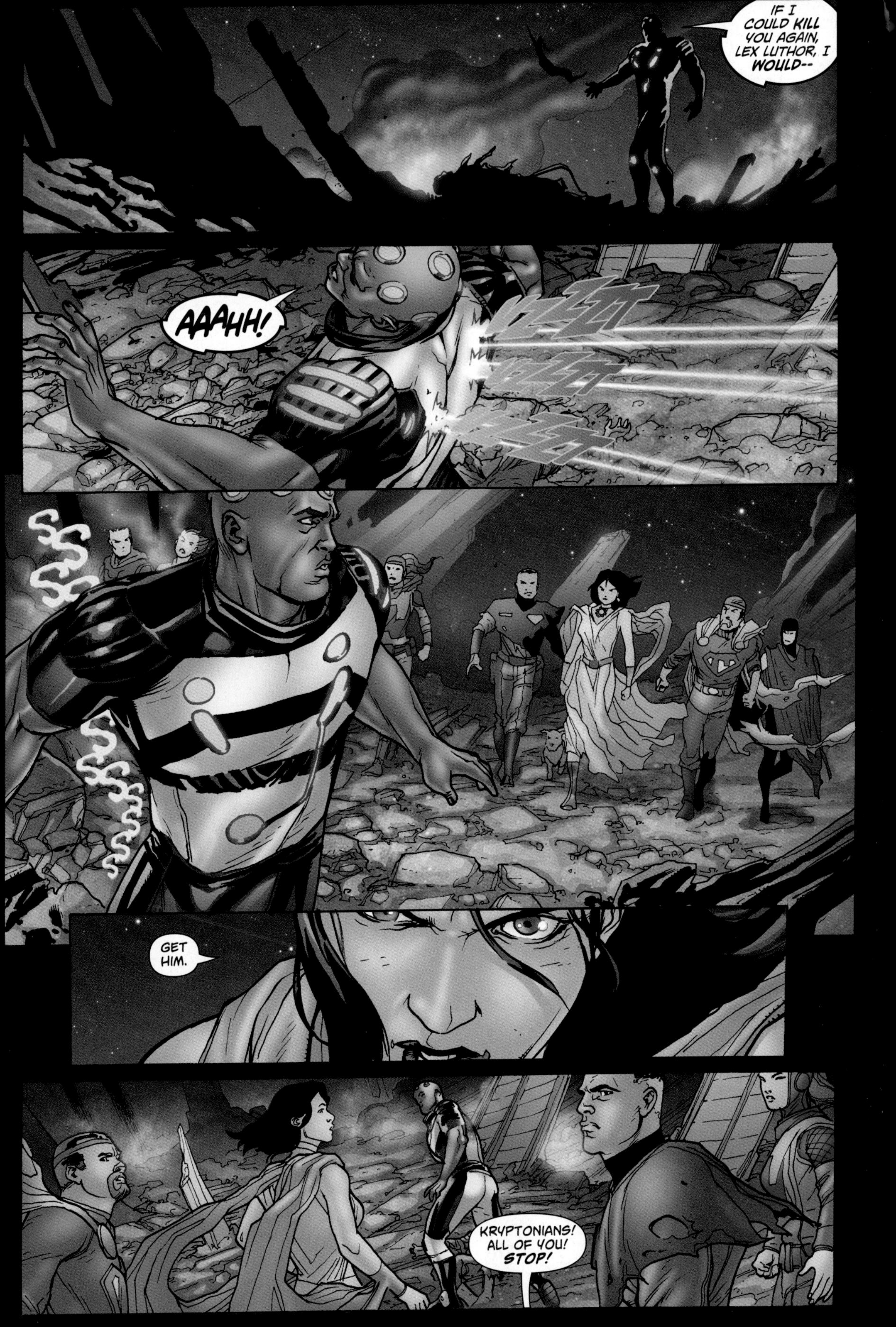
IF I COULD KILL YOU AGAIN, LEX LUTHOR, I WOULD--
AAAHH!
GET HIM.
KRYPTONIANS! ALL OF YOU! STOP!

SAY WHAT YOU WANT, COLUAN, I'M *NOT* LISTENING.

BATTLE ISN'T WORD-PLAY.

IT'S *SKILL.*

AFTER YOU TOOK KANDOR THE *FIRST* TIME...

...I SWORE AN *OATH...*

...ONE DAY YOU WOULD KNEEL BEFORE ME...

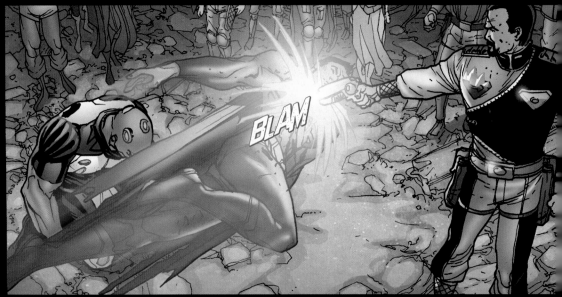

BLAM

cover by **JOE QUINONES**

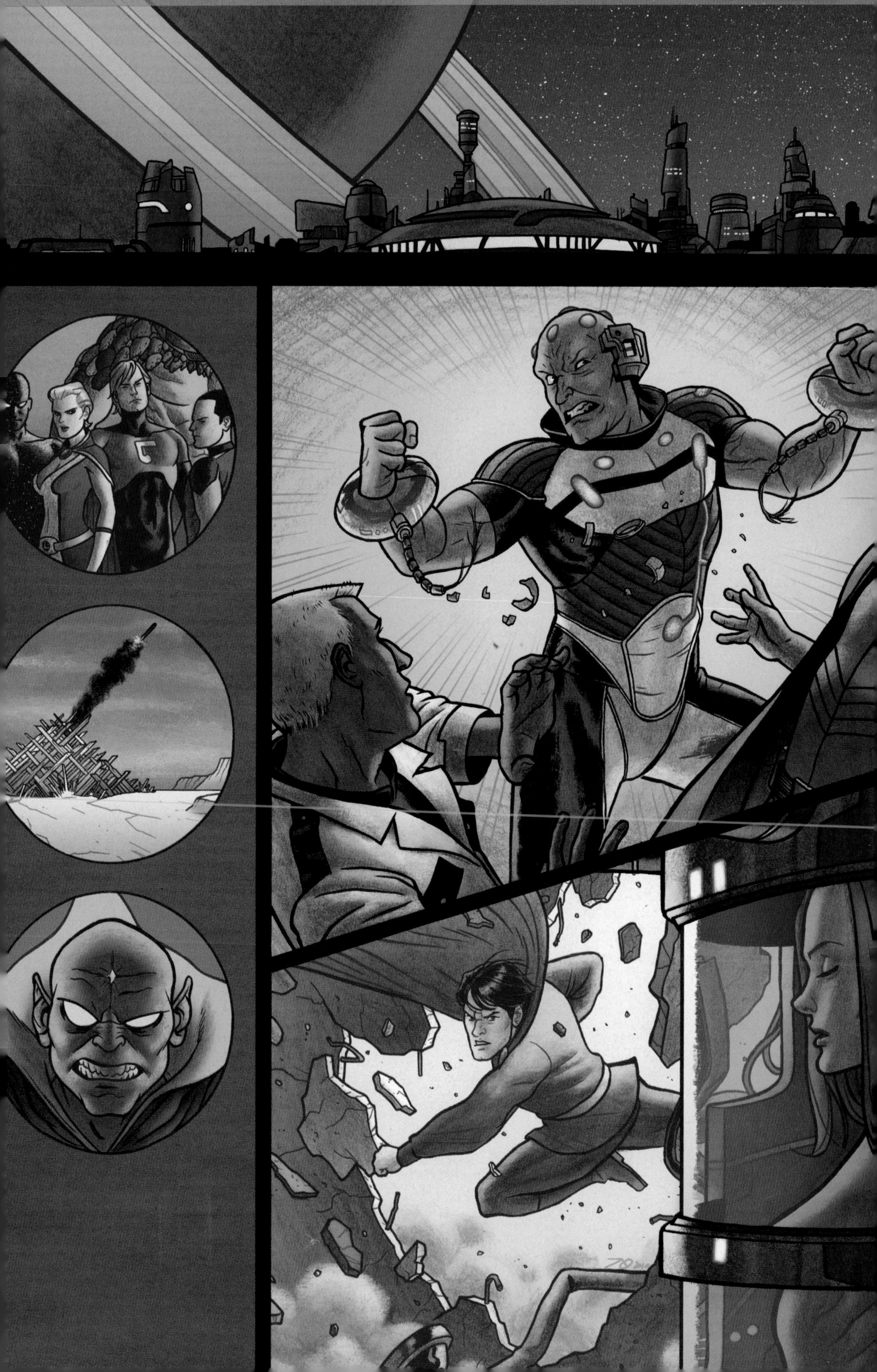

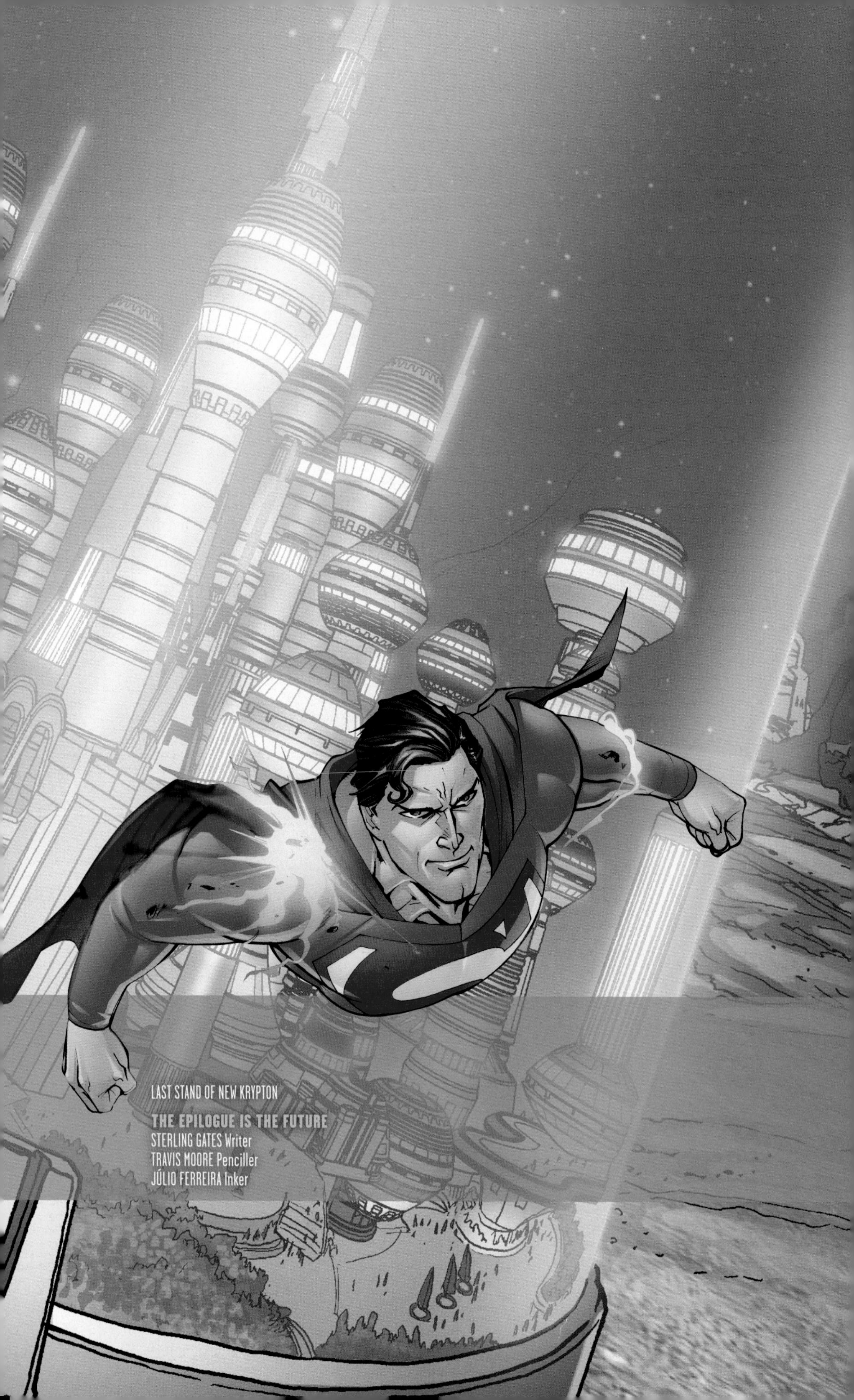
LAST STAND OF NEW KRYPTON
THE EPILOGUE IS THE FUTURE
STERLING GATES Writer
TRAVIS MOORE Penciller
JÚLIO FERREIRA Inker

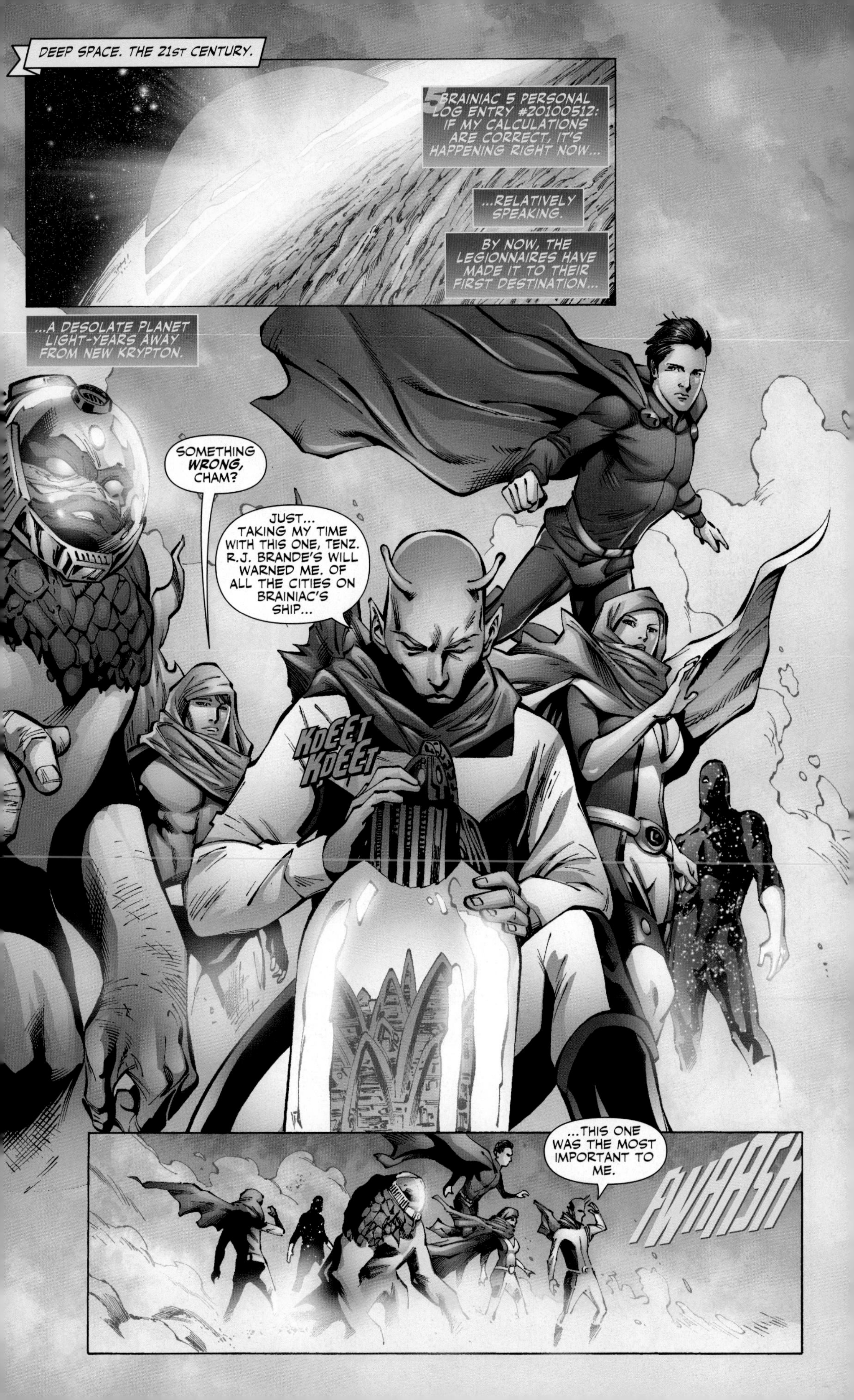
DEEP SPACE. THE 21st CENTURY.
BRAINIAC 5 PERSONAL LOG ENTRY #20100512: IF MY CALCULATIONS ARE CORRECT, IT'S HAPPENING RIGHT NOW...
...RELATIVELY SPEAKING.
BY NOW, THE LEGIONNAIRES HAVE MADE IT TO THEIR FIRST DESTINATION...
...A DESOLATE PLANET LIGHT-YEARS AWAY FROM NEW KRYPTON.
SOMETHING WRONG, CHAM?
JUST... TAKING MY TIME WITH THIS ONE, TENZ. R.J. BRANDE'S WILL WARNED ME. OF ALL THE CITIES ON BRAINIAC'S SHIP...
KDEET KDEET
...THIS ONE WAS THE MOST IMPORTANT TO ME.
FWAASH

NEW DURLA.

...I KNOW, JECKIE. I JUST...I WANT TO SAY SOMETHING...

NO. WE FOLLOW WHAT HE TOLD US TO THE LETTER.

HIS RACE--DURLANS--ARE NOMADIC BY NATURE. THERE ARE THOUSANDS OF TRIBES HIDDEN IN POCKETS ACROSS THE UNIVERSE.

CENTURIES AGO, BRAINIAC CAPTURED A LOST TRIBE OF DURLANS CALLED THE KEL'PAR. HE HELD THEM PRISONER FOR DECADES UNTIL WE FREED THEM.

...LEE-JUN...

...HOME...

LET'S GO. THERE ARE OTHER WORLDS TO COLONIZE BEFORE TIME UNLOCKS AND WE CAN GO BACK HOME.

I CAN'T IMAGINE IT WAS EASY FOR REEP DAGGLE, SEEING ALL OF THEM.

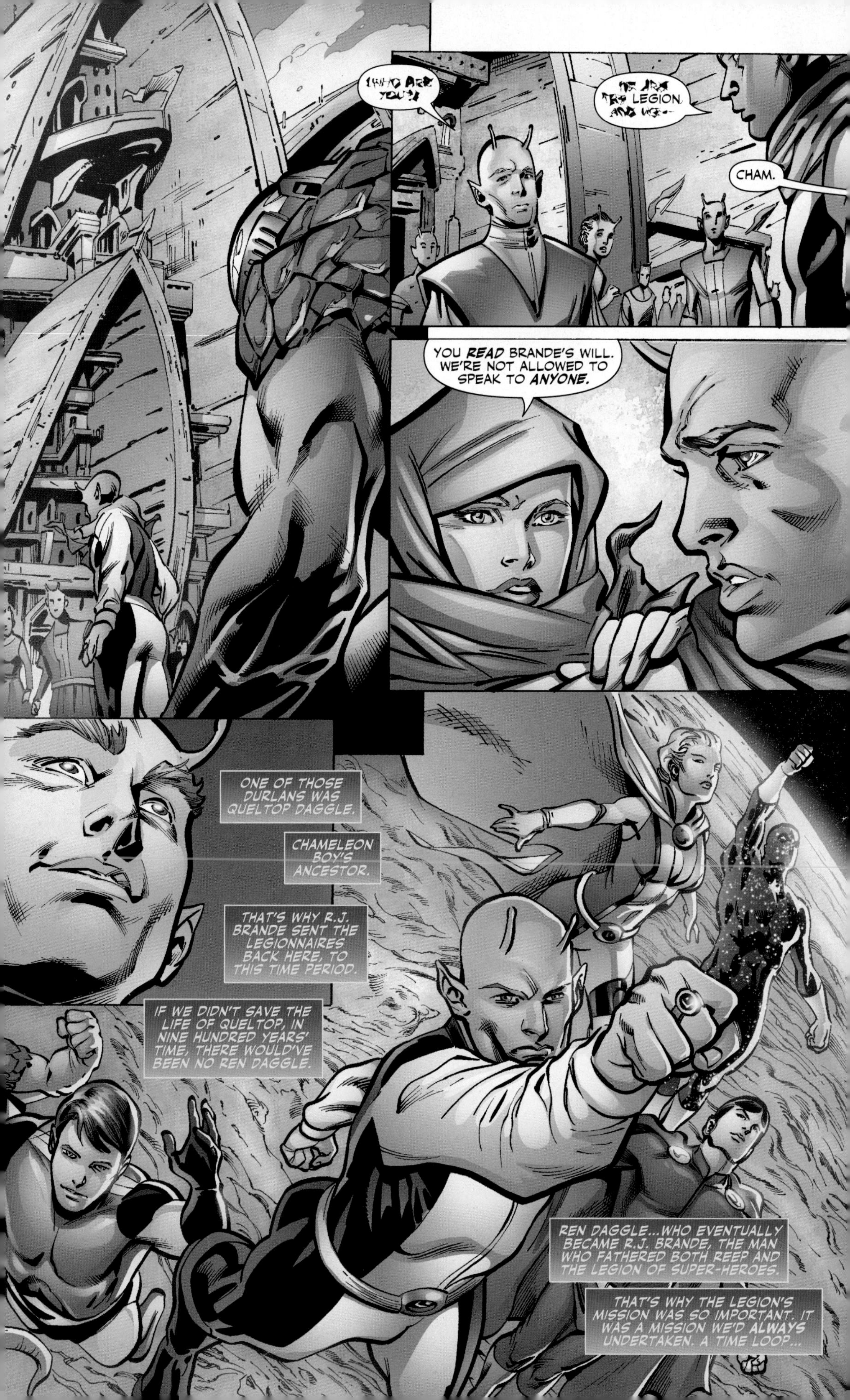
WHO ARE YOU?!
LEGION
CHAM.
YOU READ BRANDE'S WILL. WE'RE NOT ALLOWED TO SPEAK TO ANYONE.
ONE OF THOSE DURLANS WAS QUELTOP DAGGLE.
CHAMELEON BOY'S ANCESTOR.
THAT'S WHY R.J. BRANDE SENT THE LEGIONNAIRES BACK HERE, TO THIS TIME PERIOD.
IF WE DIDN'T SAVE THE LIFE OF QUELTOP, IN NINE HUNDRED YEARS' TIME, THERE WOULD'VE BEEN NO REN DAGGLE.
REN DAGGLE...WHO EVENTUALLY BECAME R.J. BRANDE, THE MAN WHO FATHERED BOTH REEP AND THE LEGION OF SUPER-HEROES.
THAT'S WHY THE LEGION'S MISSION WAS SO IMPORTANT. IT WAS A MISSION WE'D ALWAYS UNDERTAKEN. A TIME LOOP...

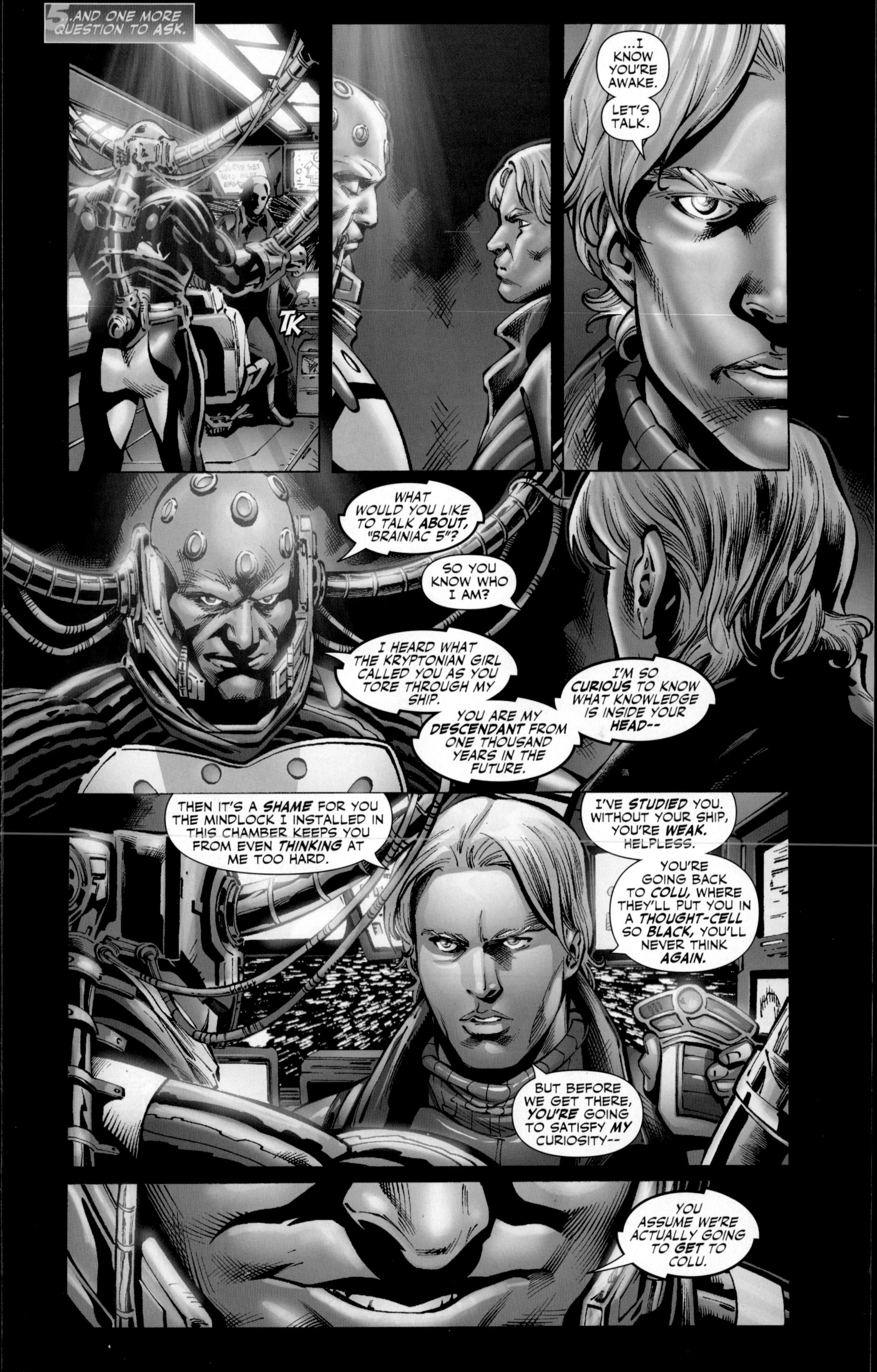
5...AND ONE MORE QUESTION TO ASK.
TK
...I KNOW YOU'RE AWAKE.
LET'S TALK.
WHAT WOULD YOU LIKE TO TALK ABOUT, "BRAINIAC 5"?
SO YOU KNOW WHO I AM?
I HEARD WHAT THE KRYPTONIAN GIRL CALLED YOU AS YOU TORE THROUGH MY SHIP.
YOU ARE MY DESCENDANT FROM ONE THOUSAND YEARS IN THE FUTURE.
I'M SO CURIOUS TO KNOW WHAT KNOWLEDGE IS INSIDE YOUR HEAD--
THEN IT'S A SHAME FOR YOU THE MINDLOCK I INSTALLED IN THIS CHAMBER KEEPS YOU FROM EVEN THINKING AT ME TOO HARD.
I'VE STUDIED YOU. WITHOUT YOUR SHIP, YOU'RE WEAK. HELPLESS.
YOU'RE GOING BACK TO COLU, WHERE THEY'LL PUT YOU IN A THOUGHT-CELL SO BLACK, YOU'LL NEVER THINK AGAIN.
BUT BEFORE WE GET THERE, YOU'RE GOING TO SATISFY MY CURIOSITY--
YOU ASSUME WE'RE ACTUALLY GOING TO GET TO COLU.

James wanted to tell a big Mon-El story over the course of it, connecting him back to the Legion, and we were both very concerned with finding a way to make the New Kryptonians stars in their own right as they rose up to help Superman stop the threat.

Throughout writing this story, James and I kept talking about how this was first and foremost a story about the New Kryptonians and their fears, and about how none of the Guilds would unite under any one person. The High Council and Alura had failed them all, as had Supergirl's attempts at unification. Obviously, they needed a hero to unite them...

...and they got one in General Zod, the man who almost kills Brainiac in the streets. The New Kryptonians are driven toward Zod's leadership over the course of Last Stand, and it's Zod — not our hero, Superman — who "wins" the hearts of the people at the end. It's a dark and unexpected ending for a Superman story, and it leads to another very dark and tragic Superman tale.

• • •

There are a few moments I'm particularly proud of across the two volumes of Last Stand, including the Military Guild member who puts the gun to his head once he sees that the city of Kandor has been rebottled, the little Kryptonian girl who can't turn off her super-hearing, and the wife of the man killed in Brainiac's opening attack coming back at the end to fry Brainiac with heat vision. I loved the way Pete Woods drew her face as she looks at Brainiac and says "Get him." Chilling stuff.

While I can't speak for James, I know I had a wonderful time co-writing this crossover with him and working with our phenomenal art teams. Pete Woods, Jamal Igle, Travis Moore, Ivan Rodriguez, Bernard Chang, Eduardo Pansica, Javier Pina, and Julian Lopez all did beautiful jobs, and my hats are off to all of them.

So. Going forward. The Legion have saved their worlds, ensuring the future. Supergirl met Brainiac 5, the man who could end up being the love of her life. Superboy got to see what a Kryptonian planet would look like, and Superman saw his friends and family unite to help save his world. Everyone got a little something out of this story, didn't they?

Oh, and General Zod got *exactly* what he wanted: With Brainiac defeated (and made to kneel before Zod!), the people of New Krypton would now follow him anywhere...

...including into a war with the planet Earth.

I hope you enjoyed SUPERMAN: THE LAST STAND OF NEW KRYPTON, Super-Reader. Get ready for the next (and final) volume in the New Krypton saga, as the 100-Minute War begins!

SJG
Los Angeles, October 2010

ADVENTURE COMICS 10 variant by **BERNARD CHANG**

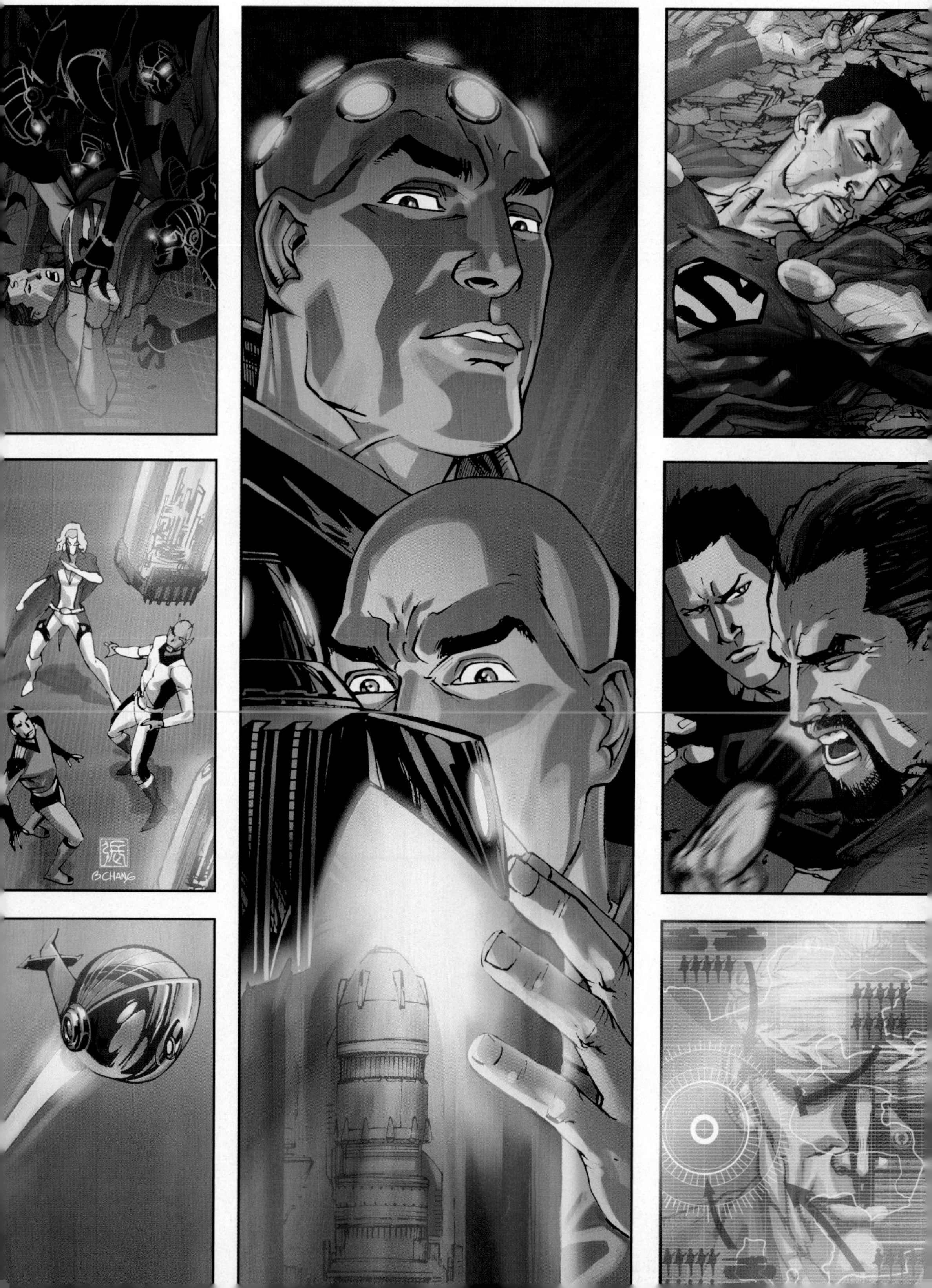
BCHANG

SUPERMAN: LAST STAND OF NEW KRYPTON 3 by **CHRIS WESTON**

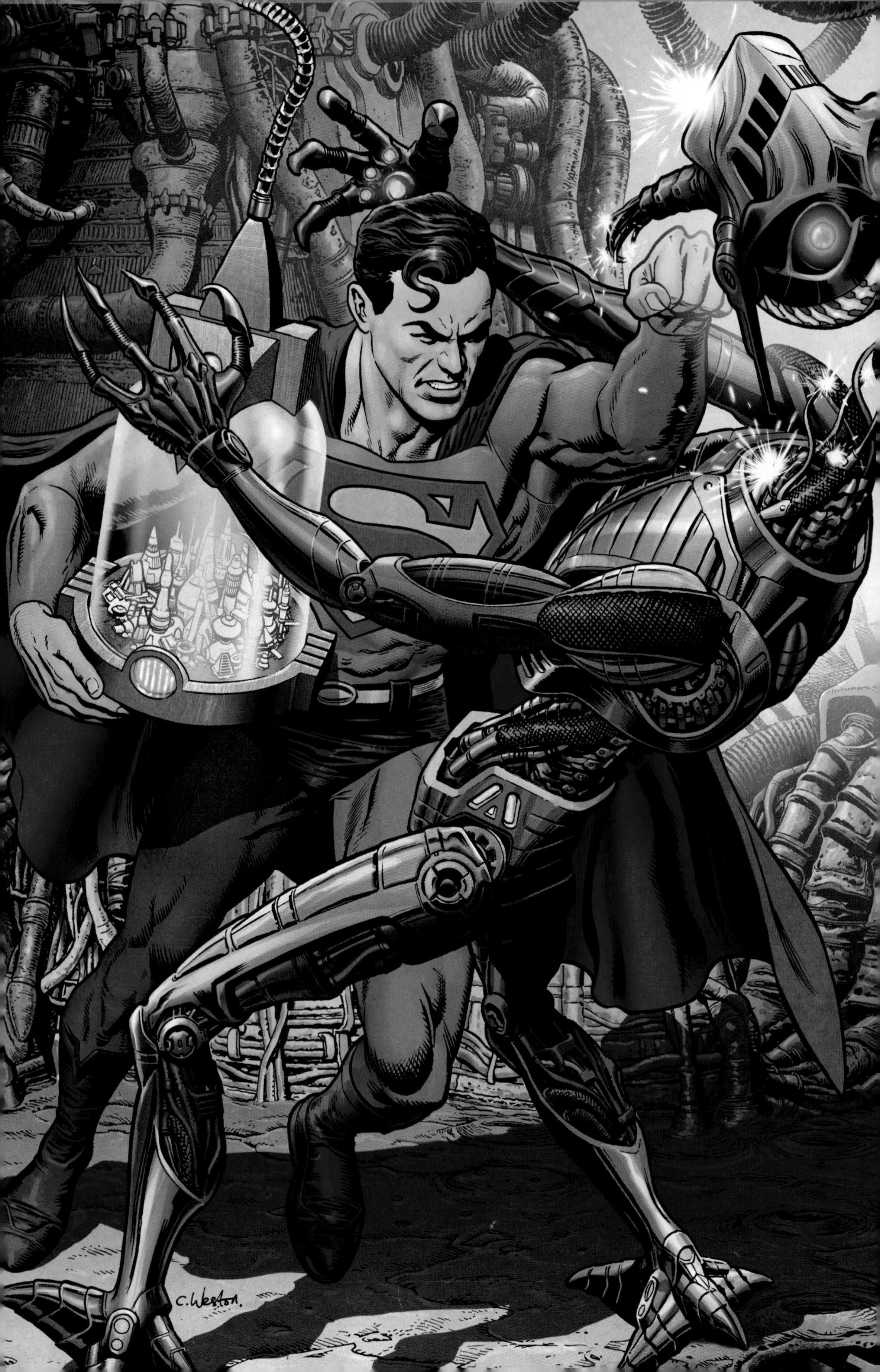
C. Weston.

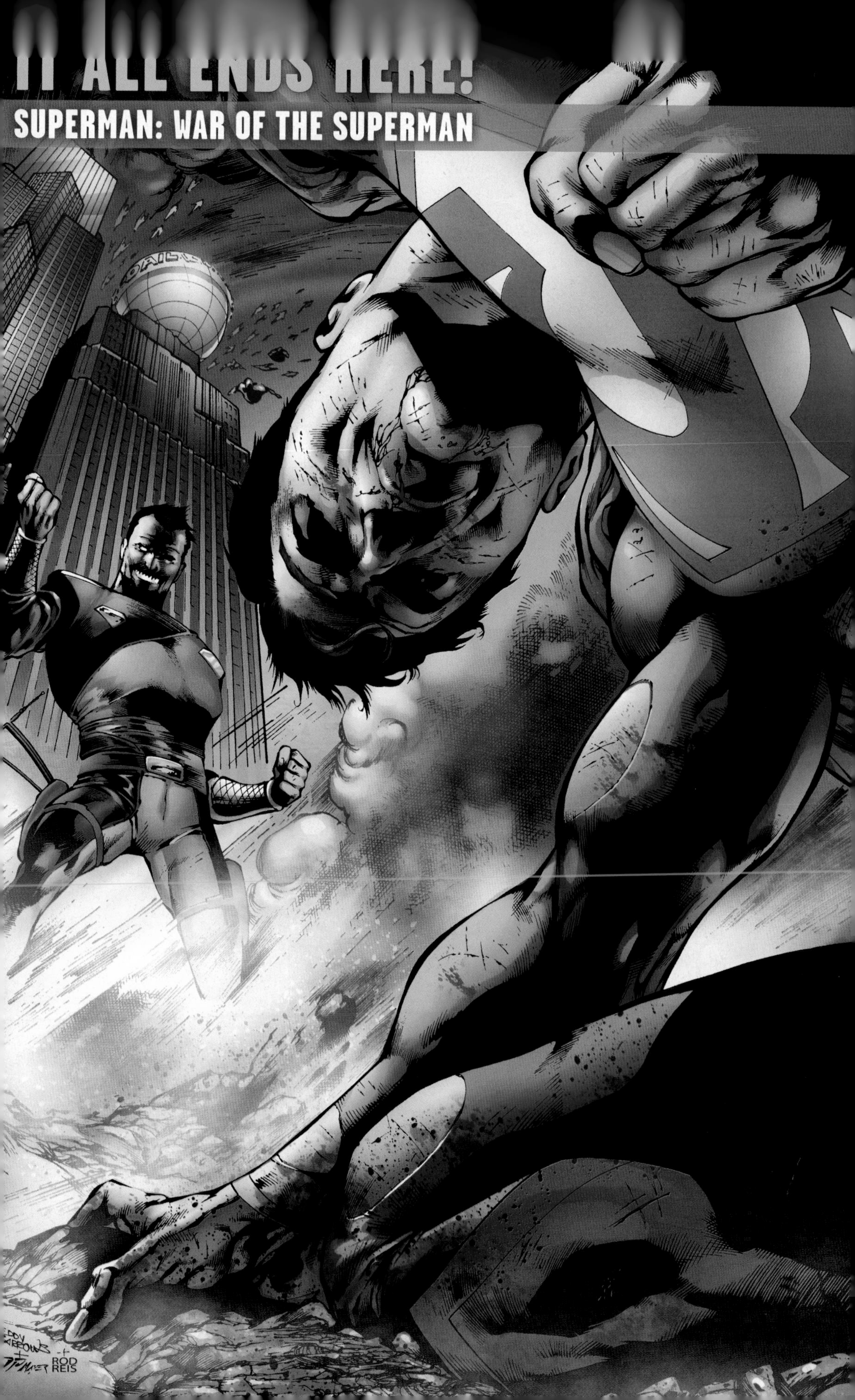
IT ALL ENDS HERE!
SUPERMAN: WAR OF THE SUPERMAN
ROD REIS

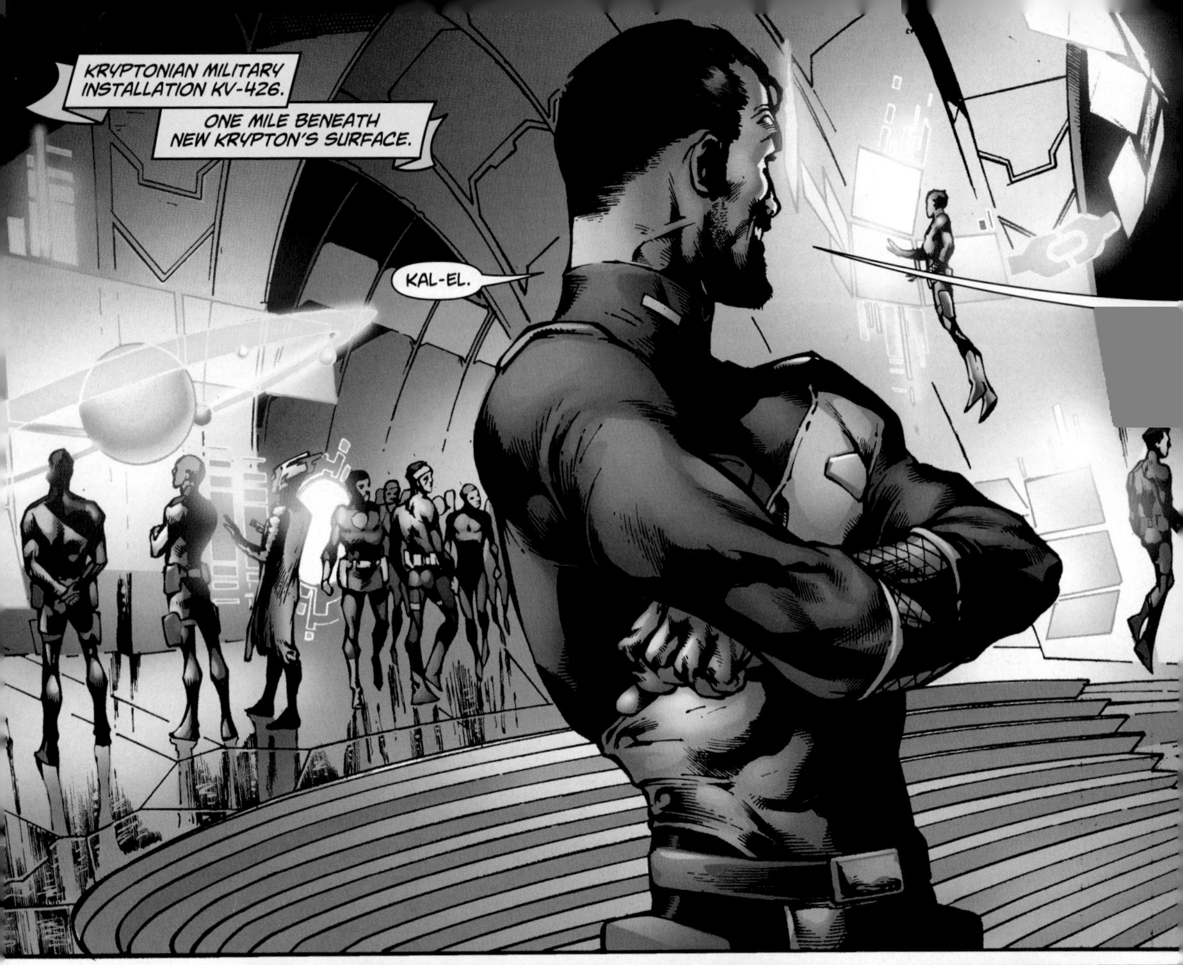
KRYPTONIAN MILITARY INSTALLATION KV-426.
ONE MILE BENEATH NEW KRYPTON'S SURFACE.
KAL-EL.

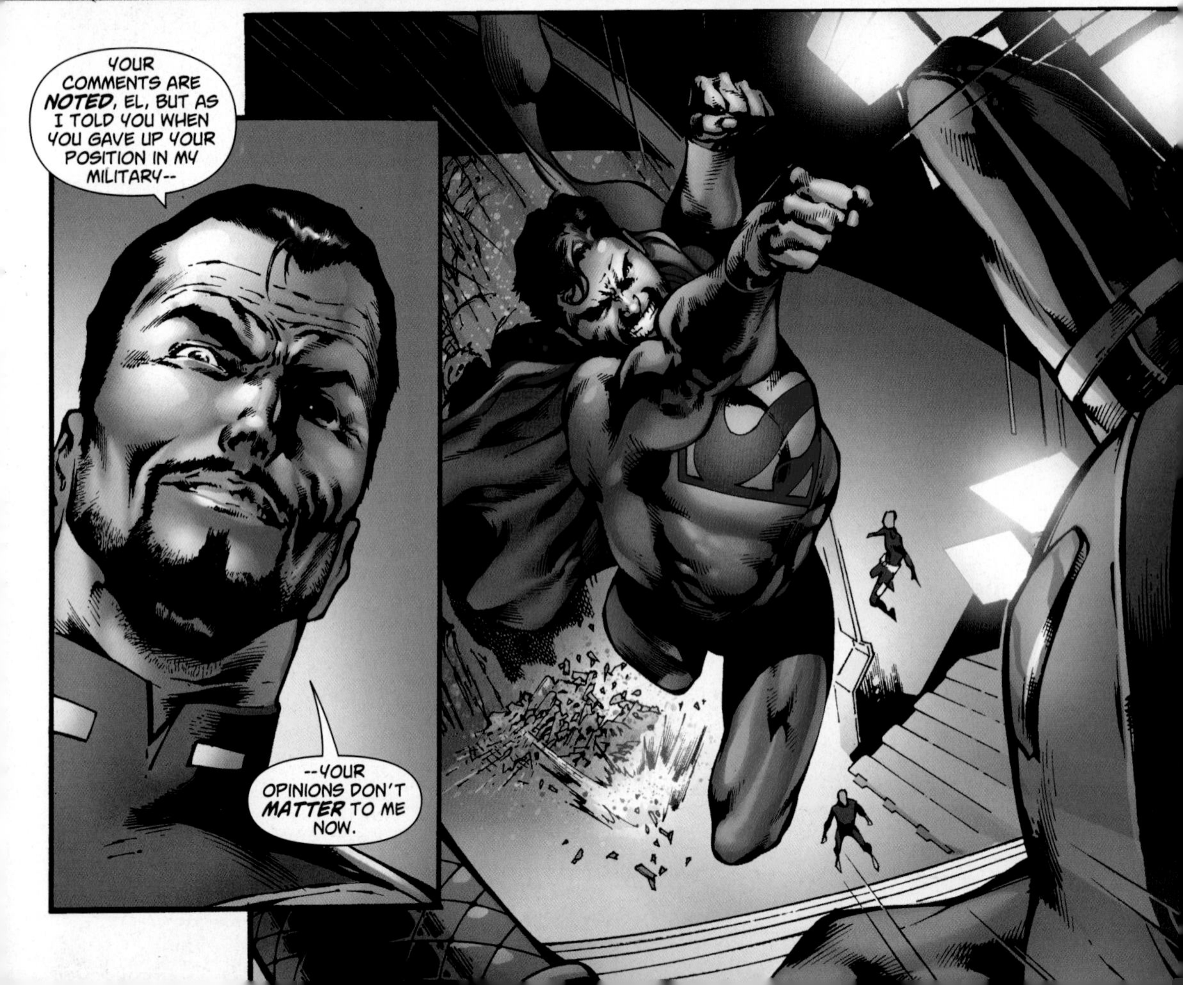
YOUR COMMENTS ARE **NOTED**, EL, BUT AS I TOLD YOU WHEN YOU GAVE UP YOUR POSITION IN MY MILITARY--
--YOUR OPINIONS DON'T **MATTER** TO ME NOW.

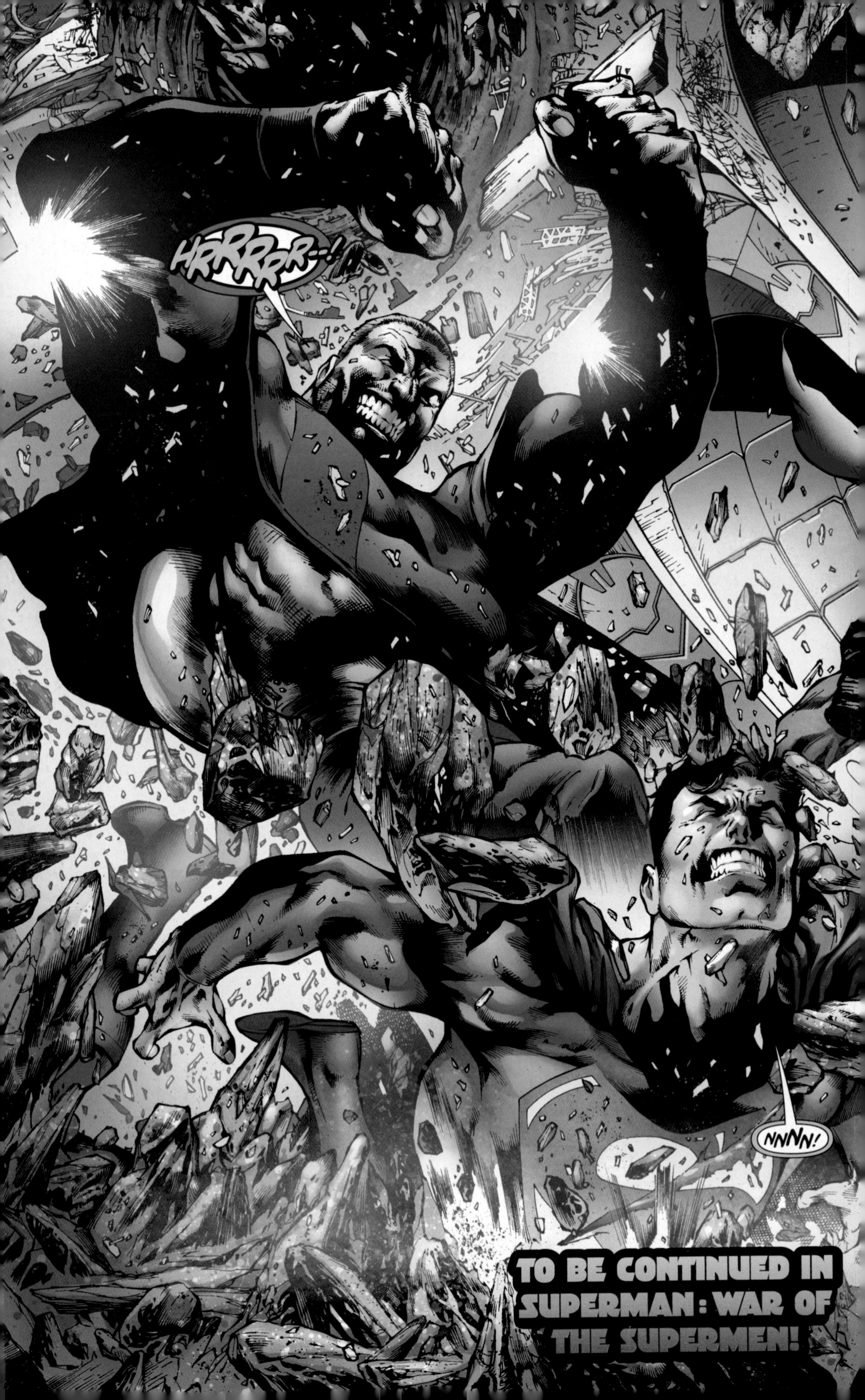
HRRRRR--!
NNNN!
TO BE CONTINUED IN SUPERMAN: WAR OF THE SUPERMEN!